Hartshorne, Process Philosophy, and Theology

HARTSHORNE, PROCESS PHILOSOPHY, AND THEOLOGY

Edited by
Robert Kane and Stephen H. Phillips

STATE UNIVERSITY OF NEW YORK PRESS

Published by
State University of New York Press, Albany

Printed in the United States of America

For information, address State University of New York Press, State University Plaza, Albany, NY 12246

Library of Congress Cataloging-in Publication Data

Hartshorne, process philosophy, and theology/edited by Robert Kane and Stephen H. Phillips.
p. cm.
Includes index.
ISBN 0-7914-0164-2. — ISBN 0-7914-0165-0 (pbk.)
1. Hartshorne, Charles, 1897- —Influence. 2. Process philosophy. 3. Process theology. I. Kane, R. (Robert), 1938- II. Phillips, Stephen H.
B945.H354H37 1989 89-4237
191—dc19 CIP

10 9 8 7 6 5 4 3 2 1

CONTENTS

Preface

This volume is an outgrowth of an international conference held in honor of Charles Hartshorne's ninetieth birthday at the University of Texas at Austin in February of 1988. The papers provide an introduction to Hartshorne's contributions to twentieth-century process philosophy and theology as well as a discussion of some of the current controversies in philosophy and theology which these contributions have spawned. Most of the essays are accessible to general readers and the opening essay by David Ray Griffin is a lucid and penetrating general introduction to Hartshorne's thought. But the essays also attempt to break new ground on issues that have concerned Hartshorne throughout his philosophical career—on the nature and methods of metaphysics, the existence and nature of God, and the place of religion and religious metaphysics in the modern world. Many of the essays survey the current state of controversies on these topics among process theorists, and other essays relate Hartshorne's work to different philosophical and religious traditions and to trends in twentieth-century thought—to postmodernism, classical Western theism, Eastern philosophies, particularly Indian theism, contemporary analytic philosophy, American pragmatism, and others.

"Process philosophy" has come to be a general designation for philosophical views which emphasize the creative and temporal aspects of reality and assert that "becoming" is an essential and primary, not a derivative, feature of whatever is real. Though traces of process thought have been discerned in some Eastern philosophies, also in the West as far back as Heraclitus, and in some idealist philosophies, Hegel's for instance, process philosophy did not attain a distinctive voice as such until about a century ago—in the writings of Henri Bergson, C. S. Peirce, William James, Samuel Alexander, and especially Alfred North Whitehead and his intellectual successors, the most notable of whom has been Charles Hartshorne. While it would be a mistake to identify process philosophy generally with Whiteheadian process philosophy, nevertheless views and reflection in the tradition of Whitehead, Hartshorne and their successors have been at the center of twentieth-century discussions of process thought, and, through Hartshorne and others, process conceptions have become a powerful force in modern theology. The following essays describe and evaluate Hartshorne's distinctive contributions to these developments.

The lead essay, "Charles Hartshorne's Postmodern Philosophy," by David Ray Griffin, is more than a lucid introduction to Hartshorne's major positions and arguments. It is an original discussion of the relevance such a process world view has for current "professional" philosophy and theology, and more broadly, for the postmodern intellectual landscape. "Modern philosophy is self destructing," Griffin suggests. "This process of self-destruction has been going on for some time, but has become more obvious in the past decade, especially through the discussions evoked by Richard Rorty, Jacques Derrida, and related thinkers. ... But from the point of view of the postmodern philosophy of Alfred North Whitehead and Charles Hartshorne—which is a *constructive* postmodernism, quite different from the deconstructive ... postmodernism—this self-immolation of modern philosophy is neither surprising or disturbing. It is not surprising because modern philosophy has from the beginning been based on faulty premises. It is not disturbing because the self-elimination of modern philosophy will create a void that may be filled by a postmodern philosophy that can perform the cultural tasks of philosophy in a more adequate way." Griffin goes on to identify what he regards as the faulty premises of modern philosophy, which include "formal dualisms" between objective facts and subjective values, and between theory and practice, as well as three substantive theories: "(i) a mechanistic materialistic, non-animistic doctrine of nature, (ii) a sensationalist doctrine of perception, and (iii) a denial that divinity is naturally present in the world." He shows how Whitehead and Hartshorne reject these modernist doctrines without falling prey to the skeptical, nihilistic or atheistic conclusions of deconstructive postmodernism. And he goes on to scrutinize Hartshorne's alternatives to these modernist doctrines, concluding with a discussion of the "practical importance of explicitly metaphysical belief" for a meaningful life and, collectively, a better society.

In the second essay, "From Modal Language to Model Language: Charles Hartshorne and Linguistic Analysis," Jan Van der Veken undertakes "a dialogue between the proponents of Hartshorne's ... metaphysics and the proponents of the analysis of religious language—such as Ian T. Ramsey, John Wisdom ... Ludwig Wittgenstein" and others in the tradition of Anglo-American linguistic philosophy. He says: "Wittgenstein has shown that we are often 'bewitched' by ordinary language: '*Behexung durch die Sprache*.' One striking case is our deeply rooted way of asking the God-question as 'Does God exist?' It seems to be a most natural way of posing the question, and yet, when taken literally, it is wholly wrong. Wisdom's famous parable [of the explorers who came upon a well-tended garden in the middle of a wilderness and asked whether there was a gardener] seems to pose the question in the same way: 'Yes or no, is there a gardener (God)?' As we shall see, however, to ask the question in this way is entirely to miss the point of parable." Taking the parable as a *point d'appui*, Van der Veken goes on to a profound meditation on the nature of faith, and integrates Hartshorne's "panentheistic" approach to the question of God with Wittgensteinian reflections on language, insights of Ramsey and Wisdom, and themes from contemporary theologians such as Schubert Ogden and Langdon Gilkey. ('Panentheism' is a term coined by Hartshorne for his own view, meaning that God is the all-encompassing Reality who—in contradistinction to the God of pantheist views—transcends the world while including it.) Finally, Van der Veken argues that religious language must include both the "modal" language of metaphysical assertion about God and the "model" languages of ordinary believers which express in historical contexts their world of values, meaning and responsibility.

Barry Whitney, in "Hartshorne and Theodicy," surveys some of the recent debates among process philosophers concerning the theologically central problem of evil (to which Whitney himself has contributed recent important books and articles): how can we reconcile the existence of a maximally powerful and good God with the existence of evil? Process theists like Hartshorne take a different approach to the problem than classical theists: process theists insist that *any* world which God might create *must* contain free creatures and hence the possibility of evil that is uneliminable by God. They also insist that God's influence on the world is primarily "persuasive," not "coercive." God is "worthy of worship" because God continually brings about the best in situations to the entire extent of divine influence, i.e. within metaphysical constraints governing all creation. Nonetheless, Whitney argues that there are problems yet to be resolved in process solutions to the problem of evil—despite the worthy efforts of Hartshorne, David Griffin, Lewis Ford and other process theorists. Whitney is himself inclined toward the Hartshornean position that "the process God acts solely persuasively," but admits that the "enabling conditions for creaturely actualization" *appear* coercive; and he urges process theists to attain greater clarity about why this should be so. He lays out the contemporary debate, identifying inadequacies in existing positions, thereby clarifying what he takes to be the principal tasks now facing process theodicy.

Among the chief disagreements between what Hartshorne sometimes calls his "neoclassical" or process theism, on the one hand, and "classical" Western theism, on the other, are disagreements about the nature of God's knowledge, and about the relation of divine omniscience to human freedom. Donald Wayne Viney discusses these issues in "God Only Knows? Hartshorne and the Mechanics of Omniscience." He begins with a brief, informative survey of the classical positions on omniscience and human freedom, discussing Boethius, Aquinas, Scotus, Molina and others. Viney gives an original twist to this historical survey by distinguishing three regnant metaphors or models for omniscience in the tradition, which he calls the practical, the innatist and the perceptual, and by showing how each model is exemplified in different theories. All this is preparatory to a sympathetic discussion of Hartshorne's views on divine omniscience and human freedom, which are contrasted with those of the classical tradition. Viney's essay also includes discussion of the Molinist theory of "middle knowledge," and responses to arguments of contemporary philosophers who defend classical accounts of divine omniscience. Pivotal to his essay is the section devoted to a reconstruction of what he calls "Hartshorne's central argument" against the possibility of divine foreknowledge of future contingent events, including free human future actions.

Since the early 1960s, the development by logicians of new techniques in modal logic (the logic of necessity and possibility) has led to a revival of interest in classical philosophical theology among analytic philosophers in the English-speaking world. Hartshorne's name is sometimes linked to this revival since he was instrumental (along with Norman Malcolm and others) in stimulating interest in the application of modal logic to St. Anselm's famous "Ontological Argument" for divine existence. Despite this fact, and despite the fact that process theism has been growing in influence during the same period in which philosophical theology has seen its "analytic" revival, there has been only a limited amount of dialogue between process theists and analytic theists. Analytic theists tend to defend the classical conception of a non-temporal and immutable God, and are suspicious of the temporal God of process theism, which they regard as "limited" or "finite." Daniel Dombrowski considers this dispute in "Must a Perfect Being Be Immutable?" He discusses the views of certain analytic theists—William Mann, Eleonore Stump, Norman Kretzmann and Alvin Plantinga—on the traditionally ascribed divine attributes of simplicity, eternity, immutability and impassibility. Though acknowledging the sophistication of the attempts to defend such traditional ascriptions, Dombrowski expresses strong reservations about their success. His main charge against these modern "classical" theologians, however, is not against their often subtle and astute reconstructions of traditional views, but against their unquestioned acceptance of a classical position he sees as decisively refuted by Hartshorne, namely, that a perfect being must in all aspects be non-temporal and immutable. These analytic theists, Dombrowski argues, have not at all taken seriously enough the arguments that a perfect being could *not possibly* be simply eternal, but must be eternal *and* temporal, could not be simply immutable, but must be immutable in some respects, changeable in others. Dombrowski adroitly presents and defends Hartshorne's arguments on these matters, and urges greater dialogue between the two camps, a dialogue to which this essay makes a substantial contribution. He also discusses briefly the work of Richard Swinburne, another recently influential analytic theist, as well as the work of Richard Creel, a contemporary "classical" theologian who *has* tried to cope with Hartshorne's arguments against divine impassibility.

In " 'Mutable God': Hartshorne and Indian Theism," Stephen Phillips expands the context of informed discussion of Hartshorne's views, by relating them to Indian theism. In an extended introductory section, he sketches the long history of Indian theology with the interests of process theologians in mind. He then focuses on the world view of Aurobindo as the modern Indian theism most interesting for its ideative consonances with process views. Aurobindo's view, as interpreted by Phillips, clearly lines up well with Hartshorne's process theism against "classical" Western theism on some issues, but there is a reverse alignment on others. Still other issues appear to take on importance largely only in an "East/West" debate. For example, Aurobindo holds, with Hartshorne, that God changes as the world changes, and that creation brings restrictions on God's power. But the Easterner argues, in opposition to Hartshornean tenets, that God need not have created anything at all (a "classical" Western position), and indeed, could retract into utter "self-absorption" (a uniquely Indian conception), destroying our world. Imagining an "engagement" between Hartshorneans and followers of Aurobindo, Phillips contrasts positions on the necessary characteristics of God, and in particular, on God's mutability. A Hartshornean argument is reconstructed against Aurobindo's thesis that God need not necessarily change—that God need not have created anything at all, but did create and does create by choice. Phillips lays out an Aurobindonist response, finds merits and weaknessness on each side, and delineates the issues he believes are pivotal for a resolution. The essay also presents, in an Eastern context, some unique twists to the questions about theodicy and omniscience—as well as immutability and divine power—that are discussed in other contributions to this volume. The overall force of the essay is to make an appeal that philosophy, and philosophic theism in particular, recognize a global inheritance.

Hartshorne has often said that he has been influenced almost as much by the American philosopher, Charles S. Peirce, as by Whitehead. Until about 1930, Peirce was a comparatively obscure figure in American philosophy, known only as a logician and mathematician, whom William James had recognized as the founder of American pragmatism. Little was known about Peirce's actual writings until, around 1930, Hartshorne and Paul Weiss completed a project of publishing the collected papers of Peirce in six volumes. This was the beginning of a general recognition of Peirce as one of America's greatest philosophers, and also the beginning of a lifelong influence of Peirce's writings upon Hartshorne. But despite this influence, Hartshorne has sometimes been critical of Peirce's metaphysical categories of Firstness, Secondness and Thirdness, and has suggested revisions to bring them closer to his own line of thinking. These criticisms of Peirce's categories are the partial subject matter of the essay, "Hartshorne and the Basis of Peirce's Categories," by the distinguished Peirce scholar, Kenneth Laine Ketner. Ketner's concern is with the "basis" of Peirce's categories, about which he says: "The distinction between the categories and the basis of them is one that some students of Peirce have missed, but which Hartshorne knows accurately: the categories are hypotheses within Peirce's metaphysics which are based upon certain suggestive results Peirce obtained in mathematics and the logic of relatives.'' Among these suggestive results are Peirce's ''Nonreduction Theorem'' for relations (''No triadic [three-termed] relation can be composed exclusively of dyadic [two-termed] relations'') and his ''Sufficiency Theorem'' (''All relations with more than three terms can be composed exclusively from combinations of monadic, dyadic and triadic relations''). These theorems have been attacked by logicians and Peirce scholars, but Ketner argues at length that the criticisms are based on misunderstandings. His painstaking defense of Peirce's basis takes him to logic and set theory as well as to philosophical issues about relations. When it is completed, he returns to Hartshorne's treatment of Peirce's categories, arguing that some of Hartshorne's criticisms are also based on misunderstanding. Ketner's essay is more than a challenge to Hartshorne's interpretation of Peirce's categories; it is, in its own right, an original and challenging contribution to Peirce scholarship and indeed to current theory of relations.

While Hartshorne is very much influenced by Whitehead, he has also distanced himself from Whitehead on a number of issues that have been in continuous dispute among process philosophers. Whitehead holds that God is a single ''actual entity'' in the technical terminology of *Process and Reality*, but Hartshorne holds that God is, in Whiteheadian terminology, a personal *society* of actual occasions. Hartshorne also disagrees with Whitehead about the nature and status of pure possibilities (Whitehead's ''eternal objects''), about the ''perishing'' of actual occasions, about the ''laws'' of nature, and other issues. Some of these differences are the subject of Lewis Ford's essay, ''Temporality and Transcendence.'' Lewis Ford is as knowledgeable as any living philosopher about disputes going on among Whiteheadian process philosophers during the past three or four decades concerning the nature and religious availability of the process God. He has himself made major contributions to the debates. In this essay, Ford focuses on philosophical differences between Whitehead and Hartshorne regarding the question of divine transcendence. But Ford does more than that. He presents his own carefully reasoned view of divine transcendence as ''future creativity,'' which is a subtle modification of views of Whitehead and Hartshorne, correcting what Ford takes to be deficiencies in them. Ford's essay is a reminder that ''process theology'' is not a static or monolithic position, but an ongoing tradition of philosophic reflection about the nature of God.

The essays by Robert Kane and Jorge Luis Nobo are responses to Ford's contribution. In ''Transcendence, Temporality and Personal Identity,'' Kane begins with comments about traditional notions of the transcendence and eternity of God, and discusses briefly Hartshorne's doctrine of ''dual transcendence.'' ''The word 'transcendence,' '' Kane argues, ''has several meanings. Roughly, it means 'being above and beyond.' But this 'above and beyond' can be taken in several senses. In one sense it may mean that God surpasses the world in the *excellence of God's nature*. In another sense, it may mean that God is above and beyond the world in the *reality of God's life*. For dual transcendence, both senses are meant and both are important.'' Kane uses this distinction to ask pertinent questions about the viability of Ford's account of transcendence. He also discusses the comparative merits of Ford's view and Hartshorne's doctrine of God as the ''World Soul,'' and concludes with suggestive remarks about the personhood of God and the notion of personal identity.

Jorge Luis Nobo, in ''God as Essentially Immutable, Imperishable and Objectifiable,'' responds to Ford from a Whiteheadian perspective. Nobo says that ''since God, according to Whitehead, is an actual entity whose concrescence never perishes, Ford concludes that God's influence on the temporal world cannot be consistently explained by Whitehead. In support of this conclusion, Ford reports that Whitehead, when confronted with this problem in a private conversation with A. H. Johnson, 'recognized that he had not solved it.' '' Nobo argues, however, that Whitehead's remarks indicate only that Whitehead had not *tried* to solve the problem of God's influence on the world, not that it is unsolvable within the Whiteheadian system. Nobo in fact thinks the problem is solvable in Whiteheadian terms, and he brings to bear on it his own provocative interpretation of Whitehead presented in his recent book, *Whitehead's Metaphysics of Extension and Solidarity*. Nobo argues that, given his interpretation of Whitehead's metaphysics, a better Whiteheadian account of God's influence on the world and of divine transcendence can be developed than both Ford's and Hartshorne's theories.

In the final essay, Charles Hartshorne responds to each of the prior contributions, and adds remarks further illuminating the issues with which they deal. We trust that these responses together with the ten other essays of this volume will be viewed as a fitting testimonial to a philosopher who has done so much to revive interest in speculative philosophy and theology in the second half of the twentieth century.

Austin, Texas
November 1988

Acknowledgments

We would like to thank the following, whose support of an international conference held in honor of Charles Hartshorne's ninetieth birthday at the University of Texas at Austin gave rise to this volume. First and foremost, we thank the Franklin J. Matchette Foundation and its director, Robert Eckles, whose generous support helped to make the conference and this book possible. Additional support came from the College of Liberal Arts of the University of Texas at Austin (Dean Robert King), the Department of Philosophy (Chair, Robert Causey), the Religious Studies Program (Director, Lester Kurtz) and the University Public Lectures Committee. We would also like to thank Douglas Browning, Professor of Philosophy and co-director of the conference. We are grateful to the Center for Process Studies of the School of Theology at Claremont, California (especially directors John Cobb and David Ray Griffin), for encouragement and work on arrangements for the conference. Concerning the preparation of the manuscript, we are indebted to the Computation Center of the University of Texas at Austin, and the staff of Michael Cerda, Director of User Services for UNIX systems. "Camera-ready copy" was prepared with their help. We are also grateful to Elizabeth Hiles (Administrative Assistant, Philosophy, University of Texas, Austin) who did admirable last-minute typing. Finally, we thank William Eastman and his fine staff at the State University of New York Press (especially Bernadine Dawes) for supporting the project and bringing it to completion.

Charles Hartshorne's Postmodern Philosophy

David Ray Griffin

Modern philosophy is self-destructing. This process of self-destruction has been going on for some time, but has become more obvious in the past decade, especially through the discussions evoked by the writings of Richard Rorty, Jacques Derrida, and related thinkers. Philosophers are not only denying that philosophy has any capacity to discover truth beyond that learned through the natural sciences; they are even saying that philosophy cannot declare the results of science to be true. This relativism is sometimes called "post-modernism." These relativistic postmodern philosophers deny that philosophy has any unique role to play in the culture. Books have recently appeared with titles such as *After Philosophy* and *Ethics Without Philosophy*.[1]

From one point of view—a view that equates modern philosophy with philosophy itself—this development is surprising and disturbing. Surely, one thinks, it is neither conceivable nor desirable that we should no longer have professional philosophers. But from the point of view of the postmodern philosophy of Alfred North Whitehead and Charles Hartshorne—which is a *constructive* postmodernism, quite different from the deconstructive, relativistic form of postmodernism—this self-immolation of modern philosophy is neither surprising nor disturbing. It is not surprising because modern philosophy has from the beginning been based on faulty premises. It is not disturbing because the self-elimination of modern philosophy will create a void that may be filled by a postmodern philosophy that can perform the cultural tasks of philosophy in a more adequate way.

In this essay, I first explain what I take to be three basic theories of modern philosophy, and how these have led to its self-destruction. I then discuss the philosophic perspective shared by Alfred North Whitehead and Charles Hartshorne, which can be called "postmodern" because it rejects these basic theories of modern philosophy without returning to premodern modes of thought. I show how this postmodern philosophy overcomes several problems that have long plagued modern philosophy and that have recently led to its self-destruction. I conclude with a brief discussion of some of the practical implications of Hartshorne's position in his own eyes.

In this exposition, I focus to a great extent on ideas that Hartshorne shares with Whitehead, namely, panexperientialism, radical empiricism, and naturalistic theism. But I also point out several respects in which Hartshorne has strengthened their common position. He has done this by defending the position against rival doctrines, by emphasizing various features of the position that were implicit or present but not prominent in Whitehead's exposition, and, most importantly, by developing ideas that differ somewhat from Whitehead's but are arguably more consistent with the basic position and otherwise more adequate. I do not in this overview try to mention all or even most of Hartshorne's original ideas, especially his more technical contributions to philosophy and philosophical theology. I deal for the most part only with those central themes that challenge basic theories of modern thought.

Modern philosophy

Because the term 'modern philosophy' covers a very diverse set of systems, schools, and tendencies, any attempt to give a brief characterization of it must be very selective and formulated in extreme generalities that do not apply equally to all examples of modern philosophy. I focus on a set of features that I take to be fundamental to the main trajectory of modern philosophy, including that part of modern philosophy now called natural science.

Formally, modern philosophy has been characterized by various dualisms. Based on its substantive dualisms between matter and mind, determinism and freedom, which I discuss shortly, modern philosophy has spawned a disciplinary dualism between facts and values, or between science on the one hand, and theology, ethics, and aesthetics on the other. As modern philosophy developed, this dualism became that between the objective and the merely subjective. The other great formal dualism is that not between the theories of different disciplines but between theory and practice—between scientific-philosophic theory on the one hand, and the presuppositions of practice on the other, whether that practice be scientific, philosophic, ethical, or simply everyday practice. For example, we presuppose in practice that our bodies and the world beyond them are real, and that they influence our experience; we presuppose that we are nevertheless partially free, and that our experiences or minds can influence our bodies and the world beyond them in turn. In other words, we presuppose the interaction of mind and matter, and the existence of both causality and freedom. We also presuppose the reality of values—that there is such a thing as truth, that some things are better than others, and that it is usually better to know the truth than to believe falsehood. Modern philosophical theory, however, has not been able to justify these presuppositions.

These formal dualisms between objective facts and subjective values, and between theory and practice, have been supported by the *substantive* character of modern philosophy. Most of this substantive character can be derived from three basic theories: (i) a mechanistic, materialistic, non-animistic doctrine of nature, (ii) a sensationist doctrine of perception, and (iii) a denial that divinity is naturally present in the world. The non-animistic doctrine of nature says that the basic units of nature have neither experience nor the power of self-movement. The sensationist doctrine of perception says that all of our experience of the world beyond ourselves is through our physical senses and hence is limited to the types of things these senses are suited to perceive, namely, physical objects. The denial of natural divine presence in the world follows from the first two theories. If natural entities have nothing like mind or experience, a cosmic mind or experience cannot be present in them. If things can enter *our* minds or experiences only through our physical senses, then a cosmic mind or experience, if one exists, would also be barred from being present in *us*. Modern philosophers (including modern natural and social scientists) have sought to understand the world on the basis of the theory that its normal processes are fully intelligible in principle apart from any reference to divine presence.

These three theories largely account for modern philosophy's inability to explain the presuppositions of human practice. The non-animistic doctrine of physical things such as atoms, molecules, and cells, according to which they have no experience and no capacity for self-motion or freedom, makes it impossible to understand how the human body can interact with its *anima* or soul. How can the experiencing and nonexperiencing interact? How can the free and the unfree interact? This latter question has led modern philosophy to deny that the human being as a whole has any freedom, most characteristically by asserting that the mind or soul is simply identical with the brain, which operates as deterministically as the rest of nature. The sensationist doctrine of perception, which was originally designed to insist that we directly perceive nothing except physical objects, soon led to the conclusion that we do not even perceive *them*. David Hume showed that sense-perception as such provides nothing but sense-data. Sensationism hence implied that we have no direct knowledge of the existence of an actual world beyond our own experience. George Santayana pointed out that this doctrine leads not only to solipsism but to "solipsism of the present moment," because sense-data by themselves give us no knowledge of the existence of the past. In not telling us of the existence of actual things beyond our present experience, sense-perception also fails to exhibit efficient causality, the causal influence of one actual thing on another. Santayana said that the reality of the world, the past, and causality must be accepted on the basis of "animal faith," just as Hume before him had said that we must presuppose them in "practice" even though philosophical theory cannot list them as items of knowledge.

The sensationist doctrine of perception has led to an even greater divorce between theory and practice in relation to values. The reason this divorce is greater is that sense-perception's inability to give us knowledge of those non-physical things we call values is even more obvious than its failure with regard to a real world and causality. While intellectuals in general have not been led by philosophers such as Hume and Santayana to deny that we have knowledge of an actual world, the past, and causality, they *have* been led to deny knowledge of values.

This development has led to self-contradictions. Modernity has, for example, relentlessly sought to replace primitive and medieval falsehood with modern truth, while denying that we have any knowledge that truth is better than falsehood. The notion of "better than" has been taken as a purely subjective preference not capable of reflecting any relation inherent in the nature of things. Moral, aesthetic and religious assertions have been declared noncognitive, that is, incapable of being either true or false, so that arguments concerning them cannot in principle be rational. Modernity has held that the natural sciences give us truth about the physical world, but that ethics, aesthetics and theology are incapable in principle of delivering truth, because sensory perception provides us with no knowledge of their alleged, nonphysical objects. We can therefore have no objective basis for a rational discussion about those value-judgments we are constantly employing, at least implicitly—that some actions, attitudes, and ways of life are morally better than others, that some objects and actions are aesthetically more beautiful, fitting, or tasteful than others, and that our moral and aesthetic decisions are somehow really important because life has some ultimate meaning.

The recent call by relativistic postmodernism for an end to philosophy is closely related to this invidious distinction between science and the other realms of culture, especially the aesthetic-literary realm. The attack on philosophy is due in large part to modern philosophy's role in the authentication of natural science as the one source of truth, which gave it an overwhelmingly disproportionate role in determining the nature of modern culture. Relativistic postmodernism wants to bring science down to the same level as the other cultural pursuits by declaring it no more competent than they to discover truth.[2] It attempts to do this by attacking the notion of truth as such, in the sense of correspondence between idea and reality.[3]

Relativistic postmodernism's attack on the truth of the scientific world view through an attack on truth itself simply carries the three substantive doctrines of modern philosophy through to their logical conclusions. (For this reason, this movement should be called *mostmodern* philosophy instead of postmodern.) Because sensory perception reveals no "given" reality which exists independently of our perception of it, we have no basis, they say, for speaking of correspondence between our ideas and independently existing objects. Because an idea can only correspond to an idea, furthermore, it is impossible for the scientist's ideas to correspond to material objects, which are incapable of having ideas. The idea that the history of science is the history of closer and closer approximations to *the* truth, finally, was only meaningful when people could believe in a divine, nonrelativistic perspective in which the truth was lodged. The sensationism, non-animism, and atheism of modern philosophy accordingly provide three mutually supporting bases for rejecting the very notion of truth as correspondence. The willingness fully to realize this fact constitutes a large part of the self-destruction of modern philosophy.

This self-destruction, as I suggested earlier, is no surprise from the perspective of the postmodern vision of reality and philosophy shared by Alfred North Whitehead and Charles Hartshorne. From this perspective, as Hartshorne has emphasized, philosophy can be clear and consistent only insofar as it recognizes that the general principles by which we live our lives and interpret our experience are derived from a form of perception more basic than sensory perception, insofar as it affirms a postmodern animism, according to which all individuals experience and exercise self-determination, and insofar as it is explicitly theistic.[4] From this perspective, a sensationist, nonanimistic, atheistic philosophy was bound to self-destruct, and the fulfillment of this prediction provides some empirical evidence for the truth of the Whiteheadian-Hartshornean postmodern position.

In the remainder of this essay, I spell out this philosophy in terms of the three features that make it most clearly postmodern: its animism or panexperientialism, which differentiates it from the dualism, materialism, and phenomenalism among which modern thought has felt constrained to choose; its radical empiricism, in comparison with which modern sensationism is seen to be a very superficial form of empiricism; and its naturalistic theism, which differentiates it equally from the supernaturalism of early modernity and the atheism of late modernity. A philosophy based on animism, nonsensory perception, and theism will, of course, sound quaint, if not outrageous, to modern ears. But if we keep in mind the fact that modern philosophy, based on the denial of these three doctrines, is self-destructing, and that the modern world, which supports and is supported by the modern world view, is wired to self-destruct, we may be able to suspend our modern prejudices sufficiently to consider the arguments for these doctrines.

Panexperientialism and radical empiricism

In contrast with modern philosophy, which assumed the basic units of nature to be enduring substances devoid of both experience and self-movement, Whitehead and Hartshorne begin with the hypothesis that nature is comprised of creative, experiential events. The terms 'events,' 'experiential' and 'creative' indicate the three main aspects of this position. The term 'events' indicates that the basic units of reality are not enduring things, or substances, but momentary events. Each enduring thing, such as an electron, an atom, a cell, or a psyche, is a temporal *society*, comprised of a series of momentary events, each of which incorporates the previous events of that enduring individual.

The term 'experiential' indicates that the basic unit-events of the world are not "vacuous actualities," devoid of experience. Whitehead called them "occasions of experience." This doctrine does not mean that all events have conscious thoughts and sensory perceptions. It means only that they have something analogous to what we call feeling, memory, desire, and purpose in ourselves. To call this position "anthropomorphism," Hartshorne points out, is to presuppose that these experiential qualities belong uniquely to us. An animal caught in a trap does not have to become a human being in order to suffer.[5] One of the central features of Hartshorne's philosophy is the idea that the basic psychic qualities—such as feeling, memory, desire, and purpose—are "cosmic variables," capable of *infinite* scope, both above and below their human forms. Memory, for example, could include the whole past, or it might extend back only a millionth of a second.[6] Desire and purpose might be equally variable in relation to the future. To say that all events are experiences is therefore not to say that they are very similar to human experiences; it is only to say that they are not absolutely different in kind.

The term 'creative' gives special emphasis to one of these experiential variables. It says that, although all events are influenced by previous events, no event is fully determined by the past. Every event exercises at least some iota of self-determination or self-creation, and then some power to exert creative influence on the future.

Although this position could be called "panpsychism," I prefer the term 'panexperientialism.'[7] The term 'psyche' suggests a high-grade form of experience, and hence consciousness. That term also suggests that the basic units are enduring things. Also, many forms of panpsychism in which the basic units were enduring things, such as that of Leibniz, have been deterministic. By *panexperientialism* I mean the view that all the units of the actual world are experiencing, creative events.

Hartshorne has hailed this doctrine, which was first formulated with clarity by Whitehead, as one of the greatest philosophical discoveries of all time, and has spent much of his life explaining, developing, and defending it. He defends this doctrine both by bringing out its advantages and by responding to objections.

One advantage of panexperientialism, he says, is that it gives us some idea of what matter is in itself. Modern philosophy has left the nature of matter wholly mysterious,[8] saying that we cannot know what it is in itself, only how it appears to us. But, Hartshorne says, we should take advantage of the fact that in ourselves we have an individual piece of nature that we know from within as well as without.[9] If we are naturalists, and hence regard our own experience as fully natural, not as a supernatural something added to nature, should we not assume that all natural unities have two sides? The fact that it is only ourselves whose inside we know directly does not prevent us from assuming that other people have insides, that is, experiences. And most of us assume that other animals have experience of some sort. Why should we not assume that all natural entities, all the way down to subatomic events, have inside experience as well as outer behavior? We realize that a purely behavioristic approach is inadequate for human beings and other higher animals. By generalizing this insight to all levels of nature, we can have some slight intuition into what things are in themselves.[10] What we call matter is then the outer appearance of something that is, from within, analogous to our own experience.

Probably the most obvious advantage of panexperientialism is that it allows us to solve the notorious mind-body problem. By rejecting the dualistic assumption that lower individuals such as cells and molecules are absolutely different in kind, rather than merely different in degree, from our conscious experience, the problem is dissolved. In Hartshorne's words: "cells can influence our human experiences because they have feelings that we can feel. To deal with the influences of human experiences upon cells, one turns this around. *We* have feelings that *cells* can feel."[11]

By allowing us to understand our common-sense assumption that our experience is actual, that our bodies are actual, and that the two interact, panexperientialism proves itself superior to its alternatives. Materialism, by reducing mind to matter, forces us to deny that our own experience—the thing we know best in the universe—is really real and efficacious. Berkeleyan idealism, by reducing matter to mind, denies that our body is actual and efficacious. Dualism says that mind and body are both actual but leaves us in the dark about how they interact, or at least seem to interact. Panexperientialism, which is nondualistic without being reductionistic, is the only doctrine that accounts for all the things we presuppose in practice: that our bodies are real and influence our experience; that our experience is partly self-determining and influences our bodies in return.

A third advantage of panexperientialism is that it is, unlike materialism, truly nondualistic. This point, Hartshorne believes, will eventually lead science and science-oriented philosophy to embrace panexperientialism. The scientific mind, because of its drive to find universal explanatory principles, has a natural aversion to dualism.[12] The scientific community thus far, in overcoming the dualism with which modern thought began, has increasingly gravitated toward materialism. But this form of nondualism will not provide the conceptual unity science seeks, Hartshorne says, because it is really dualism in disguise. Because materialists cannot fail to believe that experiencing things exist, their assertion that nonexperiencing individuals exist means that the universe contains two fundamentally different types of individuals: experiencing and nonexperiencing.[13] This dualism is a "temporalized dualism": in its evolutionary account, it says that mere matter without a trace of experience first existed, and that then experience or mind "emerged."[14] Like other forms of dualism, this temporalized dualism has an unanswerable question. Its form of this question is: "How could mere matter produce life and minds?"[15] Panexperientialist nondualism allows us to avoid this unanswerable question by speaking of "the emergence of species of mind, not of mind as such.''[16]

If the case for panexperientialism is so strong—and there are still more advantages to come—why has it not been the most popular theory? The main reason, Hartshorne believes, is that much of the world as we perceive it does not give any evidence of animation, of having experiences and exercising self-determination. Rocks just stay where they are, unless moved by an external force. They show no sign of having feelings, desires, purposes, and the power for self-motion.[17] The difference between ourselves and a rock appears to be absolute, not merely a difference in degree. Hartshorne has a fourfold reply to this objection. Beyond the prior distinction between knowing something from within or only from without, this answer involves the indistinctness of sensory perception, the difference between aggregates and compound individuals, and the difference between high-grade and low-grade individuals. These four factors account for our idea of ''matter'' as inert, unfeeling stuff. But, Hartshorne adds, thanks to modern science we should now realize that matter in this sense is an illusion.

Ordinary sensory perception, we now know, is indistinct.[18] Even the most precise of our senses, vision, does not give us the true individuals of which the world is comprised. We see a rock, not the billions of molecules of which it is comprised, let alone its atoms and subatomic particles; we see a plant, not the billions of cells of which it is comprised. If we could see individual cells, molecules, atoms, and electrons, we would not think of any of them as inert. The increased distinctness of perception made possible by modern science has in fact shown the inertness of the microscopic world to be an illusion.[19] Scientific experience has hence confirmed what Leibniz suspected, that the unities of sensory perception, such as rocks, plants, and stars, are *pseudo*-unities, produced by blurred perception. By penetrating these pseudo-unities, modern science has undercut the main basis for dualism and materialism.[20] We can think of all the true individuals of nature by analogy with ourselves.

Blurred perception is not the only basis, however, for assuming a dualism between active, experiencing things and inert, insentient things. Leibniz's most important but largely ignored contribution, Hartshorne says, was his distinction between two types of things that can be formed when multitudes of low-grade individuals are joined together: compound individuals and mere aggregates.[21] In a compound individual, such as an animal, there is a level of experience—a mind or soul (called by Leibniz a ''dominant monad'')—which turns the multiplicity into a true individual by giving it a unity of feeling and purpose, so that it can respond as a unified whole to its environment. In mere aggregates, such as a rock, by contrast, no such dominating experience exists. The highest centers of feeling and self-determination are the molecules comprising the rock. Without a dominating center, the various movements cancel out each other, so that the rock as a whole stays put unless pushed or pulled from without. The passivity of the rock is hence a statistical effect.[22] We can thereby understand how panexperiential animism is compatible with the mechanistic approach which works so well for Galilean-Newtonian physics. Animism is true for individuals, while mechanism is true for aggregates of individuals.[23] Quantum physics supports this view, Hartshorne adds, by suggesting that the complete determinism implied by the mechanistic view of nature does not hold true for subatomic events.[24]

In summary: Hartshorne argues that the ordinary distinction between mind and matter is based on four differences: (1) We know our own "mind" or experiences from within; what we call "matter" we know from without. (2) While through introspection (or retrospection) we know an individual, our sensory perception of outer objects hides the true individuals from us. (3) What we call our mind is a true individual; what we typically call matter is a aggregate of millions or billions of individuals devoid of any overall experiential unity. (4) Our mind is a series of very high-grade experiences, with consciousness, self-consciousness, and hence very sophisticated purposes. The individuals constituting matter are very low-grade individuals, with feeling but no consciousness, let alone self-consciousness, and hence very short-range purposes.

The doctrine of the compound individual is one of Hartshorne's great contributions. Although Whitehead had suggested the Leibnizian distinction between aggregates and true individuals, it would be easy to miss it in his writings. Hartshorne has not only explained it time and time again but has also emphasized its importance. He says that, with this distinction, "Leibniz took the single greatest step in the second millennium of philosophy (in East and West) toward a rational analysis of the concept of physical reality."[25] Hartshorne did more, however, than simply draw attention to this distinction. Just as Whitehead improved on Leibniz's idea of the compound individual (by allowing real interaction between the dominant and subservient members of the society), so did Hartshorne improve upon Whitehead's formulation. Whitehead seemed to say that all occasions of experience were spatially tiny. This view made it difficult to understand how the dominant member of a society could directly influence all of its parts, and opened Whitehead to reductionistic interpretations. In Hartshorne's account, the dominant member of a society occupies the entire spatial region of the society, overlapping the regions of the lesser members.[26] Atomic occasions, for example, fill the entire region occupied by the atom, overlapping the regions of the subatomic events. The subatomic members hence live within the atomic experiences. The same principle applies to molecules, macromolecules, and cells. With regard to animals having a central nervous system, Hartshorne suggests that the mind or soul encompasses at least the region of the brain, perhaps that of the entire nervous system.

Another contribution by Hartshorne was to make clearer than Whitehead did that there is a hierarchy of compound individuals. Although which identifiable things are to be designated compound individuals is an empirical question, Hartshorne suggests that at least the following are: atoms, molecules, macromolecules, cells, multi-celled animals, and the universe as a whole. Each higher compound individual embodies lower ones, and contains the universal variables to a higher degree. Among these variables is power—the twofold power to determine oneself and to exert influence on others. Accordingly, power and breadth of experience rise proportionately.[27] Hartshorne thereby shows the relation between the human mind and its body to be simply one more form of a general principle characterizing the world. He thereby also paves the way for understanding God as the soul of the universe and thereby its supreme power.

Hartshorne's position provides, furthermore, an answer different from the two most dominant ones among modern philosophers on the relation between quantum indeterminacy and human freedom. One of these views is that quantum indeterminacy, even if interpreted realistically to mean genuine self-determination in subatomic events, is *irrelevant* for the question of freedom, because indeterminacy is canceled out with large numbers of events; for example, a billiard ball's behavior is perfectly predictable even though that of its electrons is not. This argument assumes that a human being is structurally no different from a billiard ball. The other dominant position is that indeterminacy at the quantum level *accounts* for human freedom. This position assumes that a human being is nothing but a collection of subatomic particles and the relations among them, that we contain no self-determining individuals higher than electrons and protons.

Hartshorne's position is that the world contains a great number of genuine individuals more complex than electrons and having more power of self-determination. The discovery of quantum indeterminacy is important for belief in human freedom primarily by analogy. It supports the idea that true individuals even of the most primitive sort have some degree of freedom.[28]

Having given Hartshorne's response to the major objection against panexperientialism, I return now to his list of its advantages. A fourth advantage is that it makes both *time* and *natural law* intelligible. Both of these concepts have proved unintelligible for dualists and materialists, with their idea of dead matter, meaning matter that neither remembers nor anticipates. We can only conceive the unity of the past, present and future, Hartshorne points out, through memory and anticipation.[29] Panexperientialism says that nature is comprised exhaustively of experiencing events, each of which has memory, however minimal, of a settled past, and anticipation, however short-range, of a partly open future. If an electron, a photon, an atom, a molecule and a living cell are each a temporal society of such events, then time—with its distinctions among past, present, and future, and its irreversibility—is real for such entities. For dualism and materialism, by contrast, the objective temporal order is unintelligible.[30]

The same feature of panexperientialism renders law intelligible, and hence solves the "problem of induction," that is, the problem of why we should believe the present laws of nature will hold true in the future. Materialists and dualists have assumed that the laws of physics will hold true throughout all time, while having no reason why they should hold true tomorrow. According to the Whiteheadian-Hartshornean position, the so-called laws of nature are really its most long-lasting *habits*, the habits of those low-level societies with very little spontaneity with which to diverge from the patterns inherited from the past.[31] Thinking of the laws of nature as habits, and hence as sociological laws, implies that we should not consider them eternal; they have developed in time and can continue to evolve.[32] But we can reasonably believe that the habits of photons, electrons, atoms, molecules, and even macromolecules such as DNA will not change much within the short period of a few thousand years.

A fifth important advantage of panexperientialism is that the natural sciences have been increasingly supporting it, if unintentionally, and thereby increasingly undermining both materialism and dualism. Empirical science by itself cannot prove the true metaphysical position, Hartshorne says, but it can discredit false ones, especially insofar as they are based on an earlier, less precise science.[33] And empirical science can also provide positive support for the true metaphysical position. (In this very important sense, then—to anticipate a later discussion—Hartshorne is an empiricist.) Hartshorne says that, if it is true that the actual world is comprised exclusively of experiencing events, "science will tend more and more to reveal the fact."[34]

Hartshorne provides several examples. (1) He repeatedly cites the fact, mentioned earlier, that physics undermines the view, fundamental to dualism and materialism, that the basic units of nature are inert and fully determined. (2) He also points out that physics now shows nature to be most fundamentally a complex of events, not of enduring substances.[35] (3) By showing that space and time are inseparable, twentieth-century physics also supports the basic principle of Whiteheadian-Hartshornean process philosophy, that everything is related to time.[36] (4) Science has also increasingly confirmed the assertion of panexperientialism that the difference between lifeless matter and primitive life-forms is merely a difference of degree.[37] (5) The idea that low-grade individuals, such as atoms and molecules, may have experience, even though they have no central nervous systems or specialized sensory organs, is also supported by science: physiology has revealed that paramecia can swim although they have neither motor nerves nor muscle cells, and that protozoa can digest without a stomach and can oxygenate without lungs. Accordingly, protozoa, and even molecules and atoms, may be able to feel, and even to perceive, in some lowly way. The fact that they do not have nervous systems only proves that they cannot feel and perceive to the same degree as can organisms with nervous systems. To say that it proves that they cannot feel and perceive at all, as Roger Sperry has, would be to presuppose that psychic variables, such as feeling, perceiving, and desiring, have a quite narrow range, which would be to beg the question.[38] Hartshorne's position is that the psychic variables have an infinite range. I might add that Hartshorne's position, and his prediction that science will increasingly provide evidence for panexperientialism, have recently been supported by evidence that bacteria have memory and make decisions based on it.[39]

As a way into the sixth benefit of panexperientialism, the one that Hartshorne seems to think should be the most important for those who understand the drive of science and philosophy for unification, I must discuss the epistemological side of panexperientialism, which I, following William James, call "radical empiricism."[40] The basic point, in contrast with the superficial empiricism of sensationism, is that sensory perception is not the basic form of perception. That this point follows from panexperientialism is obvious from the fact that individuals without sensory organs are said to perceive. Perception is in fact one of the universal variables, exemplified to some degree in all events. Hartshorne often uses Whitehead's term 'prehension' to refer to this primordial, root form of perception, in which the present experience feels the feelings of previous experiences, thereby taking the previous events as objectified into itself. One meaning of "radical empiricism" is that this nonsensory prehension is at the root of sensory perception. For example, my visual perception of the paper before me presupposes that my soul (my mind, my series of dominant occasions of experience) prehends those brain cells that have received the visual data from the eye. All my other sensory data likewise presuppose my direct prehensive relation to my body, as do my feelings of hunger, pain, and sexual excitement. All direct perception is prehensive.

The other clearest example of prehension is that relation we call *memory*, in which my present experience prehends some of my previous occasions of experience. This is an example of the perception of one actuality by another on the hypothesis that my mind or soul is not a continuous "stream" of experience which is simply the same through time, but is instead a temporal "society" of discrete *occasions* of experience, each of which is a distinct actuality. The hypothesis that the actual world is made up exhaustively of events, in other words, implies that memory is an example of that primordial, nonsensory perception which we share with all other actual beings.

Memory and perception may seem to differ in that memory is prehension of antecedent events whereas perception is of simultaneous events. But—Hartshorne credits Whitehead with being the first clearly to see—perception also is always of antecedent events.[41] This fact is clearest when the perceived object is remote: we know, for example, that the sun that we see is the sun as it was eight minutes ago. But even in the direct prehension of one's bodily parts, the events perceived are in the immediate past of the perceiving event, not absolutely simultaneous with it. Once this idea is accepted, perception and memory can be seen to share the same principle: direct prehension of antecedent events.[42] Looked at from the past to the present, memory and perception are both examples of the cause-effect relation, which is always a temporal relation, from past to present.[43] Given the idea that all unitary events are experiences, these causal relations all involve the sympathetic feelings by a present event of feelings of antecedent events. Through sympathy, the previous feelings are more or less repeated in the present experience, making it more or less similar to the prior ones.

The fact that memory and perception have all been explained in terms of a common principle brings us to Hartshorne's strongest basis for advocating panexperientialism to the scientific and philosophic communities. The drive of both science and philosophy, he holds, is toward conceptual integration.[44] The goal is to explain as many phenomena as possible in terms of the fewest basic categories. Through Whitehead's category of prehension—the nonsensory sympathetic perception of antecedent experiences—we are able to reduce several apparently very different types of relations to one fundamental type of relation. The category of prehension explains not only memory and perception, which seem different enough at first glance, but also temporality, space, causality, enduring individuality (or substance), the mind-body relation, the subject-object relation in general, and the God-world relation.[45]

I have already discussed the temporal relation, the mind-body relation, and "substantiality" or the relation of self-identity through time. The spatial relation is a complication of time; whereas time results from a single line of inheritance, space results from multiple lines of inheritance.[46] Given the notion that the actual world is made up exclusively of events that prehend and then are prehended, it is evident that causality in general is to be understood in the same way as the causal relations between body and mind, and between past and present events of the same mind. The subject-object relation in general is analogous to the relation between present and past in memory: a present event, which is a subject, sympathetically prehends an antecedent event, which is a subject-that-has-become-an-object. (In those subject-object relations that seem to be devoid of sympathy, or virtually so, as in the visual perception of the sun, the "object" is known only in a blurred and very indirect way. In all *direct* prehension by a subject of an object, the sympathetic feeling of feeling is evident.) Finally, the God-world relation, which is to be discussed later, can be understood in terms of God's prehension of the world and the prehension of God by the events comprising the world.

No fewer than *nine* relations, all apparently quite different from each other, have been reduced to *one*![47] Hartshorne calls this result "the most powerful metaphysical generalization ever accomplished," and "a feat comparable to Einstein's."[48] While Hartshorne is speaking primarily of Whitehead here, calling him the "greatest single creator" of this generalization (while recognizing other contributors, such as Buddhists and Bergson),[49] I want to point out that it is Hartshorne who has called attention to this achievement. One could well read through Whitehead's writings several times without realizing that such a powerful generalization had been accomplished. It is also Hartshorne who has called attention to the similarity between this accomplishment and the type of unity that scientific thinking in general seeks. For these reasons, the achievement is one in which Hartshorne shares. Fully recognizing and naming an insight of genius can be as important as the insight itself.

Thus far, I have been explaining the advantages of panexperientialism in terms of philosophic theory, especially in relation to science. I come now to the relation of theory and practice. Can we have a scientific-philosophic theory that is adequate to the notions that are presupposed in the very practice of science and philosophy, and indeed in all human practice whatsoever? The capacity of postmodern panexperientialism to do just this is a seventh advantage. I summarize here seven examples of this capacity that have been given in the foregoing discussion. (1) Panexperientialism makes intelligible the mind-body interaction we all presuppose in practice. (2) Through the distinction between aggregates and true individuals, furthermore, we can understand how the behavior of billiard balls is fully determined by external forces while our own behavior is partly self-determined. (3) Through the idea of a hierarchy of compound individuals, we can understand how we have much more freedom than an electron, an amoeba, or even a chimpanzee. (4) The idea of the priority of nonsensory perception explains how we know that there is an actual world beyond our own experience, even though sensory perception as such provides only sense-data and hence appearances, not actuality. (5) The idea that each moment of experience necessarily prehends the past as settled, hence as past, and anticipates the future as partly still to be determined, hence as future, explains our knowledge that there has been a past and that there will be a future. (6) The idea that our basic way of apprehending reality is nonsensory makes it possible to explain our assumption that we have some knowledge of moral and aesthetic values. (7) The idea that the world given to human experience is comprised of things that embody the same stuff—feelings—that is embodied in human experience itself, including its ideas, explains how our ideas can correspond to things.

An eighth advantage of panexperientialism is that, besides unifying our basic theoretical categories and reconciling philosophical theory with the necessary presuppositions of human practice, it also effects a unification of our various forms of theory. In the first place, it overcomes the bifurcation between the natural and the social sciences. Human beings, on the one hand, are declared to be fully natural, exemplifying the same principles as the rest of nature. All natural things, on the other hand, are said to be social. Reality is, to use Hartshorne's term, "social process."[50] Even the endurance of an individual electron or atom is a social process, in which each event arises out of its social relations to prior events. The idea that the statistical regularities of nature are based on habits means, furthermore, that the basic laws of nature are sociological laws. They are different in degree, not in kind, from the statistical laws applying to human societies. Mechanistic, non-statistical laws apply not to the fundamental processes of nature but only to the derivative processes between aggregates. We need not, therefore, have a dualism between the social and the natural sciences, or seek a unity of the sciences by reducing sociological to natural laws. *Natural laws have already been elevated to sociological laws.*

Besides unifying the physical, biological, and social sciences, panexperientialism provides the basis for unifying epistemology and scientific cosmology with ethics, aesthetics, and philosophy of religion or natural theology.[51] One feature of this unification is that natural science is put on the same footing with these other cultural pursuits. Unlike relativistic postmodernism, however, panexperientialist postmodernism puts the natural sciences on the same cognitive level with ethics, aesthetics and theology *not* by denying that science discovers truth, but by affirming that these other cultural pursuits are also pursuits of *truth*, that they also are *cognitive* enterprises.

Beyond putting our various cultural interests on the same level, panexperientialism allows for a real integration of them. Panexperientialism's key notion, that of sympathetic-creative value experience, most obviously suggests *aesthetic* experience, and Hartshorne indeed speaks of aesthetics as the fundamental discipline.[52] But sympathetic-creative value experience is for Hartshorne equally basic for understanding cosmology and epistemology, as we have seen, and ethics and theology, as we will see. Panexperientialism can thereby help us overcome the increasing intellectual fragmentation of modernity by moving toward a postmodern integration of our various cultural interests. The pluriversity could again become a university, in which courses in physics, biology, psychology, sociology, economics, ethics, and aesthetics would help students achieve an integrated view of themselves and the universe. Or, more radically, a postmodern university might no longer organize its approach to knowledge in terms of the modern disciplinary structure, a structure that presupposes absolute dichotomies between the supernatural and the natural, the animate and the inanimate, the sentient and the insentient, the social and the mechanistic, the human and the natural. Through this reorganization, along with the reunion of academic theory and the presuppositions of practice, the widespread custom of using the word 'academic' as a pejorative term, as in "merely academic," might be overcome.

Theism, panexperientialism, and deep empiricism

Hartshorne is probably best known and most discussed for his ideas about the divine nature and existence. Many of his most important contributions indeed come under this topic. It would be a mistake, however, to assume that his theism is separable from his panexperientialism. He says that most errors about God involve errors about the world, and vice versa.[53] His theism is in fact part and parcel of his panexperientialism, and his panexperientialism is part and parcel of his theism. Each implies the other.

To begin with panexperientialism, and then to see that it implies theism (of a nontraditional sort), was Whitehead's route. In Hartshorne's case, to the extent that any priority can be assigned—he says that one may proceed in either direction—the dominant order seems to be the reverse.[54] He characteristically portrays panexperientialism as an implication of theism, saying that "the idea of God contains implicitly the entire content of metaphysics."[55] He accordingly says: "Theism is not an adjunct to a world view; fully thought out, it is the most coherent of all explicit world views."[56] Hartshorne can even sound like the Vince Lombardi of theism, saying: "The theistic question . . . is not one more question, even the most important one. It is, on the fundamental level, and when all its implications are taken into account, the sole question."[57] Metaphysics can hence be called "the secular approach to theology."[58]

Fully thought out, Hartshorne maintains, theism implies panexperientialism, the philosophy of shared creative experience. If God is mind with infinite capacity, "then the zero of mind would be the zero of reality."[59] If God is infinite creative capacity, "the zero of this capacity which determinism posits must be the zero of the manifestation or presence of God" and hence "the zero of reality itself."[60] If God is infinite love, then "the zero case of love could only be the total absence of deity."[61]

"Theism," he maintains, sounding something like Luther and Barth, "should take its stand and not let itself be dictated to by bits of philosophy which had no origin in religious insight."[62] Regarded as implicitly atheistic are not only the ideas of determinism and insentient matter,[63] but also the idea of "self-identity as mere numerical oneness."[64] Besides making it difficult to understand how such individuals can be in God, this view takes self-identity as an irreducible, ultimate principle, not explainable in terms of spiritual categories.[65] Whitehead's idea that "society is more basic than 'substance,' " that the enduring individual is a temporal society of occasions of experience, each of which sympathizes with the feelings of earlier and later members, allows us to see how "the participation of experiences in other experiences, i.e. 'sympathy' or, in terms of its higher and happier forms, 'love,' " is truly the first principle of reality.[66]

Because (neoclassical) theism implies panexperientialism, Hartshorne can claim for theism all the virtues of panexperientialism recited earlier. The theistic insight that "love, as the relation of sympathy, . . . is the foundation of all other relations"[67] means that panexperientialism's reduction of nine categories to one is equally an achievement of theism. Hartshorne says that theism's insight into the centrality of sympathy and hence into the social structure of experience provides "the key to cosmology and epistemology, as well as ethics and religion."[68] Theism's ability to find "the key to facts and the key to values in a single idea," that of love or participation, Hartshorne hails as "an intellectual achievement than which none could be greater."[69]

Having indicated that for Hartshorne theism can be derived from panexperientialism, or panexperientialism from theism, and that for Hartshorne himself the latter direction may have been the dominant one, I return to the former order, from the world to God, showing how Hartshorne's panexperientialism supports and even implies his form of theism.

From Hartshorne's point of view, a philosophy cannot be consistent unless it is theistic.[70] Before this fact can be clearly seen, however, two major obstacles must be removed. The first of these obstacles is the fact that most people still equate theism with traditional or classical theism, which cannot be made credible. If one thinks of this traditional position as theism, then Hartshorne is an atheist. He fully agrees with the judgment of most modern philosophers that the arguments against the traditional idea of God are "as conclusive as philosophical arguments could well be."[71]

Hartshorne has in fact been one of the twentieth century's major critics of traditional theism, pointing out many ways in which it makes an intelligible, consistent and credible philosophy impossible. I mention six. (1) By asserting that God determines or at least knows the future, the traditional idea of God conflicts with our presuppositions about human freedom and responsibility. (2) By affirming an omnipotent goodness that can determine all details of the world, it conflicts with our presupposition about evil, that is, that not everything that happens is for the best. (3) By combining this idea of omnipotence with an anthropomorphic dualism, according to which only human beings have intrinsic value, supernaturalists developed a view of divine design that was disproved by the facts of evolution.[72] (4) By buttressing this doctrine of omnipotence with a doctrine of creation *ex nihilo*, supernaturalism affirmed the self-contradictory idea of a beginning of time. (5) Traditional theism attributed immutable consciousness to God, although we can think meaningfully of consciousness only as changing. (6) It spoke of God as an impassible being who could not be enriched or pained by anything happening in the world; it thereby contradicted its own injunction to serve God, and our presupposition that our lives have ultimate meaning. One reason Hartshorne is distressed by this traditional idea of God is that it has led, by reaction, to complete atheism.

Modern philosophy became atheistic, however, not only because of problems inherent in traditional theism but also because the modern world view rules out any significant idea of God. I mention four reasons. (1) A reductionism that would not allow the mind to influence the body would certainly not allow downward causation from God to the world, and would have no analogy for this. (2) The mechanistic view of nature allows for no divine influence in the world, because entities that interact only by mechanical impact make influence by a cosmic mind or soul unintelligible. According to the modern cosmology, it is impact, not love, that makes the world go 'round. (3) This mechanistic view also makes it impossible to understand how the world could be in God. (4) The sensationist theory of perception rules out any divine presence in human experience, and hence any direct awareness of God. Accordingly, portraying theism as a viable philosophy requires overcoming not only traditional theism but also the modern world view.

The obstacles to theism created by both theistic supernaturalism and mechanistic naturalism are solved by Hartshorne's postmodern panexperientialism, to which theism is integral. The theism that is integral to this panexperientialism is a naturalistic, not a supernaturalistic, theism.[73] This means that a world of finite events exists necessarily, not through the arbitrary decision of the divine will. The existence of a plurality of finite experiences is as natural as God's own existence. The nature of the relations between God and the world is therefore a natural, necessary feature of reality. The Whiteheadian-Hartshornean position hence says not only that every event has creative power—the power to shape itself in part, and the power to influence future events. It also says that the fact that every event has this twofold creative power is not *simply* a "fact," that is, not simply a contingent feature of *our* world. It is a necessary, natural feature of reality, not an arbitrary decree of the divine will that could have been otherwise and that could be overridden from time to time.

The presence of evil in our world and in every possible world is thereby explained. Evil results from multiple finite freedom, and any world God could have created would have had multiple finite freedom.[74] The possibility of evil is necessary. No particular evils are necessary, but the possibility that evil can occur is necessary. We cannot accuse God of a deficiency in goodness for not interrupting the normal cause-effect relations to prevent particularly horrendous evils. Because the normal cause-effect relations are natural, necessary, given features of reality, they cannot be interrupted. God does influence every event, but divine influence is always persuasion. It could not be unilateral determination.

This position explains not only the possibility of evil in general, Hartshorne points out, but also the possibility of the extreme horrors that human beings have caused and suffered. Freedom and danger necessarily rise proportionately. Because human beings have more freedom than other creatures, they necessarily are more dangerous and more capable of suffering.[75]

Besides explaining evil, this position makes clear that belief in God in no way denies human freedom and human responsibility for the course of human history. We cannot declare that any *status quo* has been sanctioned by divine arrangement, or that God will step in to save us from our foolish ways, such as from nuclear weapons and other ecological threats.

Besides not determining the future, God does not even know the future, beyond those abstract features of the future that are already determined by the present. God's lack of knowledge of the details of the future betokens no divine imperfection. Because all events exercise some self-determining power, the future is simply not knowable, even by omniscience. The partial openness of the future, and our own partial freedom, which we all presuppose in practice, are hence not compromised by this naturalistic theism.

This position also simultaneously overcomes the charge that the idea of God's creation of the world is self-contradictory, and the conflict between creation and evolution. Because there never was a first moment of finite existence, the creation of our world involved a creation not out of nothing but "out of an earlier world and its potentialities for transformation." Divine creative causation, analogously to ours, always involves a transformation of a previous situation. No self-contradictory idea of a beginning of time is therefore implied.[76] Also, because finite events necessarily have their own creative power, divine creative transformation is always persuasion, never unilateral rearrangement. No feature of our world in its present state of evolution is simply a divine product. Darwinian evidence that every species shows signs of "descent with modification" from earlier species is therefore no evidence against a divine creator.

Whereas the ideas about God that I have already mentioned are ones that Hartshorne shared with Whitehead (albeit with different nuances), Hartshorne went considerably beyond Whitehead in seeking to develop a coherent and fully articulate doctrine of God that is consistent with the rest of the system. Whereas Whitehead had evidently thought of God as a single, everlasting actual entity, Hartshorne conceives of God by analogy with the human soul, and hence as a temporal society of occasions of experience. Whitehead had said that God should be the chief exemplification of metaphysical principles, not an exception to them.[77] In speaking of God as a single actual entity interacting with the world, he seemed to violate this ideal, because the denial that contemporary actual entities can interact seems to be a metaphysical principle. The idea of an actual entity that "remains numerically one amidst the changes of accidental relations and of accidental qualities" is clearly called a *metaphysical error* by Whitehead,[78] and yet that description seems to fit his idea of God. Hartshorne's reconception of God overcomes this problem of coherence. God is no longer an everlasting actual entity with changing relations, but an everlasting series of divine occasions of experience; and these divine occasions of experience do not prehend contemporary occasions but immediately past ones.

This reconception also involves a revision of the doctrine of divine dipolarity. Traditional theism was, to use Hartshorne's term, monopolar. The idea that God was unchanging in some respects therefore meant that God was unchanging in all respects. This created the two problems mentioned earlier: How could an unchanging consciousness know a changing world, and how could a changing world, including our lives, contribute anything to changeless perfection? Some modern thought has been monopolar in the opposite way, saying that all is flux. At least some representatives of relativistic postmodern philosophy, which denies any unchanging principles to which all thought must conform to be adequate, portray it as a despiritualized version of Hegel's monopolar theology.[79]

Hartshorne credits Whitehead with being the first philosopher to suggest clearly that God has two natures or poles, the one changing, the other unchanging.[80] In Whitehead's version, the dipolarity of God is analogous to the bipolarity of an actual entity, that is, to its physical and mental poles. Followers of Whitehead disagree as to whether problems created by this analogy are intolerable. In any case, Hartshorne avoids these problems by making the divine dipolarity analogous to the abstract characteristics and the concrete states of a human soul. God's omniscience is an abstract feature that belongs to every divine occasion of experience; it is the unchanging feature of knowing everything that is knowable at the time. God's concrete knowing, by contrast, changes in each moment, because there are always new things to be known. While the abstract pole or nature of God is absolutely unchanging, the concrete pole is constantly changing. A similar distinction can be made for other characteristics, such as love. God's love as the abstract characteristic of loving all creatures that exist is unchanging, whereas God's concrete loving changes in each moment, because new creatures with new experiences are constantly arising. Thanks to this distinction between the two poles of God's experience, the incoherencies of traditional theism can be overcome. We can understand how God can know a changing world while having an unchanging nature. We can understand how God's experience can be enriched and therefore served by our lives even though God's character is beyond improvement.

Besides overcoming the many problems inherent in traditional theism, the panexperientialist position overcomes the distinctively modern reasons for believing divine presence in the world to be unintelligible and unnecessary. The doctrine of compound individuals, as I mentioned earlier, is generalized to the universe as a whole, with God as the soul of the universe. The general doctrine of compound individuals, in which causation runs downward as well as upward, makes downward causation from the soul of the universe to its various members an exemplification of general principles, not an exception to them. The idea that all individuals experience, and that all causation between individuals involves the sympathetic feeling of feelings, shows how God can influence the world and how the world can influence and be in God. The idea that human perception in particular is fundamentally nonsensory shows how we can have direct awareness of God's reality. The idea that power rises proportionately with breadth of experience and mentality makes it natural to think of the soul of the world as its most powerful member.[81]

Besides showing belief in God to be intelligible, panexperientialism shows it to be necessary. The idea that the actual world is comprised exhaustively of partially *free* experiences makes it clear that the order of the world can be made intelligible only through the idea of an all-inclusive soul, whose purposes order the world through becoming internalized by the creatures, somewhat as our purposes order our bodies through becoming internalized by our bodily members.[82]

The remainder of Hartshorne's arguments for the existence of God do not follow from his panexperientialism as such. These arguments do presuppose panexperientialism's demonstration that it is possible to formulate an idea of God that is self-consistent and consistent with our knowledge of ourselves and the world in general. But most of the other arguments (the ontological argument is here excluded) consist of showing that belief in God is implicit in our experience, in the sense of being "required for the interpretation of some fundamental aspect of life or experience."[83] These arguments are therefore, in a sense, empirical arguments. Because this claim is controversial, I need to defend it before coming to these arguments.

Hartshorne is often considered to be a rationalist as opposed to an empiricist. And this characterization has strong support in Hartshorne's writings. He makes a strong distinction between science, which must use the empirical method, and metaphysics, whose method should be nonempirical or *a priori*. Metaphysical or necessary truths, such as the existence of God, are to be discovered *a priori*, through an analysis of meanings.[84]

This distinction should not lead us to conclude, however, that for Hartshorne philosophy is not based on experience. In the first place, metaphysics is only one part of philosophy as a whole, which involves a synthesis of metaphysics and the special sciences.[85] In the second place, even the metaphysical part of his philosophy is based on experience. As we saw earlier, Hartshorne argues in many ways that recent science supports panexperientialism against dualism and materialism. He also says that he first came to hold panexperientialism through the recognition that nature as immediately given is essentially feeling.[86] He furthermore endorses "the whole drive of modern philosophy to relate concepts to perceptions" and endorses the empiricist principle that all meaningful ideas are derived from experience and refer to experience.[87] The empiricism he endorses, of course, is a *radical empiricism*, in which nonsensory perception is fundamental. So understood, "the principle of empiricism" is the "basis of intellectual integrity."[88] Unlike some empiricists, Hartshorne does not deny that direct perceptual experience can and must be transcended, but he insists that it should be transcended only by imaginative experience, and then only in accordance with principles given in perception.[89]

When Hartshorne calls metaphysics nonempirical, he is using 'empirical' in a narrower sense. In this narrower sense, an empirical fact is a state of affairs that might not have been. Karl Popper's criterion is used: an empirical truth is one that could in principle be falsified by conflicting with a conceivable observation.[90] Metaphysics is not empirical in this sense because the truths it seeks are necessary truths. Because necessary or metaphysical truths must be illustrated by every experience, no conceivable observation could conflict with them. A different method must therefore be used to discover them. Having accepted the narrow, Popperian definition of 'empirical,' Hartshorne uses the term '*a priori*' for the method appropriate to metaphysics.

Whether or not it was wise to refer to metaphysics as *a priori* and nonempirical,[91] Hartshorne has clearly stated that metaphysics is not unrelated to experience. To call metaphysical concepts *a priori* means they are prior not to all experience but only to particular, contingent aspects of experience. They are based instead on the strictly general traits of experience.[92] Because they are illustrated in any experience whatsoever, they need not be sought through special experiments or in special places; they can in principle be derived by reflection upon any experience.[93] Hartshorne has stated that he, at the age of seventeen, decided to "trust reason to the end."[94] He could equally well say that his method involves the decision to trust experience to the end, or, better, in its depths. The basic task of philosophical theology, says Hartshorne, is to discover, through cooperation, "what the bottom layer of our common human thought really is."[95] Instead of *a priori* and nonempirical, this approach could well be called "deep empiricism," because it seeks those universal features at the depths of every experience, beneath the fleeting superficialities.

Hartshorne points out that the ingredients of this bottom layer can be compared with what John Locke called "innate ideas."[96] A crucial difference is that for Hartshorne these ideas are not the result of a supernatural implantation at the time of the soul's creation but are directly perceived or intuited by the soul at each moment. By rejecting Locke's restriction of perception to sense-perception, Hartshorne's postmodern philosophy can give a naturalistic explanation of these universal ideas. Relativistic postmodernism, by contrast, which denies that there is any deep layer common to all people, follows from retaining Locke's sensationism while rejecting his supernaturalism. Richard Rorty, for example, claims that all the "intuitions" we have are due to tradition and education, so that "there is nothing deep down inside us except what we have put there ourselves."[97] In other words, all of our apparently deep ideas are culturally conditioned. By affirming nonsensory perception as fundamental, Hartshorne's postmodern philosophy rejects supernaturalism without falling into relativism. Through our nonsensory apprehension we all share a common set of beliefs. These beliefs, in their preconceptual form, can be called knowledge, because they consist in direct apprehensions of those universal features of reality which are always present to experience.[98]

The task of metaphysics is hence simply to formulate explicitly and thereby to make us more conscious of what we all already know in an implicit, preconscious way.[99]

That everyone knows or believes in the universal truths becomes evident in their action, which is the ultimate expression of what we most deeply believe.[100] We can verbally espouse a doctrine that contradicts one of these deep truths, but we cannot live in terms of such a doctrine. For example, we all know, down deep, that the future is partly open, that it is only relatively, not absolutely, determined. Everyone, including the philosopher who professes to be a determinist, is "busily engaged in trying to decide what the future is to be as though it were *not* yet wholly fixed."[101] Even animals reveal by their behavior that they know merely relative determinism to be true.[102] With the pragmatists, Hartshorne says that, if a doctrine cannot be lived, it cannot be true, and no one *really* believes it.[103]

Hartshorne puts belief in God in the same class. If God as the all-inclusive soul of the universe exists, then God, being ubiquitous, must be "present in the experience of the most hardened skeptic or sinner."[104] The reality of God can therefore be denied only by contradicting consciously what is intended "in some underlying stratum of affirmation."[105] Hartshorne claims, for example, that all people know, "and at some point betray that they know, that the object of our total allegiance is God."[106] The difference between believers and unbelievers is therefore "nothing but a difference in self-consciousness and consistency in regard to what all believe 'at heart.' "[107] "The real argument for God," Hartshorne says, "is just that every view which tries to deny him also denies . . . some practically indispensable belief."[108]

Among these beliefs that are indispensable in practice are the beliefs in the reality of truth, the past, an inclusive ideal, and an ultimate meaning to our lives. Apart from an all-inclusive perspective, there is no locus for that complete truth whose existence is presupposed every time we criticize an inadequate perspective on reality.[109] Apart from a cosmic memory, there is no conceivable locus for truths about the past, yet historians and the rest of us constantly presuppose that assertions about the past can be true or false.[110] Apart from belief in a cosmic ideal and evaluation, we cannot account for our common conviction that there is a standard of importance and value in terms of which to criticize inadequate human desires.[111] Without belief in a cosmic and permanent receiver of value-experiences, we cannot make sense of the idea, which we all presuppose at some level, that our experiences and decisions have an ultimate meaning.[112]

Hartshorne also states his basic argument in terms of the meanings implicit in our categorical terms. Good is that "which is good in the eyes of God."[113] Truth is "conformity to what is experienced by an omnipresent 'observer.' " The past is "what unlimited or cosmic memory can never forget." Reality is "that which God knows."[114] We find God "in our fundamental meanings," Hartshorne says. Theism is hence simply "the elucidation of the full bearings of unavoidable word uses, categorical meanings . . . ."[115]

We presuppose all these ideas, Hartshorne maintains, because God not only exists necessarily but is also necessarily present in our awareness, at some level.[116] Theism is, accordingly, implicitly present in our basic beliefs and meanings. A philosophy that denies theism necessarily denies at the explicit level various beliefs that it is implicitly presupposing. An atheistic philosophy therefore can never be consistent.

The continued association of the word 'God' with the classical idea of God should not lead us to misunderstand Hartshorne's argument here. He is not saying that all people down deep believe in the God of Augustine, Thomas, or Calvin. He in fact is saying that the presuppositions of our practice show that no one really believes in this idea of God. No one can really live in terms of a doctrine of divine providence that says that all events are determined, or that everything that happens is for the best.[117] Our presupposition that what we creatures decide and experience makes some ultimate difference, furthermore, is contradicted by classical theism's doctrines of divine impassibility and immutable perfection, which say that our lives make no difference to God, the ultimate standard of truth and value. At the bottom layer of our experience, which is expressed willy-nilly in our actions, we do not believe in that God. Hartshorne means his own doctrine of God to be an explication of the God in which we all *do* at least implicitly believe.[118]

I conclude by looking briefly at some of Hartshorne's reasons for thinking that metaphysics, including metaphysical theology, has practical importance.

The practical importance of explicit metaphysical beliefs

It might be asked: If all people believe in God and the other metaphysical truths down deep, and if we all necessarily feel, think, and act in terms of this deep belief regardless of our conscious, explicit beliefs, what difference does it make what we consciously believe? Of what value is metaphysics, including philosophical theology?

We need metaphysics, in the first place, Hartshorne says, to attain integrity. We live in terms of two levels—our conscious, conceptualized beliefs as well as our deep, preconceptual beliefs. As long as there is serious tension between these two levels, we will never attain consistency and sincerity.[119]

This integrity, besides being valuable for its own sake, is important for our behavior. If our conscious symbols are inadequate to our deep beliefs, Hartshorne says, our behavior will eventually deteriorate.[120] The affirmation of atheism, nihilism, absolute determinism, absolute relativism, or absolute selfishness is self-contradictory, and cannot therefore be fully meant and lived; but it can nevertheless be very destructive.[121] Contrary to Richard Rorty's hope, the conscious affirmation of such negative doctrines cannot remain "merely philosophical";[122] it will have an effect on our behavior.

To take the example of selfishness: Hartshorne believes that a "kind of 'altruism' is the universal principle," and that all people " 'in their hearts' know that they are 'members one of another,' and do not live for themselves alone, or even essentially."[123] Absolute selfishness is therefore impossible. Absolute *un*selfishness is equally impossible for finite beings: it is given that we are all relatively selfish, necessarily caring more for ourselves and our intimates than for people in general and for all sentient beings. What is *not* given is the degree of our relative selfishness. The idea that a person is an enduring substance, which would mean that our relations to our own past and future would be absolutely different in kind from our relations to other people, makes it seem metaphysically impossible that we could in principle love our neighbors *as ourselves*. The substance-idea of identity has in fact promoted a self-interest doctrine of motivation, according to which we cannot really care at all about anyone except ourselves. If we accept this doctrine, our relative selfishness will tend to become as close to absolute selfishness as possible.

The insight that the enduring self is really a temporal society, comprised of a series of events, shows that our identification with our past is already an example of sympathy, and that our concern for our future welfare is already a form of altruism. It also shows that our relations to our own past and future are not different in kind from our relations to other people. This insight shows that we really can, in principle, love other people in the same way as we love ourselves.[124] This implication of panexperientialism is so important to Hartshorne that he says: "On this ground alone I would not give up the event doctrine without the most rigorous proofs of its erroneousness."[125]

With regard to belief in God, Hartshorne offers many ways in which conscious belief in the God of his metaphysics can have practical importance for our lives. I will mention four.

First, by explicitly recognizing that God's perfect power does not and cannot eliminate, control, or occasionally override the power of the creatures, we can retain faith in the basic goodness of life in the face of its inevitable tragedies.[126] Second, explicit belief in God will encourage us to imitate God—both God's sympathy for all feelings and desires, and God's creativity, in which the creation of new values is combined with respect for old ones.[127] The vision of God will also lead us to aspire to approximate that unity of love with knowledge and power that God alone embodies.[128] Third, theism "implies that love is the supreme good, not pleasure or knowledge or power, and those who think otherwise will be disappointed.''[129] Fourth, explicit belief in God provides an answer to the final question of human life: What is its ultimate meaning, what should be our central aim? "Be the aim Nirvana, the Classless Society, the Welfare State, Self-realization,'' Hartshorne says, "the query is never silenced, what good is it, from the cosmic and everlasting perspective, that one or the other or all of these aims be attained for a time on this ball of rock?''[130] Belief in God, as the One in whom we all live and who cherishes all good things everlastingly, provides an infinite aim for life—to contribute to the divine life. And this infinite aim strengthens rather than weakens our commitment to finite aims. I close with a statement from Hartshorne in which he seems to state in these terms the central motivation of his own life, a life that has produced close to twenty books and four hundred and fifty articles. In a gloss on the idea that all of one's life should be a "reasonable, holy, and living sacrifice'' to deity, Hartshorne says, "if I can inspire multitudes who will never see me in the flesh, then the incense I send up to God will continue to rise anew for many generations.''[131]

NOTES

1. Kenneth Baynes, James Bohman, and Thomas McCarthy, eds., *After Philosophy: End or Transformation?* (Cambridge: MIT Press, 1987); James Edwards, *Ethics Without Philosophy* (Gainesville: University Press of Florida, 1985).
2. Richard Rorty, *Consequences of Pragmatism* (Minneapolis: University of Minnesota Press, 1982), 86-87, 165, 194.
3. Ibid. xvii, xxv, xxvi, 192.
4. Charles Hartshorne, *Beyond Humanism: Essays in the Philosophy of Nature* (Lincoln: University of Nebraska Press, 1968), 86-87, 216, 226, 267-68 (henceforth BH); "Physics and Psychics: The Place of Mind in Nature,'' John B. Cobb, Jr., and David Ray Griffin, ed., *Mind in Nature: Essays on the Interface of Science and Philosophy* (Washington, D.C.: University Press of America, 1977), 89-96 (henceforth P&P).
5. BH 120.
6. BH 116-17.
7. Hartshorne at one time used the term 'panpsychism,' but later switched to 'psychicalism' (cf. BH passim and P & P 91). I have explained my reasons for eschewing both of those terms in favor of 'panexperientialism' at greater length in Cobb and Griffin, ed., *Mind in Nature*, 97-98.
8. P&P 90.
9. P&P 90; *The Logic of Perfection and Other Essays in Neoclassical Metaphysics* (Lasalle, Ill.: Open Court, 1962), 183-84 (henceforth LP).
10. BH 202, 266; LP 225; P&P 90.
11. LP 229.
12. P&P 90; *Creative Synthesis and Philosophic Method* (London: SCM Press, 1970; Lanham, Md.: University Press of America, 1983), 9 (henceforth CSPM).

13. CSPM 9, 27.
14. *Omnipotence and other Theological Mistakes* (Albany: State University of New York Press, 1984), 83-84 (henceforth OOTM).
15. P&P 92.
16. LP 125.
17. P&P 91; "Why Psychicalism? Comments on Keeling's and Shepherd's Criticisms," *Process Studies* 6/1 (Spring, 1976), 67-72, esp. 67.
18. BH 199, 304, 314.
19. LP xii; *Reality as Social Process: Studies in Metaphysics and Religion* (Glencoe, Ill.: The Free Press, 1953), 33 (henceforth RSP).
20. BH 199, 314.
21. CSPM 90; LP 213; P&P 95.
22. *Man's Vision of God and the Logic of Theism* (1941; Hamden, Conn.: 1964), xvi (henceforth MVG).
23. BH 70, 315.
24. LP 224; CSPM 203: BH 143, 144.
25. P&P 95; see also CSPM 90.
26. For a reductionistic interpretation of Whitehead, see Ivor Leclerc, *The Nature of Physical Existence* (London: George Allen & Unwin, 1972), and "Some Main Philosophical Issues Involved in Contemporary Scientific Thought," Cobb and Griffin, ed., *Mind in Nature*, 101-08. For a nonreductionistic interpretation, see David Ray Griffin, "Whitehead's Philosophy and Some General Notions of Physics and Biology," ibid. 122-34. For Hartshorne's view, see "The Compound Individual," Otis H. Lee, ed., *Philosophical Essays for Alfred North Whitehead* (New York: Longmans Green, 1936), 193-220. For a discussion of Leclerc's interpretation of Whitehead, and of Hartshorne's advance beyond Whitehead, see John B. Cobb, Jr., "Overcoming Reductionism," Cobb and Franklin I. Gamwell, ed., *Existence and Actuality: Conversations with Charles Hartshorne* (Chicago: University of Chicago Press, 1984), 149-63.
27. BH 208; OOTM 60.
28. LP 224; BH 146.
29. BH 174, 181-82, 234.
30. RSP 74; BH 138, 174, 181-82, 202, 234.
31. In a lecture delivered in 1934, Whitehead referred to "the general physical laws of inorganic nature" as "those widespread habits of nature" which "exist as average, regulative conditions because the majority of actualities are swaying each other to modes of interconnection exemplifying those laws" (*Modes of Thought* [New York: The Free Press, 1968], 154-55). In 1937, Hartshorne wrote: "But the 'laws of nature' are only the habits of the species of which nature is composed. Physics investigates the behavior of the most universally distributed species—electrons, photons, atoms, molecules, crystals. The laws of physics are the behavior patterns, the habits of these species, no more and no less" (BH 139, see also 138, 163). Rupert Sheldrake has recently emphasized this idea ("The Laws of Nature as Habits: A Postmodern Basis for Science," *The Reënchantment of Science: Postmodern Proposals*, David Ray Griffin, ed. [Albany: State University of New York Press, 1988], 79-86). Sheldrake correctly credits C.S. Peirce with suggesting this idea a century ago (80). It is interesting to note that the only passages I found in which Hartshorne uses the

language of "habits" for the laws of nature were in *Beyond Humanism*, which was published early in his career when the influence of Peirce on him was quite fresh, and which was in fact dedicated to Peirce. This side of Hartshorne's thought seems to be in some tension with his more well-known doctrine that laws of nature are imposed through divine persuasion, a doctrine which has led to the criticism that the divine persuasion in this case is really coercive imposition (Barry L. Whitney, "Process Theism: Does a Persuasive God Coerce?" *Southern Journal of Philosophy* **17** [1979], 133-43, esp. 137-39, and *Evil and the Process God* [New York and Toronto: Edwin Mellen Press, 1985], 100-11). Had Hartshorne continued to speak of the laws of nature as the habits of its various species, this criticism might have been avoided. These habits could be portrayed as the joint product of divine and creaturely causation, which seemed to be Whitehead's position (see his passage about habits, cited above, and his description in *Adventures of Ideas* [1933; New York: The Free Press, 1967] of his position on the laws of nature as intermediate between the doctrines of pure immanence and pure imposition [111-15, 129-30]). Sheldrake's idea of morphic causation provides a possible way of assigning a larger role to creaturely causation in explaining how the habits become so pervasive.

32. BH 139.
33. BH 142, 292, 293.
34. BH 260.
35. LP 218; CSPM 187, 189.
36. BH 257.
37. P&P 92.
38. RSP 54; BH 201; see Roger Sperry, *Science and Moral Priority: Merging Mind, Brain, and Human Values* (New York: Columbia University Press, 1983), 20-21, 70.
39. A. Goldbeter and D. E. Koshland, Jr., "Simple Molecular Model for Sensing and Adaptation Based on Receptor Modification with Application to Bacterial Chemotaxis," *Journal of Molecular Biology* **161/3** (1982), 395-416; Julius Adler and Wing-Wai Tse, "Decision-Making in Bacteria," *Science* **184** (June 21, 1974), 1292-94.
40. The term 'radical empiricism' has various meanings, even within William James' own writings. Given some of those meanings, Hartshorne would emphatically *not* be a radical empiricist. I am using the term only in reference to the doctrine of the priority of nonsensory perception, which allows other actualities, causal relations, and values to be directly perceived.
41. CSPM 92, 107; "Ideas and Theses of Process Philosophers," Lewis S. Ford, ed., *Two Process Philosophers: Hartshorne's Encounter with Whitehead* (Tallahassee, Fl.: American Academy of Religion, 1973), 100-03, esp. 102.
42. CSPM 91-92.
43. CSPM 107.
44. CSPM 9.
45. BH 195; CSPM 92, 107; RSP 74-75; LP 129.
46. CSPM 218-19.
47. BH 192.
48. CSPM 107, 92.

49. CSPM 107.
50. See *Reality as Social Process.*
51. CS xviii; P&P 92.
52. CSPM 303-21.
53. LP xiii, 138-39, 144.
54. Besides CSPM 40-41, see xvii, where Hartshorne says that the firmest residuum from his early pious if liberal Christian outlook "is summed up in the phrase *Deus est caritas*, together with the two 'Great Commandments': total love for God, and love for neighbor comparable to love for self. . . . If there are central intuitive convictions back of my acceptance or rejection of philosophical doctrines, these may be the ones." His "natural theology" should therefore probably be called "a Christian natural theology" in John Cobb's sense of this term as explained in the final chapter of *A Christian Natural Theology: Based on the Thought of Alfred North Whitehead* (Philadelphia: Westminster Press, 1965).
55. CSPM 55; see also 44.
56. LP 126.
57. LP 131.
58. CSPM 24, 28.
59. LP 123.
60. LP 126.
61. LP 126.
62. LP 122.
63. LP 122-23, 143; OOTM 62-63.
64. LP 120.
65. LP 120-21.
66. CSPM xvii-xviii.
67. BH 26.
68. LP xviii.
69. LP 129.
70. BH 86-87.
71. MVG 58.
72. LP 205; P&P 94. Given Hartshorne's distinction between metaphysical and empirical (in the narrow sense) issues, which is discussed later, one must be careful in saying that Hartshorne believes the traditional doctrine of God to have been disproved by the "facts" of evil and evolution. Hartshorne insists that contingent facts could not disprove a God-idea that was not already inherently incoherent, even apart from these facts (LP 157; CSPM 19-22, 292). What is inconsistent with traditional theism is not simply the great amount of evil in our world, and some of the details of the evolutionary process, but the very reality of processes not controllable by a supreme agent. The reality of creaturely creativity or freedom is not simply a contingent fact about our particular world but a necessary feature of any world. Particular evils and particular facts about the evolutionary process may be important in focusing our attention on the incompatibility of traditional theism and the nature of the world, but the proper lesson to be drawn, Hartshorne says, is that the traditional idea of God, including God's relation to the world, is an incoherent idea.
73. See LP xiii: "a Neoclassical Theism belongs in a Neoclassical Metaphysics." Hartshorne had at one time used the term 'naturalistic theism' (BH 25, 56, 253,

263). But he later gave it up, conceding the term 'naturalism' to the ontological doctrine that all knowledge is empirically testable, in the narrow sense of 'empirical' defined in the text below. In relation to naturalism thus understood, he has said, "I am an unabashed supernaturalist" (BH viii, which is in the Preface written for the 1968 edition). In terms of the meaning I am giving to the contrast between naturalistic and supernaturalistic theism, however, Hartshorne is unabashedly a naturalistic theist. As he points out, his theism is "about equally distinct from the old naturalism and the old supernaturalism" (RSP 23).

74. OOTM 15, 21; LP 209; CSPM 237-38; MVG xvi, 14, 30-31, 36, 89.
75. CSPM 13-14; RSP 107; LP 13-14; *The Divine Relativity: A Social Conception of God* (1948; New Haven: Yale University Press, 1964), 136; *Whitehead's Philosophy: Selected Essays, 1935-1970* (Lincoln: University of Nebraska Press, 1972), 93-94; *A Natural Theology for our Time* (Lasalle, Ill.: Open Court, 1967), 81-82.
76. MVG 230, 231, 233.
77. Alfred North Whitehead, *Process and Reality*, corrected edition, David Ray Griffin and Donald W. Sherburne, ed. (New York: The Free Press, 1978), 343.
78. Ibid., 79.
79. Richard Rorty, "Postmodernist Bourgeois Liberalism," *Journal of Philosophy* **80** (1983), 583-89.
80. "Ideas and Theses of Process Philosophers," 102.
81. BH 209, 308; LP 120.
82. LP 157, 285; CSPM 284-85; BH 285.
83. CSPM 280. Hartshorne points out in this passage that the ontological argument does not share this feature of the remainder of his arguments. I do not deal with it in this essay, in spite of the fact that it has been extremely important to Hartshorne, partly because of this difference, partly because its discussion would require too much space, and partly because I have never found it convincing. (It seems to me to prove only that *something* exists necessarily, not also that this something has other divine attributes, such as perfect love, knowledge, and power.)
84. CSPM 29-31, 85; LP ix, 157; MVG 62.
85. MVG 72.
86. BH 233; RSP 19; CSPM 76; "Why Psychicalism?" 67; George Wolf, "The Place of the Brain in an Ocean of Feeling," Cobb and Gamwell, ed., *Existence and Actuality*, 167-84, esp. 167.
87. BH 229; MVG 79, 86; RSP 44; BH 135.
88. BH 321. On Hartshorne as a "radical empiricist," see note 40 above.
89. BH 231, 229.
90. LP 150, 208; CSPM 215, 278.
91. It seems to me that Hartshorne's decision to refer to his method as "*a priori*" and "nonempirical" was unfortunate. No matter how many times he or his commentators may explain that these terms do not mean "prior to all experience" and/or "deductive," these connotations seem to be inevitably suggested. For example, most of Eric von der Luft's review of Donald Wayne Viney's book, *Charles Hartshorne and the Existence of God* (Albany: State University of New York Press, 1985) (*Process Studies* **15**/3 [Fall, 1986], 207-12), is devoted to demonstrating that Hartshorne's arguments for God's existence are inductive

arguments, from which it is concluded that they are not, in spite of claims of Viney and Hartshorne to the contrary, really *a priori* or nonempirical arguments. Neither Viney's discussion of what Hartshorne means by nonempirical, nor Hartshorne's statement in the Foreward of his "preference for not giving the arguments a deductive form" could forestall the assumption that *a priori* and nonempirical *mean* deductive.

92. MVG 29, 63; BH 263.
93. CSPM 31, 93, 284-85.
94. LP viii. In stressing that Hartshorne is a "deep empiricist," I am not denying that he is a rationalist. I am only pointing out that his rationalism is based on this deep empiricism, which seeks to bring to consciousness and to formulate all the elements comprising the bottom layer of experience which are always presupposed in practice. Hartshorne in fact describes his rationalism as one that has learned from empiricism (LP viii). Whitehead's view of rationalism, according to which it is the "search for the coherence of the presuppositions of civilized living," is endorsed by Hartshorne (LP viii; CSPM xvi). Hartshorne makes the same point by characterizing philosophy at its best as "an agonizing struggle for balanced definiteness" (CSPM 93). Animals are said to have the deep truths in a balanced way, but vaguely, whereas any bright person will become definite about such truths, but in a one-sided way. The reason to have a philosophic profession is to struggle for "the sharp vision of the whole truth" (idem.).
95. MVG 80.
96. CSPM 31.
97. Richard Rorty, *Consequences of Pragmatism*, xxix, xxx, xlii.
98. BH 274. Hartshorne distinguishes between our intuitions as such and the verbalization of them, stressing that the latter is an art and a very fallible one (CSPM xvi, 31-32).
99. BH 274; MVG 152.
100. MVG 79.
101. BH 137; see also BH 157, CSPM 204.
102. CSPM 93.
103. CSPM xvi, 291.
104. MVG 79; see also BH 86-87.
105. MVG 80.
106. BH 37.
107. MVG 79.
108. BH 164.
109. LP 152; CSPM 286-88.
110. LP 152; OOTM 33-34; CSPM 287.
111. MVG 59; BH 89, 103, 261; LP 292; CSPM 286-88.
112. BH 13-16; OOTM 15; LP 286.
113. LP 257.
114. LP 153.
115. LP 153.
116. BH 37, 86-87; MVG 80.
117. LP 12; OOTM 19, 25.
118. Hartshorne says that "each of the arguments points not simply to the theistic conclusion, but to the neo-classical form of the conclusion" (LP 296).

119. MVG 80-81.
120. BH 72.
121. LP 12, 189.
122. Rorty, "Postmodernist Bourgeois Liberalism," 588-89.
123. LP 18, 16.
124. CSPM 191; LP 16-18.
125. CSPM 198.
126. LP 11-14.
127. BH 316; MVG 116, 229.
128. BH 208-09.
129. BH 256.
130. LP 132.
131. LP 257-58.

From Modal Language to Model Language: Charles Hartshorne and Linguistic Analysis

J. Van der Veken

"Redefining God"[1] has always been Charles Hartshorne's main concern. According to Hartshorne, to understand the *meaning* of God—as necessary being—is to establish God's existence. This is a consequence of the all-important thesis of the "modal existence" of God, according to which his existence is not a matter of fact, but a matter of logical necessity (or impossibility): the very possibility, or meaningfulness, of God entails his existence. Since Hartshorne places so much stress upon meaning, it is amazing that there has been no sustained dialogue between those who sympathize with his ideas and the proponents of that other philosophical tradition that has devoted so much attention to the problem of meaning, namely, Anglo-Saxon linguistic analysis—especially as applied to religious language.

It seems to me that a dialogue between the proponents of Hartshorne's panentheistic metaphysics and the proponents of the analysis of religious language—such as Ian T. Ramsey, John Wisdom, and Ludwig Wittgenstein—would prove most fruitful for both parties. As far as the *modal* status of God-language is concerned, Hartshorne is on the right track. On the other hand, much of what, for Hartshorne, are "theological mistakes" can be better understood if they are seen as *model* or evocative, expressions. I would like to show that if Hartshornean metaphysics can be combined with an understanding of the idiosyncrasy of religious language, as suggested by Wittgenstein and elaborated by Ramsey, then a most beautiful and irenic philosophy of religion would result. It must be admitted, however, that Hartshorne's redefinition of God is far more radical than he himself suggests in labeling his metaphysics "neoclassical." In fact, Hartshorne's God is closer to the "Absolute" of Idealistic philosophy than to the God of classical theism. As such, his affirmation of God escapes the logical positivist's critique of religious propositions (the criticism that existence is not a predicate; that the existence of God cannot be verified, etc.). On the other hand, an insight into the way religious propositions in fact "function" should mitigate Hartshorne's criticism of traditional theism.

Wittgenstein has shown that we are often "bewitched" by ordinary language: "*Behexung durch die Sprache*." One striking case is our deeply rooted way of asking the God-question as "Does God exist?" It *seems* to be a most natural way of posing the question, and yet, when taken literally, it is wholly wrong. Wisdom's famous parable[2] seems to pose the question in the same way: "Yes or no, is there a gardener (God)?" As we shall see, however, to ask the question in this way is to entirely miss the point of the parable.

I

What is wrong with the question "Does God exist?"? I see three fallacies:

1. The "fallacy of the proper name." The question "Does God exist?" seems to ask about the existence or nonexistence of an entity—like a unicorn—of which we know already what it would be like if it did exist, and hence about which we could answer the question of its existence if only we could come into contact with it. For many persons, God is such an entity—a person—whose proper name is 'God' (or 'Yahweh' or 'Allah,' etc.). R. Collingwood has pointed out the fallacy of the proper name by talking about "un certain nommé Dieu."

2. The "fallacy of factual existence." The question also suggests that a negative answer is possible. One need not be a fool to say "No, there is no God." The discussion between Wisdom's two explorers seems to be formulated in precisely these terms: "is there or is there not a gardener." But if the God-question is a question about meaning, or logical possibility, then it is completely misconstrued by turning it into a factual question. Hartshorne's main concern is to combat this way of asking the God-question.

3. The "fallacy of one among many." Hartshorne famously redefines God as "the One Who is Worshipped."[3] "The One" is an expression deeply rooted in the monotheistic tradition. However it can be readily misunderstood to mean that there is only one God (and *we* are happy to know his *proper name*), but many realities "outside" of him. The language of divine transcendence encourages the idea that God is "above" all other realities. For this reason Hartshorne makes it clear that there is only one Reality and that only inclusive Wholeness can be the referent of absolute devotion.

The fallacy of the proper name can be avoided by redefining 'God' very much in the same way as Hartshorne has done it so successfully. We should not just say that "God is worshipful," but that "only that which is worthy of complete devotion may be called God." All else are idols. As a religious term, however, 'God' does function as a proper name: in our culture, the expression 'God' is a shortcut for talking about the God of the Christians, or at least the God of the great monotheistic religions. Let us accept this *religious usage* of the word 'God.' It is only really misleading when combined with the fallacy of factual existence.

Hartshorne has never been impressed by Kant's assertion that existence is not a predicate. Kant's assertion runs as follows: if we say that x has the properties a and b, and then add "and what's more, x does exist," we add nothing at all to the meaning of x. "Otherwise stated, the real contains no more than the merely possible. A hundred real thalers do not contain the least coin more than a hundred possible thalers."[4] Russell, Carnap, and most analytic philosophers accept this without question. Carnap argues that the proposition "God exists" must be logically translated into "There is (at least) one x with the property 'God.' " "There is a God" implies the elementary proposition "x is a God." And, according to Carnap, the theologian should reject this way of speaking of God.[5]

This is a most insightful criticism. But Carnap sees no alternative and that is the reason why he rejects God-talk altogether. There is a second difficulty. Even if we answer the question "Does God exist?" in the affirmative ("Yes, there is an x called God"), we might not be talking about God at all. A god affirmed in this way cannot escape Heidegger's charge against the onto-theological structure of Western metaphysics, according to which metaphysics has dealt with beings and has "forgotten" Being. Indeed a god who is "an x" is still one being among beings, not Being in the "verbal" sense of the Event of coming-into-Unconcealment.

Hartshorne's God is surely not one being amongst beings: rather he is all-inclusive Reality (of which nonexistence cannot reasonably be asserted). Although his identification of God with all-inclusive Reality may be open to other criticisms, it is not open to the worn-out Kantian objection that existence is not a predicate. Kant's comparison with the one hundred *Reichstahler* has been a very influential one, but is it not scandalous (as Hegel labeled it) to compare the existence of the Absolute—and God is surely no less than the Absolute—with the contingent existence of *Reichstahler*? Not existence, but *necessary existence* is asserted of God. And necessity of existence is a predicate.

The modal status of the God-question (meaning the logical necessity or impossibility of God) has attracted Hartshorne's attention to Anselm's argument. But Anselm is more ambiguous here than Hartshorne. Anselm, after all, tends to conceive God as the Supreme Being, which points over against himself the multitude of created beings. How can such a being exist necessarily? No individual being, not even the highest, can exist necessarily. It would, indeed, always be a being among beings, and only Reality as a whole cannot fail to exist. Anselm has not seen that talking about "*id quo majus cogitari nequit*" (or IQM) he was moving from the realm of beings to the realm of Being. Only Being or all-inclusive Reality can be said to be IQM. Only IQM can without arrogance or logical slip be said to exist necessarily. That was Parmenides' intuition, which has been underscored by all great metaphysicians—by Spinoza, Hegel, and Hartshorne.

It is puzzling that, although linguistic analysis so clearly helps us overcome the very objections of the logical positivists to God-talk, only the traditional conception of God has had influence in analytical circles. Yet there are a few exceptions. For example, although it has often been overlooked, the point of Wisdom's parable in fact transcends the controversial affirmation/denial of "a gardener." Wisdom, too, suggests that the God-question is *not* a factual one—all the facts "are in"—but a matter of *evaluating* the "garden with weeds." This evaluation is not a factual question in the ordinary sense of the word (although Hartshorne criticizes Wisdom for suggesting that it is[6]). Anthony Flew has in a shrewd way twisted the very point of Wisdom's parable, suggesting that the question is indeed about the existence or nonexistence of a gardener.[7] The initial affirmation of the traditional believer ("Yes, there is a gardener") has died "the death of a thousand qualifications," so that, in the end, the believer no longer says anything at all. Now we would be seriously misguided if we were to defend the believer and, in spite of all the ambiguities of the situation, assert, "Yes, there is a gardener, after all." In doing so we would commit both the fallacy of the proper name and of factual existence: "Yes there is an x, called 'God.' " Such a God would be "metaphysically out there" (J. A. T. Robinson). Admittedly, Wisdom's parable encourages just such a conception of God—a God who is no real element in the picture, but who *intervenes* from time to time in a most uncontrollable way. But the weight of the picture is not there.

Hartshorne has convincingly proven that there is a way out of Carnap's—and Kant's—difficulty. If we see the universe as a possible value for x and drop the indefinite article 'a' in the expression 'a being, called "God," ' then the real question would be as follows: can the universe be called "divine" in any acceptable sense of the word? Or in the language of Wisdom's parable, can the *whole* situation—the jungle, the clearance of the woods, the flowers and the weeds, and, more importantly, the two explorers themselves—be *evaluated* with good reason as the manifestation of loving care at work in a reality that in itself has also the features of "wild" creativity?[8]

What is gained by a refinement of the God-question along these lines can be summarized as follows. *In no sense whatsoever* does the question ask about the existence of *a* being among beings, called "God." What is at stake is the *evaluation* of *R*eality as a *W*hole. (Hence the use of capitals.) Asking the God-question is asking whether Reality as a Whole has such characteristics as would allow us to reasonably call it "divine" (in the religious sense of the word), or, in the least, whether there is in Reality itself an Instance or an Agency at work that deserves the believers total commitment. The most important point, powerfully advocated by Hartshorne, is that the God-question cannot be about what is "less" than Reality as a Whole. Yet, to conclude from this that "God is the all-inclusive reality"[9] seems to me an unjustified step.[10] And it is exactly on this delicate point that analytic philosophy—mostly in a Wittgensteinian fashion—can contribute to a refinement of Hartshorne's position.

To qualify all-inclusive Reality as God is to *see* it in a very specific way, i.e. *as* worshipful. To "see as" is to interpret. Other interpretations are possible, and thus have to be considered, i.e. they are not logically excluded from our considerations regarding ultimate meaning or non-meaning. Is all-inclusive Reality such that it should be called "divine," or are other ways of "seeing as" equally appropriate? Could not all-inclusive Reality just as well be called "Matter" or "Spirit" or "Evolutionary Life?" Even the "heathens," you see, use Instances with capitals. All such talk is already about all-inclusive Reality. And it is not God-talk in the religious sense of the word. God-talk adequately expresses our seeing reality this way rather than that, i.e. as qualified by divine characteristics rather than by impersonal traits (anonymous fate, or even Chaos, all of which are nontheistic interpretations of all-inclusive Reality). God-talk adequately describes Reality *as* believers *see* it. Believers do not simply assert the necessary existence of all-inclusive Reality (who would want to quarrel with that?), but they *interpret* it as supported by divine presence, as permeated by divine love.

To understand the logic of interpretive language, which expresses a certain outlook on reality, a well-known passage from Wittgenstein's *Philosophical Investigations* may prove helpful. In considering the duck-rabbit figure, Wittgenstein expresses the fact that we do not merely see, but *see as*.[11] At first we see the figure as a duck, but when we turn the page a quarter of a full circle, we see it as a rabbit. What was the duck's beak becomes the rabbit's ears. Or we may enjoy recalling the "puzzle pictures" of our childhood: first there were only branches, then suddenly one sees a face—or whatever else may be on a man's mind (consider the famous Freud drawing). What changes? *Our* way of seeing? *Our* interpretation? *Our* way of structuring the chaos? Who can tell? One cannot see whatever one wishes. And once one sees something, one cannot dismiss it either.

And what do we see? One is tempted to say that we continue to see the same picture, but that only our attitude changes. The same spots on the paper, the same lines, represent completely different realities. But would it not be more accurate to say that we saw something rather different, although represented by the same ambiguous symbolic traits? "To see" and "to see as" are not two independent activities: we do see something only because we *see* that which is given *as* this rather than that. To see is always to structure, to interpret, to grasp a "Gestalt," which brings the manifold and ambiguous world to a sufficient unity so that we can see something at all.

This insight is especially exciting when applied to reality as a whole.[12] Should we not say that metaphysics is a picture of the world, literally a "Welt-Anschauung?" And with Wittgenstein we would like to say that "The whole *weight* may be in the picture."[13] Is not every philosophy a means of ordering and structuring all given realities so that Reality becomes meaningful, so that we can find our way about it? The metaphysician seeks patterns that account for the world *as he sees it.* A system (*sun-titenai*) is a linguistic rendering of an outlook on reality. To be sure, such a rendering is a rational enterprise: "to account for" presupposes that the suggested pattern offers some insights into the coherence of the world, explaining what would otherwise be left obscure.

And yet, such a metaphysical system—such a picture of the world—is not a compelling argument: it is always a picture of the world as the metaphysician sees it. According to Wittgenstein such a picture need not even pretend to be reasonable.[14] Regarding the status of such pictures, of course, Hartshorne would be more demanding. Whereas Hartshorne argues, Wittgenstein bows his head.

Let us consider whether and how a metaphysical outlook on Reality might be justified. Here again Hartshorne's contribution to meeting the challenge addressed to religion by logical positivism is most instructive. Logical positivism has made *one* specific mode of justification the criterion of cognitive meaningfulness, viz. verification through sense experience. A large part of the early debate about the meaningfulness of religious language revolved around the verification issue.[15] But it has not always been understood this way. Wisdom, for instance, has distanced himself from logical positivism regarding precisely this point. His main concern has been to draw attention to the fact that from a certain perspective, the God-question ceases to be a question that can be decided along empirical lines, but that it is still a question that can be discussed in a rational way (Wittgenstein notwithstanding), much like the question whether someone has exercised "reasonable care," or whether someone is to be declared "guilty of a crime." Questions about "reasonable care" or "criminal guilt" are not questions about the facts, not questions about what is the case, but questions about the *evaluation* of facts—in short, questions of "seeing as." And—the examples make this abundantly clear—they are not questions of taste either. For Wisdom, on the contrary, those questions that really matter, say, in a courtroom, are nonempirical ones: "Is he guilty after all?"[16] Although the two explorers learn the same facts about the garden, and although they do not disagree about what happens to untended gardens (their disagreement is not over the facts, nor over what one should reasonably expect), yet they speak about the garden in quite different ways. They speak differently about the garden(er) because they see the garden differently. With Wittgenstein, we might say that they see the garden as one thing rather than as another. For Wisdom, the God-question is not an empirical question (contrary to Hartshorne's reading of Wisdom's position), but it is not completely nonfactual either (which explains Hartshorne's reaction). In his rereading of the parable, Flew reaches a conclusion opposite to that of Wisdom because he twists the real point of the parable. According to Flew (a true logical positivist), questions that cannot be answered on the basis of further investigation cease to be meaningful. Wisdom hopes to convince us of the existence of real questions, meaningful for the way persons live their lives, that cannot be decided by further investigation. What happens in the courtroom provides a good illustration: when the judge decides whether a document is a valid will or whether a defendant is guilty of a crime, his inquiry reaches beyond questions about "what has happened." He structures the factual evidence, interpreting and evaluating it. Of course, his final judgment does have important "factual" consequences; it would be to completely miss the point to call such judgments irrational or mere expressions of feeling on the part of the judge. What Wisdom has shown is that, although such questions are real and important, they cannot be decided upon the basis of further empirical investigation.

Wisdom's parable has captured so much attention that much of the rest of his philosophy of religion has gone unnoticed. We must still ask why the explorers are talking about a gardener *at all*. Wisdom suggests that deep within us there are forces of which we have always been aware. In antiquity these forces were given mythical names: "Eve said: 'The serpent beguiled me.' Helen says to Menelaus: '. . . Surely it was not I, but Cypris there.' "[17] Such mythical words should not be seen merely as a means of escape. Up to a certain point they are "true": there are evil forces at work in the world; there is more evil than the sum-total of evil human deeds. Freud wrote, "Obscure, unfeeling and unloving powers determine men's fate."[18] On the other hand, there is always a power working for goodness—a tender Force, a Love that permeates our very being. If we recognize this ambiguity, we begin to understand why the Greeks—and Wisdom—speak of "gods." Thus there are good reasons to believe in gods. "Do gods exist?" and "Do demons exist?" are not meaningless questions.[19] To speak of them is not irrational insofar as we take such language "seriously, not literally" (Niebuhr's phrase). There are good and evil forces at work in our lives. A new form of Manichaeism seems unavoidable: there are good reasons for accepting that there are man-transcending forces, *both* good and evil.

Why then should we talk of "God," as Hartshorne so confidently does? It is not enough to talk of a transcendent dimension, even of all-encompassing Reality, which is clearly "greater than ourselves." Here we touch the exact point where many of the traditional proofs for God's existence have gone astray. Although they do prove the existence of "something" beyond human reality, still they miss the point: they prove the existence of "something Necessary," "something Unmoved," but they do not prove the existence of God. Granted that there is "More" than just human reality, should this More be called "God?" Thus the God-question is not simply "Are there forces greater than ourselves?" but "Are these forces to be called God?" The two questions should be carefully distinguished. First, are there forces that transcend man? That there are such forces can hardly be denied. Call them the forces of cosmic evolution, psychological dynamisms, social structures, archetypes, or gods (idols). That there is more than just human reality is all too obvious. The title of one of Hartshorne's first books is *Beyond Humanism*. Post-war humanism (Camus, Sartre) now strikes us as exaggerated and false. The reality expressed in their stories about the gods is still with us: "We have eaten of the fruit of the garden and we cannot forget it, though we never were there."[20] The question about the existence of forces transcending man is today answered in the affirmative. Atheists are far more willing to recognize these "anonymous structures" than during the high tide of humanistic atheism. This is an additional argument for my thesis that at this level (that is, at the level of asking about transcendent Reality) the God-question is not yet decided. That it can no longer be reasonably denied that there are forces transcending man—although these forces cannot be pointed out empirically—is, during these anti-metaphysical times, a quite significant result. At the same time, it is not enough to justify *God*-talk.

II

To claim that all-inclusive Wholeness is God is clearly to claim more than the existence of transcendent Reality. To talk of God is to express a certain conviction about the very character of the Real, about the way in which all-encompassing Reality *eventually* should be conceived. And we express this in the claim that what exists is to be called God.

What can be said about transcendent Reality? The least that can be said is that it is highly ambiguous. Reality is threatening as well as hope-inspiring. There is good as well as evil, and neither is entirely man's own invention. The explorers' question, which at the outset seemed merely to be "Is there a gardener?" needs badly to be reformulated. The difference between the two explorers is not that one affirms the existence of a reality transcending his own powers (i.e. a gardener who "works at night"), while the other denies it. Both agree regarding the existence of a non-man-made jungle: there are flowers and weeds. Nor does their disagreement consist in the one's cherishing what for the other is merely weeds (like tourists who see "mere stones" where the archeologist sees an untarnished source of investigation). They agree about the ambiguity of the situation. The exact measure of their disagreement lies, rather, in the way they transcend its ambiguity. And this happens by *naming* the situation as a whole. This naming activity subordinates some elements to the overall picture, accounting for the way the ultimate character of the Whole is eventually evaluated. The believer finds that Loving Care is the predominant feature, although he recognizes that there is also evil and conflict. The so-called nonbeliever does not go so far—although he might believe in gods. He accepts the ambiguity of Reality: there are flowers and there are weeds. "Nature" has been at work here: man-transcending powers are not necessarily denied, but they receive an impersonal name—"Cosmic Force,"

"Fate," "Chance"—or no name at all. The nonbeliever does not dare to "see" more, to recognize Loving Care. In short, he does not believe in God.

God-talk is appropriate when we judge or decide about the ultimate nature of reality, when we break through the ambiguities of life and express our belief in Loving Care, *despite* conflict, chance, disorder. We express our belief in the future, despite an evident trend toward degradation; we believe in Love, even though there is also hate.

On this level, God-talk is clearly "convictional" (W. Zuurdeeg). We do not simply "see" reality; we see it *as* ambiguous—threatening *and* hospitable. But this ambiguity is ultimately pierced on the existential as well as reflective level: we evaluate the ultimate "character" (Whitehead's expression) of Reality. Evil is finally judged subordinate to the good: in one way or another, evil does not have the last word ('hate' is not written in capitals).

Language that describes the more-than-ourselves, which is clearly modal language, seems to move in the direction of confessional language, or of what I propose to call "valuational language." But valuational language is no longer modal language: it expresses our belief that Ultimate Reality will eventually be characterized by what we experience as the very best. Our experience of worth becomes our guiding principle. Our finite and ambiguous experience of worth is now the *model* for our confessed characterization of Ultimate Reality.

That our modal language (i.e. language about ultimate reality) becomes model language means that we express our hope that Reality as a Whole is permeated by the best that *we* experience in our lives: love, tender care, hope, and forgiveness. *All* that we experience as worthwhile can be attributed to God. During epochs when human sensibility is not very refined, God will be spontaneously depicted as the mighty Lord of Hosts, or as the God-Warrior, or as the God of Revenge. As modal language this would be scandalous, of course, but as model language it reveals very well the values experienced during certain times.

The subjective, interpretive, and historical character of God-language should not be denied. If, however, we were to interpret religious language merely as the expression of a respectable opinion—and bow our heads—then we would not account for the way believers themselves see religious language.[21] The very heart of the logic of religious language seems rather to be this: although believers know that what they express is a conviction and an evaluation, they claim to express a *true* outlook on reality: they claim to express how Ultimate Reality *should* be conceived. This truth claim is essential to the logic of God-talk. It is not merely a subjective cry, but the expression of the conviction that Reality comes to life and that it reveals a coherence and a trustworthiness without which our lives would be nothing more than a mere transient fake. The language of "stability" most suitably expresses that trustworthiness. As Hartshorne has put it: "The changeless character of God is his absolute loyalty. 'Without a shadow of turning,' as the Bible says." Often, however, Hartshorne conceives model language as if it were modal language; then, of course, it is very difficult to characterize Ultimate Reality as changeless. In fact, nothing could happen if all-inclusive Reality were unable to move in a new concrete state of itself. But this is not what religious language denies—and has never denied (unless perhaps in some extreme forms of Eastern monism).

Because his interpretation of reality is "bestowed upon" the believer, he is a messenger to those around him: he wants to convince others, not about his convictions, but about the truth of his convictions. The choice of words is itself revealing: the fact that we talk about "disclosure" and "revelation" suggests that something not of our own making is manifested. However, the disclosure is linked to existential experience: what is revealed is not just a private affair; it must in principle be accessible to all. A believer cannot but be an evangelist: "The conversion of the Gentiles is both the effect of truth and the test of truth."[22] A disclosure is fundamentally different from a subjective "blik," and therein lies the difference between Ramsey and R. Hare. The fact that the believer professes his conviction does not negate the claim that he *intends* to express reality as it really is. Again, convictional language turns into cognitive language, with the added characteristic of being a "truth claim." One must understand the logic of a truth claim to understand the language of religion. Ramsey has much to say about this matter, although, as far as I recall, he does not develop it explicitly. Religious language rests upon an insight (a discernment) that itself is based upon the experience of the More (than the visible and tangible realities) in a "cosmic disclosure."

No one has done more than Ramsey to clarify the logic of religious language. He has shown in a very convincing way that *all* our talk about heaven and earth can be meaningful insofar as it is conceived as model language. But it is less clear what, according to Ramsey, the referent of God-language is. The referent of God-language is the More that is revealed in a cosmic disclosure. But is it more than the cosmos?

In a sense, I am more than my observable behavior. Analogously, there is more than the material universe. The more-than-the-material-universe is related to the Universe, as I am related to my objective behavior. But how is the more-than-observable-reality related to Reality as a Whole? Is there more than the Universe? Ramsey wavers on this point, offering two different interpretations. At times he suggests that there is more than the observable universe (when he speaks of the universe and its "more"), while at other times he suggests that there is only the all-encompassing Universe (i.e. the material universe and its "More"). It is thrilling to see how Hartshorne's panentheism can clarify and undergird Ramsey's intuitions. And once we have seen the beauty of the Hartshorne-Ramsey combination, we can never forget it. Of course, to speak of "the universe and its More" is a theistic interpretation; to speak of this More as the all-inclusive Universe is clearly panentheistic.

The key problem is the shifting meaning of "the Universe." The word 'God,' just as the word 'I,' can refer to the Whole of "the observable *and* its more." More commonly, however, it is suitable to interpret Ramsey's God-talk as if God refers to the more-than-the-visible, insofar as it transcends the visible and is distinguished from it.

If Ramsey identifies God and the More (than the visible Universe), then he is close to a traditional, theistic understanding of God (even if Ramsey's More is seen *in* the visible, not just *tamquam causa in effectu*). If, however, Ramsey speaks of "a total commitment to the whole universe" (which he does in a text dating back to 1957[23]), then he is extremely close to Hartshorne, who defines the object of religion as all-inclusive Reality. Ramsey once used the daring expression, "the universe—which is God."[24] It is clear that here the Universe is the object of total commitment, or worship, which is precisely Hartshorne's view.

Let me return to the way Ramsey makes the transition from the disclosure of the More to the affirmation of God and to the problems related to this transition. Ramsey's procedure takes the following logical steps:

1. The empirical anchorage of all God-talk is the experience of a disclosure (just as all language about the "I" is rooted in the disclosure of the more-than-the-observable).

2. All cosmic disclosures have by necessity the *same* referent, just as in the many disclosures of the more-than-observable-behavior one unique "I" manifests itself.

3. The one referent of all cosmic disclosures is God. The word 'God' functions as an "integrater," which bundles the different forms of cosmic disclosure into a unity. Reality as experienced in the creativity of life, the trustworthiness of nature, the moral appeal—all are models of the one divine Reality. Hence Ramsey strongly advocates a multi-model discourse.

It is surely a worthwhile insight to see God-talk as the integration of what becomes transparent in the many cosmic disclosures. To comprehend means to bring together. The affirmation of God is a pre-eminent case of bringing together, and hence illuminating, all that is given to us in experience—in the most encompassing sense of "experience": experience as given both directly and by implication (what Whitehead calls the "formative elements").

Ramsey convincingly describes the experiences of the More. The array of examples is inexhaustible. In this way Ramsey's analysis of religious language functions as an eye-opener. Yet we have to recognize that his analysis moves within the hermeneutical circle. Or to put it more simply, one must have already heard the word of faith in order to "see." A nonbeliever will say that Ramsey moves too readily from the experience of the More to the affirmation of God. In a sharp analysis of Ramsey's philosophy, Donald

Evans emphasizes the difficulty of making Ramsey's transition. It is exactly the same difficulty found to plague the transition from the many transcendent forces (Wisdom's gods) to God. Ramsey correctly argues for the necessity of multi-model discourse. But a basic problem remains unsolved. What leads Ramsey to affirm that the many models can be integrated, that they ultimately converge in the direction of one and the same More of the Universe, which is God? Cannot that which is disclosed as Blind Fate, Concealedness, Brute Force, or even Wickedness—which are all more-than-human realities—as well be integrated into a language about the one More? Why a Universe rather than a "Pluriverse," or even Chaos? I do not hold that Ramsey is wrong to claim that the function of the word 'God' is precisely to integrate what is disclosed in the myriad of cosmic disclosures. But there is more to integrate than those discourses that all point in the same direction (creativity, care, moral appeal). There is also the threat of contingency, of futility, of suffering, of failure—all the stumbling blocks to traditional theism. In Ramsey we find a few hints about a love that is, although suffering, mightier than the powers of the world. Yet Ramsey's analyses of religious language would gain enormously by integrating into his vision a metaphysical concept such as Creativity, or Ongoingness, with God as its innermost qualification, which would allow for the integration of dissonant disclosures. Such, of course, is the concept we find in the philosophy of Whitehead. Precisely because Whitehead's God does not coïncide with Creativity as such, he can overcome the negative and the suffering; he can accept it into his own life and heal it.

Among the many cosmic disclosures, Ramsey selects those that are likely to move the person who is able and willing to "see" to the disclosure of the one More; so the trustworthiness of nature will reveal something about God's care. The moral appeal that goes out from the other person readily leads to the disclosure of a cosmic Ought. But what about the experience of the absence of God in a silent universe? Again, Ramsey's analysis of religious language would gain tremendously if it included the distinction between "that which transcends man" and "God," i.e. the transition from the More to God.

On exactly this point Langdon Gilkey has made an important contribution in his *Naming the Whirlwind: The Renewal of God-language.*[25] The title itself suggests the necessity of distinguishing between the Whirlwind and God. On the level of existential analysis, Gilkey is concerned with leaving the options open. The Ultimate can be experienced—but as the Void as well as God. The truth-question and hence the God-question arise only within a community of faith, within a cultural context, where particular answers to the ultimate questions are received, lived, and celebrated. "You shall know them by their fruits." If in a given community a received answer fruitfully contributes to the possibility of a meaningful life, i.e. if it allows those who accept it to overcome the dread of meaninglessness and futility, then this answer has delivered its credentials and may be called "religious." Then that community has decided in favor of the God-option.

To have shown that a disclosure, revelation, and celebration of the Ultimate is possible—and even unavoidable—in a secular age is Gilkey's great contribution. As far as the justification of religious language is concerned, however, he, too, seems in need of a solid metaphysics. According to Gilkey's analysis of the dimensions of ultimacy, meaning and meaninglessness reveal themselves as equally possible. Hence there is talk about the Void as well as talk about God.

At this point, I would like to raise a decisive question: Are belief in the Void and belief in God *equally* justifiable? I do not think so. And this moves us close to the Process-conceptuality, wherein God "is not the whole story" (he allows for other creative agents over against him; he is truly a God who takes into his own life that which would otherwise have been lost forever), but in the end is victorious. The problem of the justification of God-talk is pushed far enough only if we come to avoid the conclusion that there are *not* as many reasons for despair as for hope. Gilkey himself gives a hint: "Religious symbols and preeminently that of God, are meaningful, therefore, as thematizing answers to our ultimate questions; in symbolic form, they thus express, if they express anything at all, that unconditional answer which is essential if we are to live with serenity, intelligibility, meaning, courage, and love in the face of our contingency, relativity, temporality, and the ambiguities of our freedom."[26]

To be sure, ambiguity is a characteristic of the situation in which we live in this world. But can we cope with this ambiguity in any way we choose? Is faith merely one "option" (H. Kung)? Gilkey suggests that some kind of religious answer is essential if we are to live with serenity, meaning, and love. This way of putting it should receive its full weight. It is not entirely true that "any possible answer to an ultimate question is always correlated with and so can be balanced by a corresponding 'No' as another possible answer."[27] In fact, the belief in the greater worth of Love is not yet extinguished. Scientists accept that the universe is open to rational exploration, and the dream of a more humane and just world has not yet altogether been given up as an illusion. How can such a preferential belief in meaning and Love be justified? I think this question lies at the heart of religion.

To my knowledge, no Process thinker has clarified this logic of "faith *in spite of* the evident threat of meaninglessness" better than Schubert Ogden in his *The Reality of God.* It is in the affirmation of the worth of our earthly lives that we find the reality of God in our times. In the experience of the intelligibility of the cosmos, in the exigency of the ethical appeal, in the struggle for justice, the answer to the question of meaning has, in fact, already been given. Religious faith is not at the origin of this basic trust; rather, it is the explication of this trust. According to Ogden, religious assertions point "to the objective ground in reality itself of our ineradicable confidence in the final worth of existence.''[28] In that confidence itself its Ground, or basis, is already implicitly co-affirmed. Otherwise, that confidence would be unjustified. The affirmation of this basic confidence logically precedes any specific religious assertion. In this sense, belief in God is already present wherever such confidence is justified. Atheism, according to Ogden, is not the absence of faith, but faith in a deficient manner, which does not allow for the ultimate clarification of its presuppositions. To behave in a truly human way is only existentially possible because it is already rooted in the belief in the deep worth of our existence, however precarious and endangered this belief may be. For Ogden, there is a logical link between our existential confidence in the worth of our lives and the affirmation of the Ground of this confidence, which is called ''God.'' God-language makes explicit what is implicitly taken for granted: that *eventually*, or *after all*, our confidence in the meaning of life, our basic trust in love and justice, *are* justified.[29] To say that only a theistic metaphysics fully accounts for the meaning and values that are in fact accepted implies that nonreligious accounts of Reality ultimately fall short of accounting for the way we in fact experience our lives. Such accounts leave their ''background'' (Whitehead) partially or wholly unexplained.

That God is the basis of our ultimate confidence in the meaning of our finite lives implies that God truly relates to our lives, that our struggle for justice is also His struggle, that our successes and failures add to and take away from God. Such a conception of deity is implied in all that has been said. It underscores the point that a solid analysis of religious language requires a metaphysical backing.

In fact what can we say in light of all this about the very status of God-talk? It far exceeds the affirmation of the necessary being (modal language). It seeks models with which to illumine the very nature of ultimate Reality—models borrowed from what is most dear to us: our world of values, meaning, and responsibility. God-talk is both meaningful and true to the same measure that the best that we experience in life is not an illusion and cannot be without a foundation in reality itself. In fact we wish to *account* for the conviction that our belief in love, rationality, and the future is justified, *in spite of* the ambiguities of the present situation. That this belief is justified cannot be reasonably denied, unless we wish to destroy nearly everything that man has achieved and negate all that is most worthwhile to him. The belief in the ultimate worth of Love can be justified only if that worth has shown itself in everyday life, e.g. in the loving care shown by the persons around us. Such experience will quite understandably function as a *model* for the expression of what we wish to say about the ultimate nature of Reality, which supports us in our existence. According to this account, value-language is always—and justifiably so—''theandric'': it is as much about God as about ourselves. In the *ordo cognoscendi* (the order in which we know things) such language is—as is all language—anthropomorphic. In the *ordo essendi* (the order of the nature of things) it is theo-logical—model language about modal Reality. Should love never have appeared, there would have been no reason to speak theologically about Reality. Neutral words, such as Nature or Fate, would have sufficed. But in fact we live *as if* our lives are meaningful, so that we have to account for our ineradicable confidence, which is *more* than "animal faith" (Santayana). We have to give a rational account of this confidence. In fact, we—or most of us—accept life; we are open to the moral appeal; we are able to discover scientific truth; we appreciate beauty. And yet we know that all rationality, all goodness, all beauty is threatened—unless there is Someone greater then ourselves, Someone who is not less intelligent, moral, and loving than we are, but *more* so. Why should human model language about the ultimate source of meaning, intelligibility, and value not be adequate, provided that we realize that it is model language describing that which is modally different from ourselves? Hartshorne has even argued that love, understanding, care, and memory have their first analogue (*analogon princeps*) in God. This is very congenial to the above-proposed approach. Religious language is to be taken both literally and as pointing to what is modally different. So God literally loves us, but his love is all-encompassing. God literally knows, but his knowledge is modally co-extensive with Reality; hence he knows all there is to know—the actual as actual and the possible as possible, as Hartshorne has so clearly and convincingly expressed it.

Through religion man wishes to express and undergird his confidence in Reality as a whole, his faith in the meaning of life, in rationality, in the future, in humanity, and to make it clear that these are *not* illusory. Man has in fact already solved this problem: he does believe in the truths of science (the skeptical theoreticians notwithstanding) and he is touched by the claims of justice and love. Because the basic question of the meaning of life is already answered, it is meaningful to seek the Ground of this lived certitude, in much the same way as Kant sought the conditions of possibility of moral behavior. Reality must be such that our experiences of reality—our best and richest experiences included—are neither futile nor irrational (in the Kantian sense).

God-talk presents itself as the true word about the ultimate questions concerning our place in Reality as a whole (or more philosophically speaking, concerning the relation between the finite and the infinite), because such is the way we live. Yet the justifiability of God-talk is always threatened by the realities of concrete life, and in exactly the same way as the very meaning of our lives is threatened. Ogden's "Merrick Lectures" were delivered at Wesley University (Ohio) in the mid-1960s, a time when it was fashionable to claim that there is no opposition between the modern secular mentality and belief in God. "World-acceptance" was almost synonymous with secularized faith. God was seen as the Ground of the best values of the Secular City. For some reason, such ideas are no longer widely held. Hartshorne's philosophy seems likewise overly optimistic, too "panentheistic." World-acceptance is no longer evident; nor does it seem, as such, compatible with Christian faith. For this reason the most vivid religious language of our day—the theologies of liberation, faith, Wholeness, and ecology—has shifted toward the ethics of responsibility. The logic of theological discourse has to shift from the justification of the present to the expression of the final hope of mankind: that God *will be* all in all.[30] Talk of God is meaningful only in association with the hope that eventually love will not fail.

God-talk along these lines should be seen not so much as a justification of what is, but as a promise of the kingdom to come, adding yet another chapter to the dialogue between Process thought and new strands of theology. Let me conclude by expressing my hope that it has become clear that the logic of religious language cannot be tackled in isolation from a metaphysical outlook on reality and a world-transforming praxis. Hartshorne has developed most powerfully the modal aspect of God-talk. It is the task of those who take their inspiration from his ideas to discover new models for action, developing these insights, taking into account the concreteness of the world in which the kingdom of God is already present and into which it is yet to come.

NOTES

1. Charles Hartshorne, "Redefining God" in *The New Humanist* 7/4 (July-Aug. 1934), p. 8-15.
2. Wisdom's article has first been published in *Proceedings of the Aristotelian Society*, 1944. It has been reprinted in *Logic and Language* I, edited by Antony Flew, Oxford 1951, pp. 187-207 (I refer to this text) and in J. Wisdom, *Philosophy and Psychoanalysis*, Oxford 1953. About Wisdom's philosophy of religion, see D. Z. Phillips, "Wisdom's Gods," in *Faith and Philosophical Enquiry*, London, Routledge and Kegan Paul, 1970, 170-203.
3. "In theistic religions God is the One Who is Worshipped," Charles Hartshorne, *A Natural Theology for Our Time*, La Salle, Illinois, Open Court, 1967, p. 3.
4. "Und so enthält das Wirkliche nichts mehr als das bloss Mögliche. Hundert wirkliche Thaler enthalten nicht das Mindeste Mehr, als hundert mögliche," Immanuel Kant, *Kritik der reinen Vernunft*, Zweite Auflage 1787, Die transcendentale Dialektik. Von der Unmöglichkeit eines ontologischen Beweises vom Dasein Gottes, Berlin, Preusische Akademie, 1911, p. 401.
5. R. Carnap, "Berwindung der Metaphysik durch logische Analyse der Sprache" in *Erkenntnis* **2** (1931), p. 219-241, and more in general "On the Character of Philosophical Problems" in *Philosophy of Science* **1**, 1934, pp. 5-19. See Hartshorne's comments in *Beyond Humanism: Essays in the Philosophy of Nature*, Lincoln, University of Nebraska Press, 1969 (1937/1), p. 255.
6. Hartshorne, "John Wisdom on 'Gods,' " in *Downside Review* (Bath, England), 1959, pp. 5-17. Hartshorne interprets even "He exercised reasonable care" as a statement about a contingent truth. But the point in Wisdom's parable is that the "reasonable care"-question is asked after "all the facts are in." Wisdom is more in agreement with Hartshorne than he seems to accept in his article devoted

to Wisdom's "Gods."

7. A. Flew, "Theology and Falsification," in *New Essays in Philosophical Theology*, edited by Antony Flew and Alaisdair MacIntyre, London, SCM, 1963 (1955/1), p. 97. The point is now no longer that the issue has to be debated on another level, but that the original assertion has died "the death by a thousand qualifications."
8. I suggest the expression "wild" creativity, in analogy with what for Merleau-Ponty is "*l'être brut et la pensée sauvage.*" Brute or savage being suggests very well what I want to say: being as such is not fully permeated by reason. Of course, those expressions are influenced by the title of Cl. Lévi-Strauss' book *La pensée sauvage.*
9. Hartshorne, *A Natural Theology for Our Time*, p. 12.
10. See my "Ultimate Reality and God: the Same?" in the Hartshorne volume of the Library of Living Philosophers.
11. L. Wittgenstein, *Philosophical Investigations*, Oxford, Blackwell 1953, Part II, XI, pp. 193-195.
12. Wittgenstein has not done it explicitly, but his insights can be elaborated along that line. My colleague I. Verhack has a most inspiring passage about what he calls Wittgenstein's "deictic metaphysics": "Similarly for the Higher (the sense of the world) and our disclosure-feeling of the value-face of the world: the sense of the world is not discovered through one of our descriptions of the world, but it is the all-embracing 'character' of the world as a whole—the way in which the world looks to us as a whole. It is that which makes of it an enjoyable (or an unhappy) world. The givenness of such a character implicitly points to a disclosure-feeling in and to which the value-face of the world is given. In Wittgenstein's conception it points to the existence of the ethical will which is capable of good and evil (6.34)" (Ignace Verhack, "Wittgenstein's Deictic† Metaphysics: An Uncommon Reading of the Tractatus," in *International Philosophical Quarterly*, December 1978, p. 442. †(Verhack explains the term as follows: "Deictic: a philological term accepted by *The Concise Oxford Dictionary*, with the meaning of 'pointing, demonstrative.' ") This text is clearly also inspired by Ramsey, and it is, of course, very congenial to Hartshorne's approach. To make the basic similarity with the position here defended even more striking, I like to quote Hartshorne's phrase: "The 'Ostentation' here required is not far from the whole of philosophy," in "John Wisdom on 'Gods,' " p. 13. 'Deictic,' of course, has the same meaning as 'Ostentation.'
13. L. Wittgenstein, *Lectures and Conversations on Aesthetics, Psychology and Religious Belief*, edited by Cyril Barrett, Blackwell, 1966, p. 71.
14. L. Wittgenstein, o.c., p. 58, in his discussion with O'Hara: "Not only it is not reasonable, but it doesn't pretend to be." See Peter Winch, "Wittgenstein: Picture and Representation," in *Tijdschrift voor Filosofie* (Leuven) **49** (1987), pp. 3-20.
15. See *Religious Language and the Problems of Religious Knowledge*, edited with an introduction by Ronald E. Santoni, Bloomington-London, Indiana University Press, 1968. He offers a good selection of the most important texts for and against the possibility of verification of religious assertions.
16. The "after all" is the indication of a logical shift, just as in the reported example of note 29 the mother says "everything" is all right.

17. J. Wisdom, a.c., p. 204. The quote is from Euripides, *The Trojan Women*, Gilbert Murray's translation.
18. S. Freud, *New Introductory Lectures on Psychoanalysis*, Lecture XXXV, "The Question of a Weltanschauung," *Complete Psychological Works of Sigmund Freud*, trans. James Strachey, 1964, p. 167. Quoted by D. Z. Phillips, "Wisdom's Gods," in *Faith and Philosophical Enquiry*, London, Routledge & Kegan Paul, 1970, p. 184.
19. In Heidegger there is also a strange interest in "the gods." He wants to revive the pre-christian experience of the sacred, as Hölderlin, Heidegger's favorite poet, has done before him. Today there is, also in France, a strange attraction of a kind of new paganism.
20. J. Wisdom, a.c., p. 205.
21. It is remarkable that this is exactly Antony Flew's objection against Hare's "blik-theory of faith": Any attempt to analyse Christian religious utterances as expressions or affirmations of a *blik* rather than as (at least would-be) assertions about the cosmos is fundamentally misguided. First, because thus interpreted they would be entirely unorthodox. If Hare's religion really is a blik, involving no cosmological assertions about the nature and activities of a supposed personal creator, then surely he is not a Christian at all? Second, because thus interpreted, they would scarcely do the job they do" in *New Essays in Philosophical Theology*, pp. 107-108. Wisdom also rejects a non-cognitive interpretation of religious language: "For it tries to take from the doctrines of religion, not merely something without which they would not strictly speaking be religious, but something without which they would no longer be themselves" ("Religious Belief," in *Paradox and Discovery*, Oxford, Blackwell, 1965, p. 55).
22. A. N. Whitehead, *Religion in the Making*, p. 133, New York, The World Publishing Company, Meridian Books, 1971.
23. *Religious Language*. An Empirical Placing of Theological Phrases, New York, Macmillan 1963, (1957/1), p. 41.
24. Ramsey said this in a never published lecture held at Tilburg (the Netherlands) on the 11th of March 1971. I owe this reference—and many insights in Ramsey—to my colleague W. de Pater, who has written extensively and competently about Ramsey, and brings the above quoted text in his article: "De empirische basis van godsdienstige taal," *Vox Theologica* **42** (1972), p. 25.
25. Langdon Gilkey, *Naming the Whirlwind: The Renewal of God-Language*, Indianapolis-New York, Bobbs-Merrill, 1969.
26. Langdon Gilkey, o.c., p. 442.
27. o.c., p. 450.
28. Schubert M. Ogden, o.c., p. 137: "I hold that the primary use or function of 'God' is to refer to the objective ground in reality itself of our ineradicable confidence in the final worth of our existence."
29. Peter Berger in fact asks the same question: has the mother the right to say to her crying child in the night: "Don't be afraid—everything is in order, everything is all right?" Is the mother lying to the child? The answer, in the most profound sense, can be "no" only if there is some truth in the religious interpretations of human existence.
30. Because of the "will be," I propose to talk about eschatological panentheism, or even more correctly, about eschatological theo-en-pantism. Although I do not

think that it is necessary to frame neologisms ''eschatological theo-en-pantism'' would express nicely what I want to say. It makes clear that at present ''God'' and ''All there is'' do not coincide, but that there is hope that God more and more will permeate all there is (God and his kingdom).

Hartshorne and Theodicy

Barry L. Whitney

There are few theological issues as significant and few as perplexing as the theodicy question. For centuries, Christian theologians have sought to explain how the devastating reality of evil in the world is consistent with belief in an all-powerful and all-loving God. Historical consideration of this issue, however, has been dominated by Saint Augustine, whose writings on theodicy have been overwhelmingly influential in both Catholic and Protestant circles.[1] It has been only in the past few decades that clearly defined alternatives to Augustine's traditional theodicy have been proposed. Foremost among these innovators are theologians like John Hick (who has constructed an "Irenaean" theodicy), philosophers Alvin Plantinga and Austin Farrer (who have done significant work on the free will defense), and a number of others, including Whiteheadian-Hartshornean process theists.[2]

The theodicy issue undeniably is an exceptionally complex problem; yet it can be understood essentially as addressing two principal questions and as providing two main types of answers. The *questions* are to explain how God's existence is consistent with both "moral evil" (sin, envy, greed, deceit, etc.) and "physical evil" (droughts, famines, disease, birth defects, etc.). The two types of *answers* commonly are referred to as the "existential" and "theoretical" approaches. The existential (or practical approach) appeals to "faith" as the only (or, at least, the ultimate) solution; human beings, we are told, are incapable of comprehending fully why God permits or perhaps causes evil, and it is thought to be pointless, if indeed not also impious and blasphemous, to question God's ways. We must cope with the evil as best we can, proponents of the faith solution advise, and persevere in our belief that everything happens for a "morally justifiable reason," known only to God.[3]

Many of our greatest theological minds throughout the centuries, nevertheless, have felt a pressing intellectual and religious obligation to pursue the theodicy problem rationally; indeed, it is the very nature of "theology" to seek a rational understanding of religious beliefs. This theoretical (or rational) approach concedes that our finite human perspective is limited, but at the same time insists that we must seek some understanding of the reasons *why* God would cause or permit evil and suffering in the first place, and indeed *why* God apparently allows such miseries to continue unabated. Yet Hartshorne has observed what unfortunately what is all too true: we have a general populace which, for the most part, inclines to be religious, yet which "shies away from any attempt at rational discussion of religious issues" (OOTM,13-14). This attitude seems incredibly cavalier, for while rational reflection on the theodicy problem may not be able to create faith where none existed, it most assuredly is indispensable in helping to "preserve an already existing faith from being overcome by this dark mystery."[4] Religious leaders, I respectfully submit, have an obligation to apprise themselves of current theological deliberations on such issues and to disperse this information (in an appropriate manner) to the people under their care.

Over a decade ago, I complained that there was an unjustifiable lack of critical scholarly attention to Hartshorne's substantial contributions to the theodicy issue and, indeed, to process theodicy in general.[5] This situation fortunately has changed somewhat, as growing numbers of commentators (both sympathetic and antagonistic) have begun to discuss seriously and assess critically the various aspects of process theodicy. Griffin's notable book, *God, Power, and Evil* (1976), deserves much of the credit for this belated scholarly interest: by means of his meticulous analyses of the dominant traditional Christian theodicies (generally understood by process theists to be such prominent figures as Augustine, Luther, Calvin, Barth, etc., and especially Aquinas and the influential tradition he inspired), Griffin has demonstrated conclusively that process theodicy not only is fully cognizant of the traditional perspectives, but has constructed an innovative approach which challenges the very essence of the traditional Christian theodicy.[6]

It is disconcerting, however, that many of the current discussions of process theodicy have become bogged down in superfluous arguments, the most common of which attacks the supposed "religious inadequacy" of the "limited" God of process thought. Hartshorne and other process theists have responded persistently and (to my mind) convincingly to this objection; yet they have done so apparently without overwhelming success. It must be acknowledged, to be sure, that resistance to the process conception of God is understandable (to a point), since process theism certainly has proposed a major shift in theological thinking. Griffin recently has noted that the acceptance of the "change from a doctrine of coercive agency to one of persuasive agency would not be a minor change in Christian thought: it could be the most radical change ever made."[7] It is precisely this issue upon which I wish to focus and to expose some of the reasons why it has contributed so significantly to the continued opposition toward the process enterprise.

The key to the process solution to the theodicy question centers about this issue of divine power: the traditional interpretation of God as "omnipotent" is rejected by process thinkers as seriously inadequate and in need of major revisions. Hartshorne insists that "no worse falsehood was ever perpetrated than the traditional concept of omnipotence. It is a piece of unconscious blasphemy, condemning God to a dead world, probably not distinguishable from no world at all" (OOTM,18). This understanding of divine power has been "so fearfully misdefined" and has so "catastrophically misled so many thinkers" that the word is now virtually meaningless and ought to be dropped from theological discourse (OOTM,26). The "idea of omnipotence, as it figures in the classical [formulation of the] problem of evil, is a pseudo-idea" (NLPE,203). Classical theism "had a confused idea, really a self-contradictory one . . . of the meaning of the term 'God,' " and therefore also "confused ideas about what is to be meant by 'creature,' or being other than God" (NLPE,202). Hartshorne believes that the traditional understanding of God gives to God absolute power in the sense that God supposedly would "be able to prevent anything undesirable from occurring." (NLPE,202). Hartshorne's point, of course, is that this idea is "an absurdity": "For [God] to have power to prevent anything undesirable from occurring is for [God] to have a monopoly on decision-making power," (NLPE,202) and if this were in fact the case, the very reality of freely creative creatures would be threatened. An absolute determinism, whether it be divinely imposed or the result of worldly factors (environmental or attributed to our characters), is an impossible position to defend (OOTM,19-23).[8]

Hartshorne's "metaphysics of freedom" has argued the case thoroughly that all reality, including the most minute and trivial levels, has some degree of genuine creativity (although this does not imply a conscious freedom, except for the higher forms of life on this planet). The "minimal solution" to the problem of evil, then, is to comprehend that it is not God who determines all events, but "the creaturely freedom from which evils spring" (NTT,81). Indeed, "since all creatures have some freedom, all evil can and should be viewed as involving unfortunate ... cases of creaturely decision" (NLPE,205). "This is the sole, but sufficient reason for evil as such and in general" (NTT,81). With "a multiplicity of creative agents, some risk of conflict and suffering is inevitable" (CSPM,237-8). God's role is not to decide unilaterally the details of earthly life—even if this were possible—but rather to provide a world order in which freedom is possible, and hence the prospects for great aesthetic goods, despite the inevitable evil and destruction which also occur.

Hartshorne makes the value judgement, shared by most theists (classical and process) that "the chance for these good things was divinely judged worth the risk of the evil things" (NLPE,208). God lures and persuades the world's creatures toward free decisions which, if actualized, promote the most value possible for every creature and the world at large. For all levels of creaturely life, "there is a balance of unity in diversity which is ideally satisfying" (CSPM,304), an appropriate degree of aesthetic value to be sought. We aspire to experiences which contain "a balance of unity and variety" (CSPM,304), a "harmony in diversity" (BS,8), experiences which contain both variety and intensity, and which avoid not only absolute order (regularity, predictability) but also too much discord, too much complexity and too much superficiality (triviality). It is simply not the case, despite the protests of many skeptics, that belief in God is consistent only with a world of absolute order. "To escape the evil of triviality necessarily means to risk discord,"[9] and with each new stage in the advancement of life, from the primordial chaos to the evolution of human beings, more aesthetic value was required, and with it the risk of ever greater evils.[10]

This aesthetic motif is the means by which Hartshorne is able to answer various critics who have argued that it is not evil *per se* which is irreconcilable with belief in God, but rather gratuitous evil.[11] Hartshorne contends that there is no "utterly senseless" or "unredeemed evil." "Any evil has some value from some perspective, for even to know it exists is to make it contributory to a good, knowledge itself being a good" (NTT,80). This is not to say, of course, that Hartshorne believes that all evils are really parts of a good whole or means to a good end (as the traditional aesthetic view holds), nor indeed that evil is not genuinely evil, seen from God's ultimate perspective (as much of traditional theodicy holds). Nor does Hartshorne believe that the world is a perfect whole, ordained by God in its details as such. Hartshorne's point, rather, is that it is not the task of theodicy to try to justify individual evils; the reason for evils in general can be explained as the result of the creativity of the world's creatures, but particular evils "have no ultimate reason" and are simply "nonrational." "Risk of evil and opportunity for good are two aspects of just one thing, multiple freedom" (NTT,81).

These and other important aspects of Hartshorne's theodicy (his argument that evil is "overcome" by God; his defense of "objective immortality"; his utilization of the increasingly popular vision of a suffering God; and his revised versions of the theistic proofs, etc.)[12] merit and demand far more serious critical attention than they have received to date. In this essay, however, I wish to confine my discussion to the one particular aspect of Hartshorne's theodicy which seems especially troublesome and controversial: *the question of divine power*. I have no illusions, to be sure, that the complex and unresolved problems which center about this question can be settled in a short essay; even the most rudimentary overtures toward a solution will necessitate the concentrated efforts of many thinkers. My intention here is to expose some of the problems which must be addressed and to clarify and advance some of the arguments I have made previously.

One of the most common protests against Hartshorne's theodicy is that the process God is "too weak," "too limited" in power. Stephen Ely was among the first to lodge this complaint several decades ago,[13] and it has been reiterated by most critical commentators since then. John Hick, for example, (after virtually ignoring process theodicy in his classic book, *Evil and the God of Love* and in the first two editions of his *Philosophy of Religion*) recently has insisted that "the fundamental criticism of a process theodicy must be a criticism of the doctrine of a limited God,''[14] and Frederick Sontag, Stephen Davis and John Roth all have expressed a similar concern in their assessments of David Griffin's process theodicy.[15] Even writers sympathetic to process thought have found this issue particularly troublesome. Daniel Day Williams, for example, was concerned that Whitehead's God is ''too weak,'' a criticism he did not extend to Hartshorne, interestingly enough, since he believed that Hartshorne's God exerts some measure of coercive power (a point we shall address later).[16]

Hartshorne and other process theists, of course, have contested this critique. ''Instead of saying that God's power is limited,'' Hartshorne insists, ''suggesting that it is less than some conceivable power, we should rather say: [God's] power is absolutely maximal, the greatest possible, but even the greatest possible power is still one power among others, is not the only power'' (DR,138). The solution to the problem of evil is not to be found in the traditional strategies which seek to explain why an all-powerful God has caused or (at the very least) permitted so much suffering and anguish in the world (for example, as tests of faith, as punishment for sin, as having redemptive or educational value, etc.);[17] the solution lies in the realization that God does not cause the details of earthly events, but rather provides a world order which contains the opportunity for aesthetic value and also, unavoidably, the evil and suffering which arises from this creaturely potential.

The fundamental point made by process theists is that the classical conception of an all-powerful God is seriously deficient. Griffin has demonstrated convincingly and indisputably (in my opinion) that traditional theologians credited the deity with ''coercive omnipotence. Nothing could resist God's transitive power. No cooperation by creatures was needed for God to produce effects in the world.''[18] It matters not, I wish to emphasize, whether God unilaterally controls all events or whether God voluntarily has given creatures some degree of genuine free will: in either case God has controlling power and could (and perhaps should) have suppressed creaturely decisions and actions *intermittently* to prevent catastrophes like the holocaust, devastating famines and birth defects, etc., all of which cause such appallingly gratuitous and apparently avoidable misery and distress. It does not seem unreasonable that the God conceived by classical theism could have prevented the worst of these miseries and, indeed, could have done so without significantly altering genuine creaturely freedom.[19]

Relevant to this point are the recent writings of David Basinger who has argued that while this particular criticism has been directed by process theists against classical theodicy, the same criticism holds against process theism. Basinger's contention, that process theists ''have failed to demonstrate that a being with the acknowledged powers of the God of process theism *could* not coerce,''[20] can be maintained, however, only if his provocative and controversial critique of process theism is accepted. Otherwise, the process challenge holds: it is the classical theist who must explain why God has not intervened to prevent the most horrific of earthly miseries, not the process theist who must do so.

Another issue, relevant to the point, has been raised by a number of recent commentators. Nancy Frankenberry, for example, suggests that there is ''a fundamental distortion'' in the common practice of process theists in pitting their vision of a persuasive God against the coercive God of traditional theism.[21] Lewis Ford likewise has cautioned that while Whitehead contrasted the terms, ''persuasion'' and ''coercion,'' the latter is used only once in Whitehead's entire corpus, despite the current widespread use of the contrasting terms in the process literature. Ford maintains that the term ''coercion'' is a poor description of classical omnipotence, although he concedes that the persuasion-coercion rhetoric ''may have some usefulness within the context of theodicy.'' Ford insists, moreover, that few classical theists would admit that their conception of God's omnipotence entails a divine determinism.[22]

My suggestion, nevertheless, is that rather than trying to circumvent the contrast, persuasion and coercion, we ought to seek a far more explicit clarification of its meaning. Process theists will continue to ascribe ''solely persuasive power'' to God, and it seems indisputable that the God of traditional theism has coercive power, whether or not this power is exercised. The term ''persuasion,'' moreover, necessitates an understanding of its antithesis, ''coercion,'' a point confirmed by Morris Cohen's ''law of polarity'' (accepted and utilized by Hartshorne): ''ultimate contraries are correlatives, mutually interdependent, so that nothing real can be described . . . devoid and independent of [its polar opposite]'' (PSG,2).

Some of my own recent writings[23] have focused upon the persuasive-coercive rhetoric, and while certainly I recognize that even to begin to understand divine causal power is to take up a perplexing and undeniably complicated task, I believe that the persuasion-coercion contrast is indispensable for a proper appreciation of process theodicy and, indeed, for a reasonable assessment of classical theodicy. My primary concern is that explicit and precise definitions of persuasive and coercive power have not been forthcoming in the process literature to date. As such, the language Hartshorne and other process theists have used to describe divine persuasive power often is ambiguous and misleading. Ford (and several others) have conceded this much to me, acknowledging that I have ''shown Hartshorne's language to be imprecise.''[24] Robert Mesle, for example, has acknowledged that ''Whitney is correct in asserting that Hartshorne describes God's law-establishing activity in terms which cannot be distinguished from coercion.''[25] Indeed, my contention is that many of Hartshorne's references to divine persuasion ambiguously imply what *could* just as easily be understood as coercion, despite the fact that this clearly is *not* what he has wished to imply. Hartshorne has responded (in private correspondence)[26] that my concern may be merely a matter of semantics, yet I respectfully submit that the issue is far more serious than this. I have given detailed examples elsewhere, but a quick overview here seems appropriate, since the points I have made formerly are central to the issue under discussion. I am convinced that until a resolution of the issue is forthcoming, it will impede a full appreciation of the process vision of God and contribute to the persistent wave of resistance to the entire process enterprise. Critics, as we have noted, long have argued that the process God is too limited and too weak; yet my concern is that the process God can be indicted, with some justification, as being virtually indistinguishable from the all-powerful classical God, a concern recently corroborated by Basinger and Davaney, among others.

The divine lure, according to Hartshorne, is prehended by creatures as an element in our antecedent causal world, with God as the "supreme" or eminent "stimulus" therein (RPP,262; PSG,274). All creatures have some awareness of God, although this perception is not often "clear and distinct" (DR,140). Our discernment of the divine lure most often is unconscious (RPP,257), and in this sense, "irresistible" (WP,164), for "there must be some mode of divine power which cannot simply be disregarded" (RPP,258). God's lure, moreover, is "uniquely eloquent and appealing," since "it offers to each creature what the creature most wants or appreciates in the way of intrinsic value" (RPP,261). For God "to alter us he has only to alter himself. God's unique power over us is his partly self-determined being as our inclusive object of awareness." Indeed, "as this object changes, we are compelled to change in response" (DR,139). "God molds us, by presenting at each moment a partly new ideal or order of preference which our unselfconscious awareness takes as object, and thus renders influential upon our entire activity" (DR,142). God inspires us with an "appeal, attractiveness, or "charm" (RPP,258), with a lure so relevant to our natures and needs that we cannot "even wish not to respond": we "cannot choose but hear" (RPP,261). We do not only hear the divine lure but "in the depths of consciousness we feel and accept the divine ordering" (ANLPE,211).

I submit that these references (and others in Hartshorne's imposing corpus, as well as in the writings of other process theists) are not *unambiguously* supportive of divine persuasive power. Without a more precise rhetoric and a more substantial justification, they could be understood to imply divine coerciveness, for they seem (cumulatively, as well as individually) to suggest a divine causation which is unilaterally effective. The reference cited at the end of the former paragraph, to note but one example, does not make the necessary distinction between our *feeling* of the divine lure and our acceptance of it. That the divine lure is felt unconsciously and irresistibly is not in dispute, but the language used gives the impression that the lure is also accepted irresistibly, despite the fact that this is not what Hartshorne wished to convey. I do not feel that this is merely a question of semantics, nor do I feel that I have interpreted the references (cited above) out of their proper contexts. It is clear what Hartshorne's position is: what is not so clear is the rhetoric used to justify and defend his position.

Basinger recently has argued that while process theists agree that God's lure is unilaterally felt, it is not (supposedly) coercively or unilaterally actualized. This seems to me to be much the same point I have made in calling attention to the ambiguity between our *feeling* of the divine lure and our *acceptance* of it; yet Basinger has attributed to me a different point, one which I do not hold and one which he rightly rejects.[27] I am aware that the "crucial question is not whether God unilaterally lures each entity [since this is indisputable] but whether such luring ever insures (unilaterally brings it about) that God's ideal aim . . . is actualized." I am not as convinced as Basinger is, however, that the fact that God unilaterally brings it about that we have a "cognitive/effective" *feeling* of the divine lure implies that "the God of process theism is coercive in this sense."[28] The point at issue is whether God brings it about unilaterally that we *accept* the lure. Basinger postulates that it is possible (in some circumstances, which he has defined only vaguely) that the God of process theism could act coercively; my position is that the process God acts solely persuasively, but that an adequate justification of this central assertion is lacking in the process literature.

This point, I believe, is substantiated further by several additional passages in Hartshorne's writings which not merely and unambiguously *imply* coercive agency (unilateral action) by God, but seem to insist upon its *necessity*, despite the fact that this is not what Hartshorne has wished to convey. "God tolerates variety," he writes, only "up to the point beyond which it would mean chaos and not a world . . . . God prevents reality from losing all definite character" (MVG,265). Hartshorne contends, moreover, that God must continually insure that creaturely freedom does not destroy itself, a task which is accomplished by restraining our freedom: "God . . . set[s] limits by constraint to the destruction of mutuality" (MVG,173) and apparently does so coercively. Hartshorne, in fact, uses this very term: "Coercion to prevent the use of coercion to destroy freedom generally is in no way action without social awareness but one of its crucial expressions. Freedom must not be free to destroy freedom. The logic of love is not the logic of pacifism" (MVG,173).[29] "Process would come to an end," he argues, "if limits were not imposed upon the development of incompatible lines of process. The comprehensive order of the world is enjoyed, but not determined or created, by ordinary actual entities" (WP,164).

Since there certainly is no dispute that Hartshorne insists upon a vision of God as solely persuasive, I must conclude that these references are unfortunate examples of imprecise and ambiguous language. My contention has been confirmed recently by Sheila Greeve Davaney's argument that "Hartshorne's position concerning divine power as the capacity to influence is far less developed and clearly articulated than is his conception of receptive power .... his understanding of God as cause seems developed in only the most rudimentary manner."[30] I have given several examples of this point previously, but one further illustration, I propose, is the absence of a clearly defined distinction between God's imposition of the causal limits to our freedom and the divine luring of our free acts and decisions within those general limits. My point is that Hartshorne's references to the imposition of natural laws imply coercion, and not only is this contrary to what Hartshorne wished to convey, but it substantiates further the impression that the divine causal luring of creaturely acts and decisions within the limits established by the laws may also be coercive.[31]

"God decides upon the basic outlines of creaturely actions, the guaranteed limits within which freedom is to operate" (NLPE,206), according to Hartshorne. "A divine prehension can use its freedom to create, and for a suitable period maintain, a particular world order" (WP,164). "Only God can decide natural or cosmic laws" (NLPE,209); "a multitude of agents could not select a common world and must indeed simply nullify one another's efforts" (PSG, 273-4). Hartshorne, of course, does not regard the imposition of natural laws by God as a coercive act, since (among other reasons) the laws are merely "statistical and approximate" (CSPM,51,166); God, moreover, "must constantly 'persuade' things to obey the laws."[32] Yet my concern is that these are oblique and insufficient explanations of a divine causation which supposedly is solely persuasive; Whitehead's view that the laws of nature are immanent seems more obviously consistent with divine persuasion, although I am not at all certain how creatures could have fashioned natural laws on their own. I do not dismiss, accordingly, Hartshorne's contention that the natural laws are imposed by God; I see this as the more viable option. My point, however, is that this contention has not been established explicitly as being compatible with divine persuasion.

I am not fully appeased by Ford's proposal that we do not *feel* coerced by natural laws.[33] The point is not whether we *feel* coerced but whether we *are* coerced, and the fact that the natural laws limit what we can do is difficult (for me, at least, and for some others) to distinguish from coercion. I can appreciate Ford's objection to my suggestion that anything which affects us and which is beyond our control and consent is difficult to distinguish from coercion: my working definition of coercion (as such) may have been too vaguely stated. The obvious response, I realize, is that the limiting of freedom by the imposition of natural laws is not coercive, since it is the enabling condition for freedom. Freedom, moreover, is a function of creativity which God coordinates by valuing the alternatives we confront. I accept this point and have acknowledged it previously, but I suggest that a more thorough and convincing defense of it is in order. Ford himself, I would note, has argued that

Hartshorne's God appears to be too much in control, that "there is no way to respond to a law of nature, particularly if imposed by God; it must be obeyed, willy-nilly, for we have no choice in the matter" (TPP,79). Ford's further point of clarification, moreover (a point made previously by Hartshorne), that the divine aim cannot be coercive since it is apprehended so obliquely by us,[34] is not entirely convincing: I am aware that the lure is unconsciously prehended; the problem is that this unconscious apprehension is described as irresistible, compelling, etc. (as noted above), ambiguously implying coercive, unilateral control.

In noting this problem in previous writings, I have given the impression to several commentators that, despite a commitment to Hartshornean process theism, I have proposed ascribing coercive power to God. This is not an accurate assessment of my position, yet neither am I convinced that the point at issue can be easily resolved. Ford's terse comment, for example, that "the laws of nature would not be coercive, regardless of whether they were divinely imposed or . . . whether they characterize the average general behavior of past actualities, since they constitute part of the original enabling conditions,"[35] has not alleviated my concern that the imposition of such laws ambiguously implies coercion. The fact that this concern is shared by others confirms my sense of a present lack of a full and clear resolution of the issue. My apprehension is shared, as noted above, by Davaney (among others) who concluded her recent study of the theistic visions of Hartshorne and Barth with the comment that "it is difficult to discern any difference between Hartshorne's irresistible persuasion and Barth's gracious determinism at this point"; indeed, as she states, "as long as the notion of absolute irresistibility is associated with cosmic laws, then suspicions will remain concerning whether Hartshorne is offering a disguised determinism or merely an ill-conceived indeterminism."[36]

I acknowledge Hartshorne's suggestion,[37] nevertheless, that it makes no sense to talk of coercion with respect to electrons (for example): while electrons do in fact conform to natural laws, we have no reason to suppose they would want to do otherwise. I appreciate Hartshorne's point, moreover, that we are free not *in spite* of the laws imposed by God but *because* of them (for otherwise there would be only chaos and no world order): I grant that the natural laws are the enabling conditions for creaturely actualization. Nonetheless, I am not alone in wondering whether the vision of a purely persuasive God has been safeguarded adequately, and the consequences for process theism, I suggest, are significant: if God *could* coercively establish natural laws, or if God *appears* coercively at times to lure creaturely acts and decisions within the limits imposed by the laws, then it is reasonable to ask why God does not coerce at others times to eliminate evils and suffering. This is the dilemma faced by classical Christian theodicy, and one which process theists supposedly have avoided.[38]

It is significant to note that there have been thinkers sympathetic to process thought who have argued the case for divine coercion (or at least who have assumed it). Norman Pittenger, for example, has suggested that while the God of Whitehead and Hartshorne acts "primarily" persuasively, God acts coercively in a secondary way.[39] Pittenger, to my knowledge, has not followed through with respect to this brief statement, except to note, equally tersely, that the process God must use "coercion to prevent [the] cosmos from becoming anarchy or chaos."[40] This seems to me a case in point where a major commentator has been misled by imprecise language and the lack the necessary substantiation in defense of a divine causal agency which is solely persuasive.

The late Daniel Day Williams may be a further case in point: he has argued that, unlike Whitehead, "Hartshorne is right in stressing also the coercive aspects of our religious experience .... There are large coercive aspects in the divine governance of the world."[41] Williams unfortunately did not elaborate fully upon this provocative statement with respect to Hartshorne, although he has sought to provide the basis for an understanding of divine power which allows for more coercion than Whitehead was willing to concede, offering us a vision of "the divine companion," the suffering God, who acts to overcome the world's anguish and suffering. What is interesting in this argument is Williams' insistence that "the structures of life coerce us," implying that God "does exercise coercive power":[42] "coercive elements ... seem as necessary to a real universe as the persuasive aspects," he contended, and "no organism would survive five seconds on the exercise of [divine] tenderness alone." Whitehead's vision of a God which acts solely persuasively leads him, according to Williams, to ignore "the wide range of types of force, or coercion, and of mutual interaction. These would seem to have their place," however, "in the necessities of being, and therefore require us to find their place in God's being." Whitehead, although apparently not Hartshorne, according to Williams, "underestimated the disclosure of the divine initiative in religious experience" and thus "has given a partially inadequate account of the relation between God and the world."[43]

Gerald Janzen, furthermore, has argued against Ford that the "effort to conceive of God's activity solely in terms of persuasion" is misconceived. Janzen believes that divine power is better understood "in terms both of efficacy and of finality, of coercion and of persuasion."[44] This argument, however, and his contention that the argument can be shown to be consistent with Whitehead's writings, have not been substantiated (to my knowledge). The issue, of course, is whether it can be substantiated.

Griffin's contribution to the problem is helpful: God, he has suggested, is limited by metaphysical principles about the way actualities can be ordered, and since the deity has not created the world "*ex nihilo*," entities have "inherent" power which cannot be "canceled out or overridden by God." As such, God "cannot control [completely] but can only persuade what we become and how we affect others."[45] In my opinion, this argument supports the central theistic vision of process theism: God acts and indeed *must* act solely persuasively. Yet I insist that my concern is also warranted: there remains an unsettling ambiguity and an unsatisfying lack of a more complete justification of this important thesis.

The fact that Griffin's argument (just noted) has been disputed by Basinger confirms my point. Basinger contends that for Griffin to "establish that God could never control our behavior, it must be shown that there exists some eternal, necessary metaphysical principle which allows only for the existence of actualities who are free to reject God's initial aim at all times." Basinger argues, moreover, that "process theists have given us no good reason to believe that their God could not coerce, and hence that their 'persuasive' God is significantly different than the 'coercive' God of some forms of classical Christian theism."[46] Process theodicy, as such, is "no more adequate" than "the classical theism in which it is also held that God has voluntarily chosen to refrain from significant (if any) unilateral involvement in earthly affairs."[47]

Basinger's proposal is based largely upon an appeal to various examples of psychological manipulation which supposedly achieve the desired ends unilaterally; he insists that the process God has this apparently unexercised option available. I have reservations about the viability of this argument,[48] yet I have no reservations in regarding Basinger's proposal as but one further manifestation of my concern that there is far too much ambiguity in the process literature concerning the terms "persuasive" and "coercive" power, both with respect to God and to creatures. This accounts not only for the various recommendations that more coercive power be attributed to the process God and/or that such power is part of the divine causal agency, but also may account for the recurring critical assessments of process thought which find its vision of a solely persuasive God profoundly lacking in appeal.

I suggest that the most promising means of seeking a resolution to this problem is for process theists to demonstrate (far more clearly than has been accomplished to date) the vast and perhaps unlimited *range* of power available to God. Ford has referred to divine causal activity as "indirectly coercive," yet "directly persuasive,"[49] and Griffin has suggested that there is an "intertwining of elements of coercion and pure persuasion on the continuum of forms of persuasion" exercised by God; he has used the term "coercive persuasion" in contrast to "pure persuasion" in his brief explanation of this point.[50] Williams and Janzen, as noted above, have argued much the same, as have some others as well. For his part, Hartshorne has maintained that there is an unlimited range of potentiality offered by God to creatures for actualization,[51] and it does not seem unreasonable to me to suggest that there is likewise an unlimited range of divine causal influence, extending from that which constitutes a minimal degree of causal action to that which constitutes a maximum degree of such action—without it ever becoming coercive in the sense of overriding genuine creaturely freedom. Hartshorne surely is correct in acclaiming Whitehead's ascription of solely persuasive power to God as "one of the greatest of all metaphysical discoveries" (DR,142); yet the broad scope of this divine causal power, short of an absolute coercion, must be more clearly defined.

It must be acknowledged, of course, that even to begin to comprehend *how* God acts is probably the most enigmatic (and also, perhaps, the most significant) of theological questions, one which may lie forever beyond full human comprehension. Nevertheless, the metaphysical and moral *foundation* for a solely persuasive God *has* been formulated in the process literature, despite the lack of a fully justified defense of this vision. What remains to be accomplished is a more precise delineation of the range of persuasive power utilized by God, some of which is more "persuasive" and hence more "coercive."

Classical theism is aware that God has omnipotent power and yet that human beings nevertheless are free. Biblical texts assume likewise both an absolute divine sovereignty and genuine human responsibility.[52] I propose that process theism is correct in holding that it makes no sense to speak of absolute divine coercive power; yet I am left wondering whether it makes sense to speak of an absolute divine persuasive power. It seems to me that we must ascribe a mixture of persuasive and coercive power to God; that is, that there must be an infinite range of divine persuasive power, much of which is more persuasively influential, and hence more coercive, without it ever being an absolute coercion. This proposal calls for a careful and detailed justification. The task before us seems clear.

NOTES

1. See Hick, *Evil and the God of Love.*
2. For references, see Whitney, *What Are They Saying About God and Evil?*
3. See Whitney, *What Are They Saying About God and Evil?*
4. Hick, *Evil and the God of Love*, 7-9.
5. Barry Whitney, *The Question of Theodicy in the Neoclassical Metaphysics of Charles Hartshorne*, unpublished dissertation (McMaster University, 1977); see also my "Process Theism: Does a Persuasive God Coerce?" (1979) and "Hartshorne's New Look at Theodicy" (1979).
6. Griffin, *God, Power, and Evil.*
7. Griffin, "Creation *Ex Nihilo*," 111.
8. See Whitney, *Evil and the Process God*, 117-124.
9. Cobb and Griffin, *Process Theology*, 73.

10. See Griffin, "Creation Out of Chaos and the Problem of Evil," 285-291, etc.
11. See, for example, Peterson, *Evil and the Christian God.*
12. Whitney, *Evil and the Process God.*
13. Ely, *The Religious Availability of Whitehead's God.*
14. Hick, "An Irenaean Theodicy," 122.
15. See *Encountering Evil.*
16. See Daniel Day Williams, "Deity, Monarchy, and Metaphysics: Whitehead's Critique of the Theological Tradition"; "Time, Progress, and the Kingdom of God"; "How Does God Act? An Essay in Whitehead's Metaphysics"; *What Present Day Theologians are Thinking*; *The Spirit and the Forms of Love*; etc.
17. See Whitney, *What Are They Saying About God and Evil?*, Chapter 3.
18. Griffin, in *Faith and Creativity*, 97; and his *God, Power, and Evil.*
19. I concede, of course, that classical theists have arguments against the plausibility of this critique. God, it is proposed, perhaps *has* intervened and perhaps has eliminated the most horrendous of evils; any further intervention would be incompatible with genuine human freedom—an argument which is unfalsifiable.
20. Basinger, *Divine Power in Process Theism*, 113.
21. Frankenberry, "Some Problems in Process Theodicy," 180.
22. Ford, "Divine Persuasion and Coercion," 267-274.
23. See my *Evil and the Process God* and my "Process Theism."
24. Letter from Ford: February, 1987.
25. Mesle, review of *Evil and the Process God*, in *PS* (1987), 58.
26. Letter from Hartshorne: May, 1987.
27. Basinger cites my 1979 article, "Process Theism," as the reference for his claim that to assert that God never coerces "is sometimes thought to mean that God never unilaterally brings about any state of affairs" (*Divine Power in Process Theism*, 28).
28. Basinger, *Divine Power in Process Theism*, 28.
29. See my chapter on Hartshorne and pacifism, "Charles Hartshorne," in *Nonviolence—Central to Christian Spirituality*, 217-237; and Daniel Dombrowski, "Pacifism and Hartshorne's Dipolar Theism," (1987), 337-350.
30. Davaney, *Divine Power*, 170.
31. In an earlier article, I tried to show how Hartshorne's understanding of possibility could support a theory of divine persuasion, despite criticisms like Ford's: see my "Does God Influence the World's Creativity? Hartshorne's Doctrine of Possibility," 613-622.
32. Charles Hartshorne, "Process and the Nature of God," 173.
33. Letter from Ford: November, 1976; see also Ford's *The Lure of God*, 17.
34. Ford, "Divine Persuasion and Coercion," 269.
35. ——, "Divine Persuasion and Coercion," 271.
36. Davaney, *Divine Power*, 191.
37. Letter from Hartshorne: May, 1987. Griffin makes a similar point in "Creation Out of Chaos and the Problem of Evil," 112-114.
38. It is unfortunate that Robert Mesle has argued that I have fallen into this classical trap. His assessment of my position, however, is based upon a misunderstanding of what I have written: I have not ascribed coercive power to God. (See Mesle's review of my *Evil and the Process God*, in *PS* [1987], 57-81). Another commentator, Marvin Collins, argues that I rightly espouse coercive power to the process

God (*God and Evil in the Process Thought of A.N. Whitehead, Charles Hartshorne, and David Griffin: A Question of Theological Coherence*, unpublished dissertation (Fuller Theological Seminary, 1986).

39. Pittenger, "Process Theology, *Expository Times*, 107.
40. Pittenger, "Process Theology," 57.
41. Williams, "How Does God Act? An Essay in Whitehead's Metaphysics," 177.
42. Williams, "Time, Progress, and the Kingdom of God," 461.
43. Williams, "Deity, Monarchy, and Metaphysics," 370-371.
44. Janzen, "Modes of Power and the Divine Relativity," 405.
45. Griffin, "Creation Out of Chaos and the Problem of Evil," 105.
46. Basinger, *Divine Power in Process Theism*, 27.
47. Basinger, *Divine Power in Process Theism*, 39.
48. This may seem to be an unfair statement since I do not have space here to make clear what my problems are with Basinger's argument. In brief, I find problematic the assumption of a one-to-one correspondence of the uses of coercion in human experience and the meaning of the term with respect to God. Ford's point is relevant: "Coercion is readily understood on the level of social or physical behavior, but its proper metaphysical definition is difficult to ascertain" (*The Lure of God*, 17).
49. Ford, *The Lure of God*, 44.
50. Griffin, "Creation *Ex Nihilo*," 97.
51. See my *Evil and the Process God*, 109-111; and my "Does God Influence the World's Creativity? Hartshorne's Doctrine of Possibility."
52. See D. A. Carson, *Divine Sovereignty and Human Responsibility*.

BIBLIOGRAPHY

Basinger, David. *Divine Power in Process Theism*. Albany. SUNY Press, 1988.

Cobb, John and Griffin, David. *Process Theology*. Philadelphia: Westminster Press, 1976.

Davaney, Sheila Greeve. *Divine Power*. Philadelphia. Fortress Press, 1986.

Davis, Stephen T. (ed.). *Encountering Evil*. Atlanta. John Knox Press, 1981.

Dombrowski, Daniel. "Pacifism and Hartshorne's Dipolar Theism." *Encounter*, 1987: 337-350.

Ely, Stephen. *The Religious Availability of Whitehead's God*. Madison. University of Wisconsin Press, 1942.

Ford, Lewis. "Divine Persuasion and Coercion." *Encounter*, 1986: 267-274.

Ford, Lewis (ed.). *Two Process Philosophers*. Tallahassee. American Academy of Religion, 1973. Cited as TPP.

Frankenberry, Nancy. "Some Problems with Process Theodicy." *Religious Studies*, 1982: 179-197.

Griffin, David. "Creation *Ex Nihilo*, The Divine *Modus Operandi*, and The *Imitatio Dei*." *In Faith and Creativity*. George Norgulen and George Shields (eds.). St. Louis. CBP Press, 1987.

——. "Creation Out of Chaos and the Problem of Evil." In *Encountering Evil*. Stephen T. Davis (ed.).

Griffin, David. *God, Power and Evil.* Philadelphia. Westminster Press, 1976.

Hartshorne, Charles. *Omnipotence and Other Theological Mistakes.* Albany. SUNY Press, 1984. Cited as OOTM.

——. *A Natural Theology for our Time.* New Haven. Yale University Press, 1967. Cited as NTT.

——. "Process and the Nature of God." In *Traces of God in a Secular Culture.* G. F. McLean (ed.). New York. Alba House, 1978: 117-141.

——. *Creative Synthesis and Philosophic Method.* La Salle, IL. Open Court, 1970. Cited as CSPM.

—— and Reese, William. *Philosophers Speak of God.* Chicago. The University of Chicago Press, 1953. Cited as PSG.

——. "A New Look at the Problem of Evil." In *Current Philosophical Issues: Essays in Honor of Curt John Ducasse.* F. C. Dommeyer (ed.). Springfield, IL. Charles C. Thomas, 1966: 201-212. Cited as NLPE.

——. "Religion in Process Philosophy." In *Religion in Philosophical and Cultural Perspective.* Princeton. D. Van Nostrand, 1967: 246-268. Cited as RPP.

——. *Man's Vision of God and the Logic of Theism.* Hamden, CN. Archon Books, 1941. Cited as MVG.

——. *Whitehead's Philosophy.* Lincoln. University of Nebraska Press, 1972. Cited as WP.

——. *Born to Sing.* Bloomington. Indiana University Press, 1973. Cited as BS.

Hick, John. *Evil and the God of Love* (second edition). New York. Harper and Row, 1978.

——. "An Ireanean Theodicy." In *Encountering Evil.* Stephen T. Davis (ed.).

Janzen, Gerald. "Modes of Power and the Divine Relativity." *Encounter,* 1975: 379-406.

Mesle, Robert. Review of Barry L. Whitney, *Evil and the Process God.* In *Process Studies,* 1987: 57-61.

Peterson, Michael. *Evil and the Christian God.* Grand Rapids, MI. Baker Book House, 1982.

Pittenger, Norman. "Process Theology." *Expository Times,* 1973: 56-57.

Whitney, Barry. "Hartshorne's New Look at Theodicy." *Studies in Religion,* 1979: 281-291.

——. *Evil and the Process God.* New York. The Edwin Mellen Press, 1985.

——. "Does God Influence the World's Creativity? Hartshorne's Doctrine of Possibility." *Philosophy Research Archives,* 1981: 613-622.

——. *What Are They Saying About God and Evil?* New York. Paulist Press, 1989 (forthcoming).

——. "Charles Hartshorne." In *Non-Violence—Central to Christian Spirituality.* Joseph T. Culliton (ed.) New York. The Edwin Mellen Press, 1982: 217-237.

——. "Process Theism: Does a Persuasive God Coerce?" *Southern Journal of Philosophy,* 1979: 133-143.

Williams, Daniel Day. "How Does God Act? An Essay in Whitehead's Metaphysics." In *Process and Divinity.* W. L. Reese and E. Freeman (eds.). La Salle. Open Court, 1964: 161-180.

——. "Time, Progress, and the Kingdom of God." In *Process Philosophy and Christian Thought.* Delwin Brown, Ralph James and Gene Reeves (eds.). Indianapolis and New York. Bobbs-Merrill, 1971: 441-463.

———. "Deity, Monarchy, and Metaphysics: Whitehead's Critique of the Theological Tradition." In *The Relevance of Whitehead*. I. Leclerc (ed.). New York. Humanities Press, 1961: 353-372.

———. *The Spirit and the Forms of Love*. New York. Harper and Row, 1968.

———. *What Present Day Theologians are Thinking* (third edition). New York. Harper and Row, 1967.

God Only Knows?
Hartshorne and the Mechanics of Omniscience

Donald Wayne Viney

In Herman Melville's *Moby-Dick*, Captain Ahab's obsession with destroying the great white whale drives him and his crew (with the exception of the narrator) to their mutual destruction. On the second day of the chase, the first mate, sensing the disaster to come, calls the hunt impious and blasphemous. Ahab responds:

> Ahab is forever Ahab, man. This whole act's immutably decreed. 'Twas rehearsed by thee and me a billion years before this ocean rolled. Fool! I am the Fates' lieutenant; I act under orders (Melville 1967 [1851], 459).

The haunting sense that Ahab speaks for all of us finds expression in the technical literature of philosophical theology in the problem of divine foreknowledge of future contingents. As traditionally conceived, the deity has perfect awareness of what, to us, is future. Thus history would be the unfolding of what God knew all along. Discussion frequently centers on what, if any, sense of human freedom is salvageable given this divine knowledge. The field quickly divides into two camps: those who believe that either human freedom or divine foreknowledge must be sacrificed for the sake of logical consistency and those who deny this claim. Let us call these two groups epistemic incompatibilists and epistemic compatibilists respectively.[1] The seeds of epistemic incompatibilism are evident in Aristotle's *De Interpretatione* IX. The high regard with which he came to be held during the medieval period required that the scholastics address his arguments, despite the fact that, as a matter of faith and on pain of ecclesiastical censure, they disagreed with him. The less restricted intellectual climate of the Reformation encouraged more dissenters to express their views, although majority opinion remained and continues to remain with the epistemic compatibilists.

The focus of this paper is Charles Hartshorne's views on what I call the 'mechanics of omniscience.' The phrase is a *double entendre*. On the one hand, it refers to the question of how God comes to have knowledge of the world. What are the workings of omniscience? On the other hand, it refers to the persons who have offered theories about how God knows. The chief relevance of this issue for the problem of divine foreknowledge and human freedom is that there is a limited range of theories about the mechanics of omniscience compatible with the freedom of the creatures. Thus epistemic compatibilists may successfully refute an incompatibilist argument but offer a defective theory of the mechanics of omniscience and, as a consequence, be hoisted with their own petard.

I believe it can be shown, with Hartshorne's help, that the most plausible theory of the workings of God's knowledge that is compatible with creaturely freedom (properly understood) is one that does not allow divine foreknowledge of future contingents. The first section of the paper is devoted to an overview of the theories proposed by the "mechanics" of omniscience—both the compatibilists and the incompatibilists. The second section presents Hartshorne's responses to these theories. The third section discusses Hartshorne's central argument and his view of the mechanics of omniscience along with its implications for the truth value of propositions about future contingents.

Historical-topical survey

Theories about the mechanics of omniscience dealing specifically with divine knowledge of future contingents may be usefully analyzed according to their fit with three ideal types. First, a theology might model divine knowledge on knowledge of one's own intentions or actions. The regnant metaphors for omniscience on this approach would be drawn from *practical knowledge*—to know something because you produce it. A second type models divine knowledge on knowledge of eternal or necessary truths. The primary metaphors for omniscience here would be drawn from *innate knowledge*—to know something because it is already in your mind. A third type models divine knowledge on knowledge acquired through experience. The dominant metaphors for omniscience here would be drawn from *sense perception*—to know something because it entered your experience. Let us call these models respectively, practical, innatist, and perceptual. We will see that most theories of the mechanics of omniscience do not fit neatly into any single category but are a combination of these types. Nevertheless, each theory has a main focus, whether practical, innatist, or perceptual, and this is enough to make the three-fold classification useful.

One of the earliest and most illuminating discussions of divine foreknowledge and free will is in Boethius' *The Consolation of Philosophy.* Boethius leaned heavily on perceptual metaphors to illustrate God's knowledge of the future, but a careful reading of his argument shows that his theory of the mechanics of omniscience could only be innatist or practical. According to Boethius, God exists outside the temporal process in such a way that each moment of time is wholly present to God's mind. This is his famous doctrine of God's "eternity" (Boethius 1962, 115). Boethius suggested that time is to eternity as a circle to its center (ibid. 92). Just as all of the points on the circumference are equidistant from the center, so each moment of time is present to God. Because he took the analogy seriously, he denied that, properly speaking, God has foreknowledge. God simply knows eternally what, to merely temporal creatures, is in the future. Boethius modeled God's awareness of time on visual perception of the present. In this way he sought to avoid God's knowledge obtruding on the freedom of the creatures. He asks, "Does your vision impose any necessity upon things which you see present before you?" (Boethius 1962, 117). His answer is no; and by parity of reasoning, God's vision of events in time imposes no necessity on them.

Boethius' reliance on the visual analogy suggests a perceptual model of the mechanics of omniscience. However, he denied that temporal things are the cause of God's knowledge. Unlike physical beings whose knowledge of the world requires being acted upon by external stimuli, a being of pure intelligence, like God, would know by the active power of the mind (ibid. 113). Therefore, Boethius' account of how God knows is more akin to the practical or innatist approach than to the perceptual. Thomas Aquinas, who used the circle analogy (Aquinas 1955, 219; SCG Bk I, 66.7), made this explicit when he claimed that, "the knowledge of God is the cause of all things. For the knowledge of God is to all creatures what the knowledge of the artificer is to the things made by his art" (Aquinas 1945, 142; ST I, Q 14, a.8). The scriptural precedent for such a view is clear enough (Wisdom 15.7; Isaiah 29.16, 45.9; Jeremiah 18.6; Romans 9.21). Nevertheless, the underlying reason for taking this approach was that it was considered unthinkable that God should owe anything to the creatures (cf. Boethius 1962, 106). The perfection of the deity was itself premised on the idea that God is *actus purus*, pure act, with no admixture of potency (Aquinas 1955, 101, 136; SCG I, 16.5, 28.6). While Aquinas could speak of God's "knowledge of vision" encompassing all temporal events (Aquinas 1955, 221, SCG I, 67.2), suggesting, like Boethius, a perceptual model, it is clear that there was no implication that God's knowledge might arise as a result of experiencing the world. Therefore, Aquinas could say that "the creatures are really related to God," but "in God there is no real relation to creatures . . . ." (Aquinas 1945, 113; ST I, Q 13, a.7).

John Duns Scotus developed the practical model to an unsurpassed intricacy and precision, earning his sobriquet, the Subtle Doctor. Criticizing what he took to be deficiencies in Aquinas' view, Scotus argued that the divine intellect is incapable of distinguishing possible from actual creatures until the divine will has chosen which, among the possible creatures, will be actual. Scotus objected to the idea that worldly events are eternally present to God's mind. For Scotus, God knows events in time not because those events are present to God in eternity but because God wills them to come to exist in time. God knows things as they are in willed existence, not as they are in actual existence (although actual existence faithfully mirrors willed existence). To the objection that his view deprives the creatures of their freedom, Scotus responded that (a) creaturely decisions are contingent because caused by a contingent decree of the divine will, and (b) all that freedom requires, in any case, is the ability to act in opposite directions; the creatures possess this ability as a gift of God even if they never have the opportunity to defy the divine will (Langston 1986, Part I).

Scotus' view highlighted the key problem in any purely practical model of omniscience. Rejecting the Scotistic view, William of Ockham argued that creaturely decisions either follow necessarily from the divine will or they do not. If they do, then human acts are necessary and, like the burning of fire, not free. If the finite will does not necessarily obey the divine decree, then God would not have infallible awareness of what the creatures will do. Therefore, either the creatures are not free or God does not know in advance what they will decide. Of course, with the rest of medieval Christianity, neither alternative was acceptable to Ockham. The problem might have been alleviated with a perceptual model, but this was not an idea Ockham took seriously because of its implication of potency in God. Thus he made an unabashed appeal to revelation, and maintained that "it is impossible to express clearly the way in which God knows future contingents" (Ockham 1969, 49-50).[2]

Luis de Molina and his followers believed that Ockham's fideism was premature. God's knowledge of future contingents could be vouchsafed by a doctrine of middle knowledge (*scientia media*). Molina attributed three sorts of knowledge to God: (i) knowledge of all possible objects—along with their necessary relations—to which divine power extends, (ii) knowledge of the objects that have been actualized by the divine will, and (iii) middle knowledge, or knowledge of what any free creature would do under any set of circumstances (Kenny 1979, 62f). Innatist strands in Molina's theory are evident in (i) and (iii), while the practical model is evident in (ii). In support of middle knowledge, Molina invoked the authority of scripture (I Samuel 23; Wisdom 4.11; Matthew 11.21) where God is portrayed as knowing what an individual or group of individuals would have done under a hypothetical set of circumstances. Revelation aside, the appeal of Molinism was the way it seemed to guarantee the possibility of infallible awareness of future contingents. If God knows what a possible free creature would do under any set of circumstances and also places the creature in those circumstances, God knows infallibly what the creature will freely do. In line with the medieval prohibition against assigning potency to the deity, Molina avoided a perceptual model and combined elements of the practical and the innatist models in accounting for God's knowledge of future contingents.

It fell to more recent thinkers to develop the perceptual model of omniscience. Although Faustus Socinus, a contemporary of Molina, provided the central argument for a perceptual approach (Hartshorne 1953, 225-227), Jules Lequier seems to have been the first with a sufficient command of medieval philosophy to criticize practical and innatist models and to clarify the implications of denying them. In a radical departure from Aquinas and his tradition, Lequier declared the relation from God to the creatures to be as real as the relation from the creatures to God (Lequier 1952, 73). In a memorable phrase, he affirmed his faith in a God "who created me creator of myself" (ibid. 70). The very idea offends the medieval sensibility that creativity is the sole possession of the creator (Aquinas 1945, 243; ST I, Q 45, a.5). If the creatures are, to some extent, self-creators, then there is no blueprint of what they would do, for the blueprint is itself their doing (contra Molina). Moreover, what the creatures create, if it is genuinely real, qualifies in however humble a fashion the divine awareness (contra Boethius, Aquinas, Scotus, Ockham, and Molina). As Lequier says, "Terrible prodigy: man deliberates and God waits" (Lequier 1952, 71). Or again, the freedom of self-creativity "puts a stain in the absolute which destroys the absolute" (ibid. 74).

The consequence of Lequier's view for divine foreknowledge and human freedom is clear. If God must wait on human decisions to know them, then God does not know them eternally or in advance. Lequier reminds his readers that his view in no way compromises omniscience properly understood. Failure to know a creature's free decisions in advance is no more a limit on omniscience than inability to make a square circle is a limit on omnipotence (Lequier 1952, 171). He does not simply claim that God does not know future free decisions; he adds that those decisions do not exist to be known. The difference between divine and non-divine knowledge of the future is that the latter is "limited, obscure and full of errors" while God has perfect knowledge of the extent to which the future is open or closed (ibid. 205).

Lequier's influence would have been confined entirely to francophiles had it not been for his friend Charles Renouvier who instigated the publication of some of his works. Hartshorne summarizes the case well:

> Lequier's greatest influence was through Renouvier to James, and through James to Dewey, in making clear the connection of freedom (as creativity) with chance, setting limits to what even ideal or divine decisions can determine, and making causal indeterminacy almost axiomatic for later French metaphysics (personal correspondence, 7/9/88).

Nevertheless, history books continue to ignore Lequier (e.g. Copleston's volume on French philosophy makes no mention of him, 1977), and current literature on the mechanics of omniscience proceeds as if he never existed. Because of this and as a result of the perceived failure of Aquinas and Scotus to account for how God knows, debates over Molinism hold center stage. In what follows, another voice will be heard—one with which Lequier would find much to agree.[3]

Hartshorne on the mechanics of omniscience

Hartshorne's awareness of the classical theories of the mechanics of omniscience is evident from his many references to them (e.g. 1945, 284). The one theory he does not explicitly mention is Molinism. With fitting irony, we will see that it is easy enough to guess what his response to Molina would be. He mentioned the Socinians as early as *Man's Vision of God*, (1941, 5), but he did not become aware of Lequier until 1948 when his similarities with the Frenchman were pointed out to him by Jean Wahl (personal correspondence 5/21/86). Hartshorne came to his views on God's knowledge of the future by 1921 as a result of a conversation with W. E. Hocking. The professor convinced him that even God must face a partly open or indeterminate future (Hartshorne 1984b, 195; Peters 1970, 5-7).

Hartshorne says that if Lequier influenced him appreciably, "it was in what he said about God as the one who has 'created me creator of myself,' thus closely anticipating Whitehead's 'self-created creature' " (personal correspondence 7/9/88). Like Lequier and Alfred North Whitehead, Hartshorne takes "creativity" as the blade that cuts the Gordian knot of many philosophical problems. For Lequier, freedom as creativity was the "first truth," analogous to Descartes' *cogito*, from which philosophical reflection begins. For Whitehead, creativity was the category of the ultimate, a way of taking "process" rather than "fact" as the final metaphysical generalization. He says:

> The ultimate metaphysical principle is the advance from disjunction to conjunction, creating a novel entity other than the entities given in disjunction. The novel entity is at once the togetherness of the 'many' which it finds, and also it is one among the disjunctive 'many' which it leaves; it is a novel entity, disjunctively among the many entities which it synthesizes. The many become one, and are increased by one (Whitehead 1978 [1929], 21).

On this point, Hartshorne is in complete agreement with Whitehead. He says, "*To be is to create*" (1970, 1). His explanation of creativity is similar to Whitehead's. Creativity means:

> *additions to the definiteness of reality*. Every effect is in some degree, however slight, an "emergent whole." Emergence is no special case, but the general principle of process, although it may have privileged instances in which the extent of novelty (not determined by the conditions) is unusually pronounced (ibid. 3).

If there is a "proof" for taking creativity as the ultimate category of explanation, it is, so to speak, in the metaphysical pudding; that is to say, the argument for the ultimacy of creativity lies in its general usefulness in making sense of and solving problems in speculative philosophy. As far as Hartshorne's response to these theorists—to these "mechanics" of omniscience—is concerned, it is useful to see how the ultimacy of creativity figures in the concepts of time, freedom, and possibility.

Time

If creativity means additions to the definiteness of reality, and if creativity is the final truth of things, then it is impossible that there be a timeless whole of temporal events. When Boethius said that temporal events are *present* to

God in eternity, he did not simply mean that the events are registered in God's awareness; he meant that the events exist alongside God's eternal being.[4] The additions to reality that will be the future are an ever-present reality for God. If Hartshorne is correct, this is impossible since, strictly speaking, future events do not exist (1963, 604). Scotus had rejected the circle analogy saying that "time is not a standing circumference, but a flowing one" (Lewis 1988, 88). Hartshorne would go further and say that time is not like a circumference at all. He says that Aquinas [following Boethius]:

> assumes that events future are yet in themselves real and determinate, or that time is analogous to a circle and not to an endless line whose points are added to it from moment to moment and form no complete sum (1945, 284).

The concept of reality in Hartshornean metaphysics is the concept of an ever growing totality. " 'Reality' means 'as of now,' and the 'now' acquires new reference each moment. Events can be surveyed only from within some event or sequence of events. *Sub specie aeternitatis* only eternal abstractions could be contemplated" (1970, 118). If creativity is ultimate, then the Boethian view involves an untenable account of time, and hence of God's relation to time.

One occasionally hears the argument that the reality of the past is no less problematic than the reality of the future. If future events do not yet exist, past events no longer exist. But it should be noted that common ways of speaking about the past exhibit a certain ambiguity. We say that "the past is gone," or "no longer exists," but we do not simply mean that the past is nothing or that the once present reality has been annihilated. If we say, "Don't cry over spilled milk," we imply that there is a fact of the matter—not simply a propositional outline—about the milk's having been spilled. The question then is not whether past events exist but in what sense they exist. For Hartshorne, past events are an integral part of the growing totality that is reality:

> Past events do not exist, or are not present, *in the same sense* as they once did or were, but they may yet be, in a genuine sense, still real and still present. The new event cannot be in the old, but the old can be in the new. A novel whole can contain parts which are not novel .... Becoming is the creation of novel wholes with non-novel elements .... Hence [the] "cumulative" theory of process, or of process as "creative synthesis" (1970, 88).

If Hartshorne is correct, then there must be a sense in which the past, though no longer existent *as* present, nevertheless exists *in* the present. In the last section, we will see how Hartshorne uses a perceptual model of omniscience to account for the reality of the past. For now, it is enough to see that Hartshorne is not committed to a "false symmetry" (Hartshorne 1983, 242) of taking the past as being as nonexistent as the future.

Freedom

If Hartshorne finds the Boethian account of omniscience unacceptable because it implies a false concept of time, he finds the views of Aquinas and Scotus defective because they imply a false concept of freedom. He says that Scotus' account contradicts human freedom (1945, 284) and that—Aquinas' claim to the contrary notwithstanding—the deity's knowledge of itself as "cause" of creaturely decisions is not enough to guarantee knowledge of their actual decisions (1976, 11).

A minimal implication of the ultimacy of creativity is that human freedom is best understood along libertarian lines. According to the libertarian, an agent was free with respect to a decision only if the agent could have decided otherwise with all relevant antecedent conditions remaining unchanged (cf. Kane 1985, 21). Hartshorne speaks of the emergence of "novel wholes" in the creative advance not entirely prefigured in past causal conditions. In the human case—though not only in the human case since creativity is universal—some of these novel wholes are free decisions. To be free is to face a partly open future. The feeling we have of opportunities lost or gained in the making of decisions makes sense on this view. It is an oddity of a theistic non-libertarianism like Scotus's that God should have endowed the creatures with so strong a sense of alternative possibilities faithfully preceding their decisions though that sense be consistently deceptive.

The oddity of the non-libertarian view is not enough to show that it is false. However, it is instructive to see why Hartshorne rejects the views of Scotus and other non-libertarians. As Hartshorne says, non-libertarians locate freedom "in the ability to execute choice, not in the choice itself." In this way, one's decisions can be conceived as inevitable, as the "only then-and-there causally possible one" (Hartshorne 1984a, 14, 16). For Scotus, according to Hartshorne, an agent's decisions can be free *even when those decisions are unilaterally determined by God.* Two problems attend this view as far as theism is concerned. First, it aggravates the problem of evil by making God the author of evil. A non-libertarian can make no use of a free-will theodicy (cf. Moskop 1984, 23-27). As far as the freedom of the creatures is concerned, there is no theoretical advantage in the view that the creatures are self-determining and do evil—i.e. as opposed to the view that God brings it about that every creature "freely" chooses the good. A second problem with Scotus' view Hartshorne puts in the form of a dilemma: Either God is or is not free in a libertarian sense. If God has libertarian free will but the creatures do not, then we equivocate in speaking of divine and creaturely freedom and lose any basis in experience for an analogy between the two. If God does not have libertarian free will, then God's choices, including the choice of which universe to create, could not have been otherwise. This effectively eliminates the sort of contingency that Scotus and other non-libertarians attribute to God's choices (Hartshorne 1984a, 17-18). The non-libertarian view of freedom, therefore, creates at least as many problems for theism as it purports to solve.

Hartshorne is careful to argue that a libertarian view of freedom does not imply that there are uncaused events (although this has often been assumed, even by libertarians!). Libertarianism implies only that, in some cases, the causes preceding a decision do not totally determine what the decision will be (Viney 1986, 557). Hartshorne notes that the falsity of determinism is not the same as the lack of causation, and he cites a variety of arguments against traditional concepts of causation (1962, 161-190; 1973). For Hartshorne, every event is conditioned by past events and thus implies those events as antecedent causes. However, causes do not imply every detail of their effects. Consequently, Hartshorne denies the scholastic argument that God's knowledge of the divine will as cause entails God's knowledge of the world as effect (1976, 11). The ultimacy of creativity requires that, in however humble a fashion, the effect is always "more" than the cause. Hartshorne agrees with Lequier that the self-created creature adds something to reality and possesses a value that is greater than the existence of God alone.

Possibility

The most promising account of the mechanics of omniscience in classical theology is Molinism (cf. Basinger 1986). Not only is it an attractive option for classical theists, it seems to be indispensable for any theism that would affirm divine foreknowledge and human freedom in a libertarian sense. If God knows—antecedent to the creation of the universe and subsequent to the decision to create—which universe will be actual and what decisions the creatures will make, then God *must* have middle knowledge. For instance, before the creation of the universe, it could not have been true that, at age twenty-five, my brother *was going to decide* to be a biology instructor unless it was also true that he *would decide* to be a biology instructor at age twenty-five if presented with the opportunity. God could not have foreknown what he was going to do unless there was a truth about what he would do. Without middle knowledge—and on the supposition that the creatures (and not God) make their own decisions—God would have to wait, as Lequier said, until after having created the universe to find out what the creatures were going to decide. Ockham could appeal to revelation in the hope that an account of the mechanics of omniscience would emerge that preserved divine foreknowledge *and* human freedom. Molina's genius was to show us what that account must involve.

Molinism has contemporary champions (Kvanvig 1986; Basinger 1987; Craig 1987b) and contemporary enemies (Adams 1987, 77-93; Kenny 1979, 66-71; Langston 1986, 70-74; Hasker 1986). While Hartshorne is silent on middle knowledge *per se*, there can be no doubt that it is inimical to his metaphysics. He denies that there are possible but nonactual individuals. In

Hartshorne's words, "There is an unutilized possibility of individuals, but not an individuality of unutilized possibility" (1941, 308; cf. 1983, 330). Without possible individuals, there could be no truth about what a possible individual would do. More fundamentally, Hartshorne denies the theory of possible worlds on which the concept of possible individuals is predicated. In the Hartshornean theory of possibility lies an attack on the very heart of the doctrine of middle knowledge.

Standard accounts of possible worlds make the actual world one among many possible worlds (Plantinga 1974, 45). This allows one to conceive of God as scanning the realm of possible worlds in order to decide which one will be actual. Hartshorne denies that there are possible worlds in this sense (1970, 122). Hartshorne is fond of quoting Whitehead that definiteness is the "soul of actuality" (1965, 189; 1978, 409).[5] The argument for this view is that possibilities cannot be as fully definite as actualities without already being actualities:

> Before events happen, they lack nothing except a totally transparent, featureless something called "actual occurrence." To some of us this is truly an absurdity. If becoming does not create new quality and quantity, new determinateness, then, we argue, it creates nothing, and nothing ever really becomes (1962, 165).

For the Molinist, a possible world is like a play whose script is as fully detailed as the actual performance would be, leaving nothing to chance and nothing left for the players themselves to add. For Hartshorne, a possible world is at most like a stage on which the players improvise.

Hartshorne follows C. S. Peirce in thinking of possibilities as forming a continuum that allows an infinite number of divisions. A possibility is, by its nature, indeterminate regarding its realization. For example, suppose I take a stroll through an arboretum. Afterwards, one may elaborate on the infinite particularities of the stroll, the exact steps, the animals seen scurrying across my path, the sounds of the wind, the scent of the pines, and the like. *None* of this was specified in the mere possibility of "taking a stroll." Nor does it help to add possible details *ad infinitum* so as to duplicate the particularities of the actual stroll. Each possible detail will, because it is a possibility, leave unspecified some detail of its realization. James Felt draws attention to the way language reflects the difference between actuality and possibility in definite and indefinite articles (Felt 1983, 259). I may consider taking *a* stroll through an arboretum. On Hartshornean principles, and in actual fact, it is quite impossible to consider taking *the* stroll until after it has been taken.

If the divine envisagement of possibilities leaves nothing to the creatures but to mimic the infinite detail of omniscience, it is difficult to see how genuine creativity on the part of the creatures is possible. Thus the ultimacy of creativity requires that one reject Molinism. Fully definite worlds, maximally complete, existing antecedent to any temporal framework, are less than fictional—they are, in Felt's words, "impossible worlds" (1983). If, as I have argued, middle knowledge is a necessary ingredient to any theism that would affirm God's foreknowledge of future contingents, then classical theism is in serious philosophical trouble. The classical theist must deny either foreknowledge or human freedom (or, with Ockham, appeal to revelation).

Hartshorne's central argument

Hartshorne's central argument against divine foreknowledge of future contingents is found throughout the Hartshornean corpus (e.g. 1939a, 251; 1941, 98; 1945, 284; 1970, 135; 1976, 13; 1981, 15). The following statement of the argument is representative:

> Socinians said, once for all, future events, events that have not yet happened, are not there to be known, and the claim to know them could only be false. *God does not already or eternally know what we do tomorrow, for, until we decide, there are no such entities as our tomorrow's decisions* (1984a 38-39).

The argument is sometimes framed in terms of the difference between the past as actual, settled, or determinate and the future as possible, unsettled, or indeterminate. The reasoning is deceptively simple: perfect knowledge knows things as they are. The past is determinate, and the future is partly indeterminate. Therefore, perfect knowledge knows the past *as* determinate and the future *as* partly indeterminate.

Although Hartshorne is clear in his several presentations of the argument, critics do not always attend to what he says. Where Hartshorne speaks of determinateness and indeterminateness, one may be tempted to substitute the issue of the truth value of tensed propositions. For example, in articles that purport to discuss Hartshorne's position, William Lane Craig cites the passage quoted above and proceeds to criticize what he (mistakenly) takes to be Hartshorne's views on the truth value of propositions about future contingents (Craig 1987a; 1987c). A less hasty inspection of Hartshorne's argument reveals that it is more subtle and less easily refuted than Craig's analysis suggests. While the issue of truth values is important—and one on which Hartshorne has much to say—it is not the issue in the central argument. The argument turns on the nature of God's knowledge of events in time, not the nature of God's knowledge of propositions about events.

Craig's misjudgment is perhaps understandable in view of the fact that discussions of God's knowledge of the future generally address the question of whether and to what extent God knows truths about the future. Jonathan Kvanvig speaks for a host of philosophers when he says that "talk about the future [is] . . . talk about propositions and their truth values" (1986, 3). For Hartshorne, "talk about propositions and their truth values" is a related but secondary issue to his central argument. He says:

> Traditional treatments of omniscience (as "impassive," wholly independent, etc.), seem to imply that God's knowing is akin to our most abstract and indirect awareness of things, a "knowledge about" not a "knowledge by acquaintance," remote not intimate, and by implication fallible and inadequate in the highest degree (1945, 547).

Hartshorne here alludes to a distinction made famous by Bertrand Russell. Russell distinguished knowledge of things and knowledge of truths. Knowledge of things sometimes involves a direct awareness of an object. Russell calls this sort of knowledge acquaintance. Knowledge of truths does not require a direct awareness but applies solely to beliefs, convictions, or judgments about what is the case (Russell 1973 [1912], Chapter V). When Scotus said that God knows things as they are in willed existence and not as they are in actual existence, he was denying God's knowledge by acquaintance. One may detect the ghost of Scotus in contemporary discussions of omniscience that focus only on God's knowledge of truths. Hartshorne's contention is that knowledge by acquaintance must be an essential ingredient in the omniscience of God's "perfect knowledge."

Hartshorne's use of Russell's distinction should not lead one to suppose that the two would agree on the *objects* with which one could be acquainted. For instance, Russell includes among the objects of acquaintance sense data and excludes other minds. Hartshorne rejects the existence of purely private sense data, and includes among the objects of acquaintance other minds. The relevant comparison is not with Russell but with Whitehead. According to Whitehead, every actuality, including God, is constituted by its "feelings" of other actualities. Whitehead's technical term for these is *prehensions*, the "concrete facts of relatedness" that explain the interrelations among all actualities (Whitehead 1978 [1929], 22). Hartshorne explains:

> According to Whitehead, the basic relationship in reality is "prehension," which in its most concrete form (called "physical prehension") is defined as "feeling of feeling," meaning the manner in which one subject feels the feelings of one or more other subjects. In other words, "sympathy" in the most literal sense (1984a, 27).

As Hartshorne notes, physical prehensions are the most concrete form of feeling. A physical prehension is a feeling whose datum is another actuality (Whitehead also speaks of conceptual prehensions or feelings whose data are possibilities). When Hartshorne says that omniscience requires a knowledge by acquaintance, it is something like Whitehead's concept of physical prehension that he has in mind.

An important reason why Hartshorne believes that God should be conceived as having direct awareness of objects is that practical and innatist models of omniscience ignore the affective dimensions of knowledge. Kenny notes that the traditional account of omniscience "attributes to God the informational content of our perceptions without the hedonistic content'' (Kenny 1979, 32). Hartshorne sees this as an inadequate account of omniscience since it portrays God as unable to commiserate or sympathize with creaturely needs and feelings. Whitehead said that every prehension has a ''subjective form,'' which is the particular way in which a given agent unifies a feeling as a constituent of its own individuality. Prehensions are clothed, each with their own emotion, valuation, or purpose (Whitehead 1978 [1929], 24). A concept of God's knowledge modeled on the Whiteheadian view allows one to think of divine awareness as a form of participation in the feelings of the creatures. Omniscience is not merely a cosmic storehouse of information. As Grace Jantzen says, the significance of the idea that even the hairs of one's head are numbered (Matthew 10.30) does not have to do with ''a fetish about statistical data relating to baldness.'' The significance is that such information matters to God, that God could be '' 'touched with the feeling of our infirmities' '' (Jantzen 1984, 83). This is Hartshorne's meaning when he says that without some form of participation in the feelings of others, God's knowledge is ''an abstract and inadequate knowledge of the creatures'' (1970, 263).

For both Whitehead and Hartshorne, the foundational metaphor for God's knowledge is feeling. As Marjorie Suchocki says, for process thinkers, ''God knows [the world] by feeling it'' (Suchocki 1986, 73). It is *this* meaning of knowledge by acquaintance that figures in Hartshorne's central argument. If knowledge by acquaintance is a direct awareness of an object or an event, then it is impossible to have such knowledge unless the object or the event really exists. As Brian Haymes says, ''For A to know B [by acquaintance] implies B's existence. It makes no sense to say 'I know B, but it is not the case that B exists' '' (Haymes 1988, 28). We have already seen that, according to Hartshorne, there are no such things as future events. Assuming the nonreality of future events, there can be no knowledge by acquaintance of future events.

A possible criticism of Hartshorne's reasoning is that it applies equally to the past. Craig asserts that ''the idea of literally perceiving the past or future does not make sense'' (Craig 1987b, 121). The question Hartshorne would put to Craig is whether we ever perceive anything but the past. For instance, one sees a bolt of lightening even though the actual bolt is past by the time the image flashes on the retina. Because the time lapse for events near to us is small, there is the illusion that what we perceive is simultaneous with the perception (Hartshorne 1970, 109). Hartshorne also cites introspection as an example of perceiving one's own immediate past thoughts and experiences. ''That we are always a trifle behind ourselves in this is not only harmless but the only way to note our mental processes without interfering with them'' (ibid.). If anything is problematic, it is perception of the present, not perception of the past. Hartshorne goes further. We have seen that, for Hartshorne, the past exists, in some sense, in the present. His account of the reality of the past involves the concept of God's prehensions of the world. The metaphor Hartshorne uses for *divine* prehensions is human memory at its most vivid and lively. Memory, he says, "preserves the past into the present" (Hartshorne 1939a, 248). Human memory is often vague, fluctuating, and highly fallible. A perfect memory would not suffer these defects. Another metaphor of which Hartshorne is fond is that the universe is God's body (1941, 185). Thus God's memory, inclusive of the cosmic whole, can be conceived as the universe's introspection preserving the totality of the past within itself. Whereas a fallible awareness is measured by something called "reality," reality just is the content of the infallible awareness on this view (Viney 1985, Chapter VII).

Hartshorne's account of divine memory insures that objections to his central argument based on the putative unreality of the past or on an alleged inability to perceive the past are bound to misfire. The same considerations—the nature of process and of prehension—that lead Hartshorne to deny God's knowledge by acquaintance of future contingents also lead him to affirm God's knowledge by acquaintance of past contingents.

However, the underlying reason that some philosophers object to Hartshorne's view has nothing to do with his claims about human memory and perception. It is the perceptual model itself with which they take theological exception. Craig speaks for many traditional theists when he says that God is to be conceived as a "disembodied mind" (Craig 1987a, 110). Any suggestion that God might in some way be physical is greeted with charges of anthropocentrism (ibid.) Yet the fact is that Hartshorne and those who agree with him in conceiving God as, in some way, embodied do so for carefully considered reasons that, as far as anyone has shown, are not subject to the charge of anthropocentrism in the pejorative sense of the term. Jantzen produces powerful arguments, often paralleling Hartshorne's (Viney 1987b), that Christianity is best served by thinking of the world as God's body (Jantzen 1984). Until these arguments and others like them are considered with the attention they deserve, the dismay expressed by some traditional theists over the concept of an embodied deity and the perceptual model it implies remains only a curiosity.

Truth and the future

Hartshorne's central argument concerns God's knowledge of future contingents, *not* God's knowledge of truths about future contingents. His view on the latter issue is dictated by his beliefs about the nature of truths about future contingents. In brief, Hartshorne rejects the doctrine that all truths are eternal. He argues:

> If time is the order of creation of emergent becoming, and if what is determines what is true, then there must be emergent truths. Such truths, once emerged, are everlasting, and this everlastingness will yield all that we need, apart from really timeless truths about abstract entities that are themselves eternal (1984b, 247).

Hartshorne agrees with Whitehead's statement that "the truth itself is nothing else than how the composite natures of organic actualities of the world obtain adequate representation in the divine [consequent] nature" (Whitehead 1979 [1929], 12-13). Thus God's vision of the future perfectly represents whatever indeterminacy exists in the future at any time.

If new truths come into being, the only question is how *this* contingency of *truth* is to be represented in language. In an early and little known article, Hartshorne defended the Aristotelean idea (Aristotle 1963, 140) that detailed propositions about an indeterminate future have "indeterminate truth values" (1939b, 27). Within two years, however, he embraced a distinct view that he has held to the present (1941, 100f). In a recent work, he explicitly mentions Aristotle's view and rejects it on the grounds that it "seems to consist in suspending the law of excluded middle as applicable [to propositions about the future]" (1983, 45).[6] Hartshorne's preferred alternative is to replace the Aristotelean triad of 'true-false-indeterminate' regarding truth values with the triad of 'definitely-definitely not-indefinite' regarding predicates:

> We need no third truth value, but we do need a third type of predicate for future moments of process besides 'definitely P' and 'definitely not P,' namely 'indefinite with respect to P' (1970, 135).

Thus Hartshorne locates the indeterminacy of the future *linguistically*, not in the truth values of propositions but in predicates pertaining to the future.

The semantics for the three predicates is to be understood in terms of the causal openness or closedness of the future. If the future is closed with respect to a certain event p, then either *all* causal possibilities include p (definitely p) or *no* causal possibilities include p (definitely not p). If the future is open with respect to p, then *some* causal possibilities include p and some exclude p (indefinite with respect to p). Hartshorne says, "We meet once more the fundamental triad, the most childishly simple but generally neglected mathematical key to philosophical problems, of all, some, and none" (1941, 100). One can think of propositions about the future in terms of the square of opposition (combining the "I" and "O" to render Hartshorne's triad). Let 'F' be causally possible futures and let 'P' be causal possibilities that include the occurrence of p. Then we have: All F are P (definitely p); No F are P (definitely not p); Some F are and some are not P (indefinite with respect to p). If any one of the propositions is true, the other two are false.

Hartshorne's views on future tensed propositions can be related to statements framed in terms of probabilities. If 'All F are P' is true, then the probability of something's being P is 1; if 'No F are P' is true, then the probability of something's being P is 0; and if 'Some F are and some are not P' is true, then the probability of something's being P is between between 1 and 0. No violation of the law of excluded middle is entailed by this view. However, as Richard Purtill notes, the falsity of the principle of bivalence *is* entailed. That is to say, it is not the case that for all future contingents the probability of something's being P is 0 if and only if the probability of something's being P is not 1 (Purtill 1988, 188). Purtill's acute observation allows us to identify the key issue between Hartshorne and his opponents on God's knowledge of truths about the future: is the principle of bivalence true or false from the standpoint of omniscience? Or, in an alternative formulation, could probabilities ever be more to God than simply an expression of creaturely ignorance of what the future holds? For Hartshorne, when all ignorance is discounted, there remains a real indeterminacy in the freedom of the creatures—ideally expressed in terms of probabilities—of which it is God's privilege to have perfect awareness.

Further consideration of the truth value of propositions about the future would lead us into a philosophical thicket; the issue is best left for others to untangle. However, it is worth noting here that the assumption that all truths are timeless does not guarantee that even God could know contingent truths in a timeless fashion (Hartshorne 1941, 140). Again, the problem is to provide an account of the mechanics of omniscience that explains how there could be infallible knowledge of contingent propositions prior to the time when the events to which they refer become actual. Richard Swinburne is one who accepts the timelessness of all truth but denies that God knows contingent truths eternally or in advance (Swinburne 1977, 172f). Swinburne's view, like Hartshorne's, does not compromise God's omniscience. The concept of divine or perfect knowledge requires only that God know, at any time t, every truth that it is possible to know at t. Hartshorne's dispute with Swinburne concerns the timelessness of all truth, not the formal definition of omniscience. The economy of Hartshorne's theory, i.e. that at no time are there truths outside the divine awareness, is apparent, and is in my view its decisive advantage.

Conclusion

Traditional theists, wishing to preserve both the perfection of God and human freedom, struggled valiantly to develop an account of the mechanics of omniscience based on practical and innatist models of knowledge. The genius of this tradition, culminating in Molinism, was to show what such an account requires, namely middle knowledge. However, at the very time that Molina proposed his theory, Socinus was laying the groundwork for another approach, one based on a perceptual model of knowledge. In the nineteenth century, Lequier provided trenchant criticisms of traditional theories and eloquently presented and defended elements of the perceptual model.

Hartshorne's work advances the case for a perceptual model of the mechanics of omniscience through its understanding of divine knowledge as a form of feeling. Hartshorne's account preserves the freedom of the creatures while counteracting a bias of traditional accounts against the affective dimensions of knowledge. The result is a deepened sense of God's involvement with the world of creaturely concerns, a world where the creatures share with God the joy and the risk of creation.

NOTES

1. Epistemic incompatibilism (knowledge in tension with freedom) should be distinguished from causal incompatibilism (causation in tension with freedom). Some philosophers, like Molina, are causal incompatibilists and epistemic compatibilists; they hold that human decisions, to be free, must be causally indeterminate and that God can foreknow causally indeterminate events.
2. The appeal to revelation is by no means unproblematic. For contrasting Christian views, see Craig (1987b) and Rice (1985).
3. For a brief overview of Lequier's philosophical theology and other sources on Lequier, see Viney (1987a).
4. Stump and Kretzmann disagree with the analysis of the eternal present given here (1987, 227). I believe that Delmas Lewis has shown that their reason for construing the eternal present as merely epistemic is unwarranted (Lewis 1988, 80-81).
5. The entire quote from Whitehead is, "But definition is the soul of actuality; the attainment of a peculiar definiteness is the final cause which animates a particular process . . ." (1978 [1929], 223). For a discussion of the differences between Whitehead and Hartshorne on the idea of definiteness, see articles by David Ray Griffin and Lewis S. Ford (Ford 1973).
6. Craig asserts that "Hartshorne's position with regard to future contingent statements is that any such statement and its contradictory are both false" (Craig 1987a, 96). The basis of this claim is Hartshorne's view that where x is a future contingent, 'x will occur' and 'x will not occur' are both false. Craig disregards Hartshorne's repeated insistence that, technically, the two statements are contraries, not contradictories (1964, 476; 1965, 49; 1970, 16). Craig also fails to appreciate (or even mention) Hartshorne's view of indefiniteness as a predicate.

BIBLIOGRAPHY

Adams, Robert M. *The Virtue of Faith and Other Essays in Philosophical Theology.* Oxford: Oxford University Press, 1987.

Aquinas, Thomas. *Introduction to St. Thomas Aquinas.* Edited by Anton C. Pegis. New York: Modern Library, 1945.

———. *On the Truth of the Catholic Faith Summa Contra Gentiles Book One: God.* Translated by Anton C. Pegis. Garden City, New York: Image Books, 1955.

Aristotle. *Categories and De Interpretatione.* Translated by J. L. Ackrill. Oxford: Clarendon Press, 1963.

Basinger, David. "Middle Knowledge and Classical Christian Thought." *Religious*

Studies **22**/3,4 (Sept./Dec. 1986), 407-422.

——. "Middle Knowledge and Human Freedom." *Faith and Philosophy* **4**/3 (1987), 330-336.

Boethius. *The Consolation of Philosophy*. Translated by Richard Green. Indianapolis, Indiana: Bobbs-Merrill, 1962.

Brimmer, Harvey H. *Jules Lequier and Process Philosophy*. Dissertation, Emory University, 1975.

Copleston, Frederick. *A History of Philosophy*, Volume 9, in two parts. Garden City, New York: Image, 1977.

Craig, William Lane. "Divine Foreknowledge and Future Contingency." In *Process Theology*, edited by Ronald H. Nash, 91-115. Grand Rapids, Michigan: Baker Book House, 1987a.

——. *The Only Wise God: The Compatibility of Divine Foreknowledge and Human Freedom*. Grand Rapids, Michigan: Baker Book House, 1987b.

——. "Process Theology's Denial of Divine Foreknowledge." *Process Studies* **16**/3 (Fall 1987c), 198-202.

Felt, James. W. "Impossible Worlds." *International Philosophical Quarterly* **23**/2 (Sept. 1983), 251-265.

Ford, Lewis S., ed. *Two Process Philosophers: Hartshorne's Encounter with Whitehead*. Tallahassee, Florida: American Academy of Religion, 1973.

Hartshorne, Charles. *Anselm's Discovery*. La Salle, Illinois: Open Court Press, 1965.

——. *Aquinas to Whitehead: Seven Centuries of Metaphysics of Religion*. Milwaukee: Marquette University Press, 1976.

——. Articles on "Foreknowledge, Divine," 284, "Omniscience," 546-547, and "Time," 787-788. In *An Encyclopedia of Religion*, edited by Vergilius Ferm. Secaucus, New Jersey: Popular Books, 1945.

——. "Are All Propositions About the Future Either True or False?" *Program of the American Philosophical Association: Western Division*, April 20-22, 1939b, 26-32.

——. *Creative Synthesis and Philosophic Method*. La Salle, Illinois: Open Court, 1970.

——. "Creativity and the Deductive Logic of Causality." *Review of Metaphysics* **27**, (Sept. 1973), 62-74.

——. *Creativity in American Philosophy*. Albany, New York: State University of New York Press, 1984b.

——. "Deliberation and Excluded Middle." *Journal of Philosophy* **61**/6 (September 3, 1964), 476-477.

——. *The Divine Relativity A Social Conception of God*. New Haven: Yale University Press, 1948.

——. *Insights and Oversights of Great Thinkers An Evaluation of Western Philosophy*. Albany, New York: State University of New York Press, 1983.

——. *The Logic of Perfection*. La Salle, Illinois: Open Court Press, 1962.

——. *Man's Vision of God and the Logic of Theism*. Chicago: Willet, Clark Co., 1941.

——. "The Meaning of 'Is Going to Be.' " *Mind* **74**/293, (January, 1965), 46-58.

——. *Omnipotence and Other Theological Mistakes*. Albany, New York: State University of New York Press, 1984a.

——, and William L. Reese, eds. *Philosophers Speak of God*. Chicago: Chicago

University Press, 1953.
———. "Real Possibility." *The Journal of Philosophy*, **60**/21 (October 10, 1963), 593-605.
———. "The Reality of the Past, The Unreality of the Future." *Hibbert Journal* **37**/2 (January, 1939a), 246-257.
———. "Theism in Asian and Western Thought." *Philosophy East and West* **28**/4 (Oct. 1978), 401-411.
———, and Creighton Peden. *Whitehead's View of Reality*. New York: Pilgrim Press, 1981.
Hasker, William. "A Refutation of Middle Knowledge." *Nous* **20** (December, 1986), 545-557.
Haymes, Brian. *The Concept of the Knowledge of God*. New York: St. Martins Press, 1988.
Jantzen, Grace. *God's World God's Body*. Philadelphia: Westminister Press, 1984.
Kane, Robert. *Free Will and Values*. Albany, New York: State University of New York Press, 1985.
Kenny, Anthony. *The God of the Philosophers*. Oxford: Clarendon Press, 1979.
Kvanvig, Jonathan L. *The Possibility of an All-Knowing God*. New York: St. Martins Press, 1986.
Langston, Douglas C. *God's Willing Knowledge, The Influence of Scotus' Analysis of Omniscience*. University Park: Pennsylvania State University Press, 1986.
Lequier, Jules. *Oeuvres complètes*. Edited by Jean Grenier. Neuchatel, Suisse: Editions de la Baconnière, 1952.
Lewis, Delmas. "Eternity, Time and Tenselessness." *Faith and Philosophy* **5**/1 (January, 1988), 72-86.
Melville, Herman. *Moby-Dick*. Edited by Harrison Hayford and Hershel Parker. New York: W. W. Norton & Company, 1967. Originally published in 1851.
Moskop, John C. *Divine Omniscience and Human Freedom: Thomas Aquinas and Charles Hartshorne*. Macon, Georgia: Mercer University Press, 1984.
Ockham, William. *Predestination, God's Foreknowledge, and Future Contingents*. Translated by Marilyn McCord Adams and Norman Kretzmann. New York: Appleton-Century-Crofts, 1969.
Peters, Eugene H. *Hartshorne and Neoclassical Metaphysics*. Lincoln, Nebraska: University of Nebraska Press, 1970.
Plantinga, Alvin. *The Nature of Necessity*. Oxford: Clarendon Press, 1974.
Purtill, Richard L. "Fatalism and the Omnitemporality of Truth." *Faith and Philosophy* **5**/2 (April, 1988), 185-192.
Rice, Richard. *God's Foreknowledge and Man's Free Will*. Minneapolis, Minnesota: Bethany House Publishers, 1985. Originally published as *The Openness of God, The Relationship of Divine Foreknowledge and Human Free Will*. Nashville, Tennessee: Review and Herald Pub. Association, 1980.
Russell, Bertrand. *The Problems of Philosophy*. London: Oxford University Press, 1973. Originally published 1912.
Stump, Eleonore, and Norman Kretzmann. "Eternity." In *The Concept of God*, edited by Thomas V. Morris, 219-251. Oxford: Oxford University Press, 1987.
Suchocki, Marjorie Hewitt. *God Christ Church, A Practical Guide to Process Theology*. New York: Crossroads, 1986.
Swinburne, Richard. *The Coherence of Theism*. Oxford: Clarendon Press, 1977.

Viney, Donald Wayne. *Charles Hartshorne and the Existence of God*. Albany, New York: State University of New York Press, 1985.

——. "Faith as a Creative Act: Kierkegaard and Lequier on the Relation of Faith and Reason." *In Faith & Creativity Essays in Honor of Eugene H. Peters*, edited by George Nordgulen and George W. Shields, 165-177. St. Louis, Missouri: CBP Press, 1987a.

——. Review of Grace Jantzen's *God's World, God's Body*. *Process Studies* **16**/1 (Spring, 1987b), 61-63.

——. "William James on Free Will and Determinism." *The Journal of Mind and Behavior* 7/4 (1986), 555-566.

Whitehead, Alfred North. *Process and Reality*, corrected Edition. Edited by David Ray Griffin and Donald W. Sherburne. New York: Free Press, 1978.

Must a Perfect Being Be Immutable?

Daniel A. Dombrowski

Introduction

One would think that philosophical theists would have a great deal in common with each other, yet it is surprising how little theists read across the various boundaries in contemporary philosophy. This article will try to cross one such divide, that between analytic and process theism. George Lucas has recently, and appropriately, chided process philosophers for not paying careful enough attention to current debates in analytic philosophy,[1] if for no other reason than the fact that Whitehead's thought can contribute significantly to those debates. But Lucas's door can swing both ways. I am going to chide analytic theists (in particular, Mann, Stump, Kretzmann, Plantinga, and Creel) for not paying careful enough attention (or, in some cases, any attention at all) to the thought of a thinker who many think is the most original and profound philosophical theist of the twentieth century, Charles Hartshorne. I allege that they could learn from Hartshorne (just as Hartshorne could learn from them, as is evidenced by his regret that he does not know more about developments in modal logic).

For example, two recent articles in the philosophy of religion have appeared whose theses hinge on the assumption that a perfect being is not subject to change—Eleonore Stump and Norman Kretzmann's "Eternity"[2] and William Mann's "Simplicity and Immutability in God."[3] Since both of these important articles are carefully argued, it is surprising that such a fundamental assumption should go unexamined.[4] In both articles, the authors make Herculean efforts to show that the orthodox conception of God does not lead to incoherence when the following issues are considered: the logical relationship between eternity and time, the problem of showing how an eternal and immutable God can act in time, and whether God's immutable omniscience precludes human freedom, et al. Anyone familiar with these issues realizes that Herculean efforts are the only ones that could be successful—when such difficult matters are considered from the perspective of the traditional conception of God. (The efforts might be more appropriately described as "Sisyphean.")

Now that many analytic philosophers are showing an interest in questions about God, it is surprising that many of them should do so on the assumptions of old-style metaphysics. One such assumption is precisely that a perfect being is not subject to change. Since the 1930s, Hartshorne has been challenging this assumption, but his work has hardly received detailed criticism from analytic philosophers. One generation of analytic philosophers apparently dismissed his work as meaningless just because it was metaphysical. It is hoped that another generation will not ignore him merely because he is not thought to write in one of the styles considered appropriate by analytic philosophers. This hope is intensified when one notices Hartshorne's eminent clarity.

The general purpose of the next few sections of this article is to show why analytic metaphysicians should examine Hartshorne's work in detail, even though he is not usually thought of as an analytic philosopher. Since one way to view Hartshorne's philosophy is as a lifelong, consistent search for a coherent *meaning* to the term "God," his thoughts should be of special interest to contemporary analytic philosophers of religion. One interpreter even goes so far as to call him a revisionary metaphysician in the Strawsonian sense.[5] Eventually, I will also treat the thought of Alvin Plantinga and Richard Creel.

Mann and immutability

This author's article opens with the statement that:

> Steadfastness is a virtue we prize in persons. All other things being equal, we disapprove of those who break their promises, forsake their covenants, or change their minds capriciously. We regard as childish those who are easily deflected from the pursuit of their goals. We pity those who suffer radical transformations of character. It is not surprising, then, that many theists believe that no such fickle flickerings of human inconstancy could characterize God. Many theists—especially those infected with a bit of philosophy—carry these speculations a step further. God is supremely steadfast, but he is also insusceptible to ceasing to be the being he is. A steadfast mortal is still mortal. . . . Many orthodox theologians and philosophers have taken yet a further step. For example, the great medieval philosophers argued that God is utterly and completely immutable, that no change of any kind can befall him. (267)

It is this most extreme form of the doctrine of divine immutability (DDI), held by St. Thomas Aquinas and others, that Mann defends.

The defense proceeds by way of showing that an immutable God can be a personal and active being. Mann is not deterred by those who accuse him of building the temple of Elea in Jerusalem (268). He argues that God can be both immutable and active through an appeal to another doctrine, that of divine simplicity (DDS). God has no parts, nor does God have temporal extension. The divine attributes are coextensive: the omniscience of God *is* the omnipotence of God, etc. This is what makes God simple, and it is also what makes it possible for Mann to argue that God is immutable and active. God's immutability *is* God's activity. Likewise it is possible for God to be immutable and a person because God's immutability *is* God's eternal knowing and willing. This means that, although God can know and will, God cannot come to know, forget, calculate, have *fore*knowledge, or engage in inductive reasoning; nor can God fall in love, grow in love, become angry, or the like, for these entail dreaded divine change.

Mann admits that his list of divine attributes is a "curtailed repertoire" (270), but this does not bother him. Some peculiar conclusions follow from his views. The activity by which God wills punishment at what is from a human perspective $time_1$ *is* the activity by which God is "reconciled" to the punished ones at what is from a human perspective $time_2$. One is led, on Mann's reasoning, to conclude that divine anger, expressed in hailstorms and locusts, *is* divine joy. One is also led to believe that if God's care is equally present "from" eternity to $time_1$ and $time_2$, then there is no increase in God's love when human beings respond to God's call, nor does God *respond* to our sufferings. All of this is on the assumption that a perfect being does not change or respond. What unresponsive love is like we are not told. Presumably, for Mann, God eternally knows and cares about our sufferings even before, from a human perspective, they occur. Why, since divinity is also omnipotent for Mann, God does not *do* something to prevent human suffering is a question, not too surprisingly, which Mann does not treat. That is, theodicy is as much a problem as ever; traditional assumptions still yield traditional problems.

What is to be noticed is that all of Mann's efforts are needed *only if* one starts, as he does, with an analysis of the virtue of steadfastness to the exclusion of an analysis of other virtues. None of the four objections to his views that he considers even implicitly raise the possibility that a perfect being may be allowed to (or better, be required to) change. Mann is intent on refuting the views that: (1) DDI can be established without the DDS; (2) divine foreknowledge of proposition P cannot be identical to knowledge of proposition L; (3) DDS is incompatible with human freedom; and (4) DDS precludes God's freedom of will. The degree to which Mann succeeds in refuting these four views is not my prime concern here (although it is hard to see how he overcomes 3 and 4). The point I want to make is that the very need to respond to these sorts of objections (not to mention the theodicy problem, et al.) is worthy of our attention. Paradoxically, Mann says that it is "the logic of perfection" (272) (the phrase Hartshorne popularized in the title of one of his books) which leads Mann to his conclusions. For, on Hartshorne's view, as we will see shortly, it is the logic of perfection which should lead us to be suspicious of the doctrine of divine immutability rather than to assume it, as Mann does.

Stump and Kretzmann on eternity

Although these authors' article antedates Mann's, and supplies the basis for many of Mann's views (although not DDS), it is much more clandestine in its assumption that a perfect being is not subject to change. But the assumption is made nonetheless. The authors ably distinguish sempiternity (or what Hartshorne would call everlastingness) from eternity. The former consists in limitless duration in time (430). The latter, as developed primarily by Boethius, but also by St. Thomas and others, and defended by Stump and Kretzmann, consists in "the complete possession all at once of illimitable life" (431). The authors initially state that they are not claiming that if God exists God must be eternal; they are only elucidating what the concept of eternity means (431). But later they are not so coy (455-456). In an analysis of an argument which has as its first three premises the following:

1. A perfect being is not subject to change.
2. A perfect being knows everything.
3. A being that knows everything always knows what time it is.

Stump and Kretzmann state that (my emphasis): "it is clear that *the* weak point in the proof is premise (3)." Premise (1) is assumed to be true and is operative throughout their article. It is the assumption of premise (1) that requires them to defend the following views: that there is only an apparent incoherence between divine eternity and temporality, or between divine atemporality and divine life; that God knows simultaneously that Nixon is alive and dead; and that:

> If such an entity (God) atemporally wills that Hannah conceive on a certain day after the day of her prayer (to get pregnant), then such an entity's bringing it about that Hannah conceives on that day is clearly a response to her prayer. (451)

Once again, my prime intent here is not to evaluate these defenses, but to question the authors' unargued assumption that a perfect being is not subject to change. It is worth mentioning, however, that this assumption forces them to some questionable claims. Consider the Hannah example. If God eternally wills that the woman conceive, can she freely engage in the sexual relation which brought about her pregnancy? Is it really *her* prayer? Should not the word "respond" above be put in quotation marks, at the very least, if not dropped altogether? And how can God's "response" to the woman's prayer be an expression of God's concern for *her*, if God's decision were made eternally? In addition to pp. 455-456, treated above, the authors make it clear that their aim is to show the plausibility of the attributes given to the God by orthodox Christian theology, who is immutable (457-458), and to show the plausibility of Christ eternally having both a divine and a human nature (453). What eternally having a *human* nature is I do not know, but once the fetish for permanence gets rolling it is quite hard to stop.

I should not give the impression that there is nothing of worth in these two articles. The authors are all extremely intelligent and do the best job imaginable of making what sense can be made of the doctrine of divine immutability and eternity. Stump and Kretzmann in particular are ingenious in their clever use of Einstein's theory of simultaneity to explain relations between the eternal and the temporal. But they should have paid attention to the assumption on which these relations rest, that a perfect being must be immutable. Because Hartshorne is a prolific writer, only a few of his insights on this topic will be treated,[6] but they should be sufficient to point out what the analytic metaphysicians under consideration here could learn from him. At the very least I will show that one must *argue* for the claim that a perfect being is not subject to change; the claim cannot be assumed with equanimity, as our authors do.

Hartshorne's dipolar theism

One of the major complaints Hartshorne has with classical theism (in philosophy and theology, as opposed to biblical theism) is that it either explicitly or implicitly identifies God as permanent and not changing. St. Thomas's unmoved mover is the most obvious example of this tendency, but, in general, classical theists see God as a timeless, supernatural being who does not change.

For Hartshorne, the term "God" refers to the supremely excellent or all-worshipful being. As is well known, Hartshorne has been the most important defender of the ontological argument in this century, and his debt to St. Anselm is evident in this preliminary definition. It closely resembles St. Anselm's "that than which no greater can be conceived." Yet the ontological argument is not what is at stake here. Even if the argument fails, which Hartshorne would doubt, the preliminary definition of God as the supremely excellent being, the all-worshipful being, or the greatest conceivable being seems unobjectionable. To say that God can be defined in these ways still leaves open the possibility that God is even more excellent or worshipful than our ability to conceive. This allows one to avoid objections from Thomists or Wittgensteinian fideists who fear that by defining God we are limiting God to human language. All Hartshorne is suggesting is that when we think of God we must be thinking of a being who surpasses all others, or we are not thinking of God. Even the atheist or agnostic would admit this much. When the atheist says "There is no God," he is denying that a supremely excellent, all-worshipful, greatest conceivable being exists.

The contrast excellent-inferior is the truly invidious contrast when applied to God. If to be invidious is to be injurious, then this contrast is the most invidious one of all when applied to God because God is only excellent. God is inferior in no way. Period. To suggest that God is in some small way inferior to some other being is no longer to speak about God, but about some being that is not supremely excellent, all-worshipful, or the greatest conceivable. Hartshorne criticizes classical theism because it assumes that all contrasts, or most of them, when applied to God are invidious.

Let me assume from now on that God exists.[7] What attributes does God possess? Consider the following two columns of attributes in polar contrast to each other:

permanence	change
one	many
activity	passivity
necessity	contingency
self-sufficient	dependent
actual	potential
absolute	relative
abstract	concrete

Classical theism tends toward oversimplification. It is comparatively easy to say "God is strong rather than weak, so in all relations God is eternally active, not passive." In each case, the classical theist decides which member of the contrasting pair is good (on the left) then attributes it to God, while wholly denying the contrasting term (on the right). Hence, God is one, but not many; permanent but not changing, etc. This leads to what Hartshorne calls the monopolar prejudice. Monopolarity is common to both classical theism and pantheism, with the major difference between the two being the fact that classical theism admits the reality of plurality, potentiality, and becoming as a secondary form of existence "outside" God (on the right), whereas in pantheism God includes all reality within itself. Common to both classical theism and pantheism is the belief that the above categorical contrasts are invidious. The dilemma these two positions face is that either the deity is only one constituent of the whole (classical theism) or else the alleged inferior pole in each contrast (on the right) is illusory (pantheism).

For Hartshorne this dilemma is artificial. It is produced by the assumption that excellence is found by separating and purifying one pole (on the left) and denigrating the other (on the right). That this is not the case can be seen by analyzing some of the attributes on the right side. At least since St. Augustine, classical theists have been convinced that God's eternity meant not that God endured through all time, but that God was outside of time altogether and did not, could not, be receptive to temporal change. St. Thomas identified God, following Aristotle, who was the greatest predecessor to classical theism, as unmoved. Yet both activity and passivity can be either good or bad. Good passivity is likely to be called sensitivity, responsiveness, adaptability, sympathy, and the like. Insufficiently subtle or defective passivity is called wooden inflexibility, mulish stubbornness, inadaptability, unresponsiveness, and the like. Passivity *per se* refers to the way in which an individual's activity takes account of, and renders itself appropriate to, the activities of others. To deny God passivity altogether is to deny God those aspects of passivity which are excellences. Or again, to deny altogether God the ability to change does avoid fickleness, but at the expense of the ability to *react* lovingly to the sufferings of others.

The terms on the left side have both good and bad aspects as well. Oneness can mean wholeness, as Mann notices, but also it can mean monotony or triviality. Actuality can mean definiteness, but it can mean non-relatedness to others. What happens to divine love when God, according to St. Thomas, is claimed to be *pure* actuality? God ends up loving the world, but is not internally related to it, whatever sort of love that may be. Self-sufficiency can, at times, be selfishness.

The trick when thinking of God, for Hartshorne, is to attribute to God all excellences (left *and* right sides) and not to attribute to God any inferiorities (right *and* left sides). In short, excellent-inferior or good-evil are invidious contrasts; that is, they cannot be applied (both terms) to supreme goodness because it makes no sense to bifurcate evil into good-evil (a contradiction, not a contrast) and evil-evil (a redundancy). But permanence-change, being-becoming, etc., are non-invidious contrasts. Unlike classical theism and pantheism, Hartshorne's theism is dipolar. To be specific, within *each* pole of a non-invidious contrast (e.g. permanence-change) there are invidious elements (inferior permanence or inferior change), but also non-invidious, good elements (excellent permanence or excellent change).

Some objections

It may be helpful at this point to respond to some possible criticisms from Mann, Stump, and Kretzmann. First, Hartshorne does not believe in two gods, one unified and the other plural, etc. Rather, he believes that what are often thought to be contraries are really mutually interdependent correlatives:

> The good as we know it is unity-in-variety, or variety-in-unity; if the variety overbalances, we have chaos or discord; if the unity, we have monotony or triviality (PSG, 3).

Supreme excellence, if it is truly supreme excellence, *must* somehow be able to integrate all the *complexity* there is in the world into itself as one spiritual whole. The word "must" indicates divine necessity, along with God's essence, which is to exist necessarily. And the word "complexity" indicates the contingency which affects God through creaturely decisions. But in the classical theistic view God is solely identified with the stony immobility of the absolute. For Hartshorne, in God's abstract nature—God's being—God may in a way escape from the temporal flux, but a living God is related to the world of becoming, a fact which entails divine becoming as well, if the world in some way is internally related to God. The classical theist's alternative to this view suggests that all relationships to God are external to divinity, once again threatening not only God's love, but also God's nobility. A dog's being behind a particular rock affects the dog in certain ways, thus this relation is an internal relation to the dog. But it does not affect the rock, whose relationship with the dog is external to the rock's nature. Does this not show the superiority of canine consciousness, which is aware of the rock, to rocklike existence, which is unaware of the dog? Is it not therefore peculiar that God has been described solely in rocklike terms: unmoved, permanent, only having external relations, being not becoming?

It might be wondered at this point why classical theism has been so popular among theists, yet has these defects. Hartshorne suggests at least four reasons, none of which establishes the case for classical theism: (1) It is simpler to accept monopolarity than dipolarity, i.e. it is simpler to accept one pole and reject the other of contrasting (or better, correlative, non-invidious) categories rather than to show how each, in its own appropriate fashion, applies to an aspect of the divine nature. Yet the simplicity of calling God "the absolute" can come back to haunt the classical theist if absoluteness precludes relativity in the sense of relatedness to the world. That is, the simplicity of accepting monopolarity eventually leads to Herculean efforts to save it. (2) If the decision to accept monopolarity has been made, it is simpler to identify God as the most permanent than to identify God as the most changing. Yet the acceptance of God as most permanent need not imply a denial of divine change, nor that God, who loves all, would therefore have to change with respect to all. That is, God may well be the most permanent of all as well as the most changing of all, in the sense that, and to the extent that, both of these are excellences. God is permanent and is changing in different aspects of the divine. There is a distinction between God's necessary *existence* (the fact *that* God exists) and God's contingent *actuality* (*how* God exists), a distinction which Hartshorne has spent a great deal of time defending, and which analytic theists have spent a great deal of time ignoring. (3) There are emotional considerations favoring divine permanence, as found in the longing to escape the risks and uncertainties of life. But even if these considerations obtain they should not blind us to other emotional considerations, like those which give us the solace which comes from knowing that the outcome of our sufferings and volitions makes a difference in the divine life which, if it is all-loving, would certainly not be unchanged by the suffering of creatures. (4) Monopolarity is seen as more easily made compatible with monotheism. But the innocent monotheistic contrast between the one and the many deals with God as an individual, not with the dogmatic claim that the divine individual itself cannot have parts or aspects of relatedness to the world.

In short:

> God's being and becoming form a single reality: there is no law of logic against attributing contrasting predicates to the same individual, provided they apply to diverse aspects of this individual (PSG, 14-15).

The remedy for "ontolatry," the worship of being, is not the contrary pole, the worship of becoming:

> God is neither being as contrasted to becoming nor becoming as contrasted to being; but categorically supreme becoming in which there is a factor of categorically supreme being, as contrasted to inferior becoming, in which there is inferior being (PSG, 24).

The divine becoming is more ultimate than the divine being in process theism only for the reason that it is more inclusive.

To the rather simple objection that if God changed God would not be perfect, for if God were perfect there would be no need to change, Hartshorne makes this reply: to be supremely excellent God must at any particular time be the greatest conceivable being, the all-worshipful being. But at a later time, or in a new situation in which some creature that previously did not suffer now suffers, God has new opportunities to exhibit supreme excellence. That is, God's perfection does not just allow God to change, but requires God to change.[8]

Finally, it might be objected that God is neither permanent nor changing, neither one nor many, etc., because no human concept whatsoever applies to God literally or univocally, but at most analogically. The classical theist would say, perhaps, that God is more unitary than unity, more permanent than permanence as humanly known. Yet one wonders how the classical theist, once he has admitted the insufficiency of human conceptions, can legitimately give a favored status to one side (the left) of conceptual contrasts at the expense of the other. Why, Hartshorne asks, if God is more simple than the one, is God not also more complex—in terms of relatedness to diverse actual occasions—than the many? Analogical predication and negative theology can just as easily fall victim to the monopolar prejudice as univocal predication.

Some preliminary conclusions

To sum up, Hartshorne's theism is, (a) *dipolar*, because excellences are found on both sides of the above contrasting categories, (b) *neoclassical*, because it relies on the belief that classical theists (especially St. Anselm) were on the right track when they described God as the supremely excellent, all-worshipful, greatest conceivable being, (c) a *process* theism, in that it posits a need for God to become in order for God to be perfect, but not at the expense of God's always (i.e. permanently) being greater than all others, and

(d) a theism, properly called *panentheism*, which means literally "all in God." God is neither completely removed from the world, nor identified with the world, as in pantheism. Rather, (i) God is world-inclusive in the sense that God cares for all the world and has sym-pathy for it; and all feelings in the world—especially suffering—are felt by God; and (ii) God is transcendent in the sense that God is greater than any other being, especially because of God's necessary existence and eminent changeability.

Although it would obviously be too much to hope that analytic classical theists would be "converted" to dipolar theism as a consequence of what I have said thus far, I hope that I have at least established two points. First, the case for dipolar theism is at the very least strong enough to force the classical theist to *argue* for the belief that God is immutable. To assume monopolarity without argument, as Mann, Stump, and Kretzmann do, is inadequate. If these authors write again on the topic under consideration here, one would hope that they would contend not only with their fellow analysts, but also with process thinkers like Hartshorne. And second, the case for dipolar theism is strong enough that the question is an open one as to where the burden of proof lies when divine attributes are considered. In that the weight of the classical theistic tradition is on the side of our three authors, it might seem that the burden of proof is on Hartshorne.[9] But since Hartshorne has assiduously tried to incorporate *all* excellences into his theory of God, both those associated with divine permanence and those associated with divine change, should not the burden of proof lie with those who would like to treat the supremely excellent being as *only* possessing the excellence of permanence or the excellence of change?[10]

Plantinga, *aseity*, and control

Perhaps it will be claimed that, although most analytic theists have simply assumed divine immutability, there is nonetheless good reason for such an assumption because if God were not immutable God's *aseity* would be compromised. Alvin Plantinga seems to make just this point. In *God and Other Minds*[11] Plantinga rightly notes that two demands of the "religious attitude" are that God exists necessarily and that God should possess "various qualities in some necessary manner." Hartshorne would agree, at least he would agree *if* one of these qualities, say, is the ability always to respond to the momentary sufferings of creatures (n.b. "always" *and* "respond"). But from this latter demand that God's character be *a se* (78), Plantinga emphasizes the necessary absence of *certain* kinds of change in God.

It might seem that Plantinga is not as committed to divine immutability as the authors previously considered, since he says that it is "surely clear" that God does undergo change, as in the change from not being worshipped by St. Paul in 100 B.C. to being so worshipped in 40 A.D. But this change for Plantinga is a relational or logical one (more precisely, an external relation); God's eternal being, he thinks, is not merely changeless but unchangeable. Plantinga sides with St. Augustine in denying Hartshorne's fundamental distinction between divine necessary existence (that God exists) and divine contingent actuality (how God exists); i.e. he denies dipolarity in God.[12] The reason why Plantinga sides with the classical theistic tradition is that there is an essential connection, as he sees it, between divine *aseity* ("his uncreatedness, self-sufficiency and independence of everything else") and omnipotence (his control over all things).

Hartshorne would agree with Plantinga that God does not depend on us for divine existence, nor does God depend on us in particular for omnibenevolence. But, if not us in particular, then some creatures or other would be needed for God to love in order for God to have the properties of omniscience and omnibenevolence. This divine dependence, as Hartshorne sees it, is more than what Plantinga would claim is "Pickwickian" (in *Does God Have a Nature?*)[13]. To claim rightly, as Plantinga does, that even the rebel's existence is dependent on God does not establish the case, as Plantinga thinks, that the rebel has no significant affect on God (2-3).

For various reasons, Plantinga (along with Stump and Kretzmann) disagrees with Mann's thesis regarding divine simplicity, but this denial also, he thinks, poses a threat to divine *aseity* because if abstract objects of a Platonic sort (e.g. necessary truths) are different from God's nature they threaten the notion of divine control. But it is important to notice that Plantinga himself admits that *his* notion of sovereignty-*aseity* is (merely) an intuition (34, 68), or as I have used the term, an assumption.

There are, at the very least, plausible grounds for believing that abstract objects do not threaten God's *aseity*, hence do not conflict with the denial of divine immutability. That is, one can criticize divine immutability and still preserve some sense of *aseity* (see again the terms on the left side of the above diagram) as well as allow for the sorts of abstract objects Plantinga believes in. "X is independent of Y" minimally implies that it could be the case that X exists while Y does not, which implies that Y is contingent. If X stands for abstract objects and Y for God, then the nonexistence of God is being taken as possible. But this "possibility" conflicts not only with Hartshorne's defense of arguments in favor of God's existence but also with Plantinga's. If one asks Hartshorne whether abstract objects have supremacy over God, he would respond that the issue is secondary and largely verbal (PSG, 56-57) because both abstract objects and God are eternal (or better, everlasting) and independence has no clear meaning between everlasting things.

In two significant respects Plantinga's theism is like that of Richard Swinburne.[14] First, he assumes that God could not be embodied in any sense; he thinks that theists have always held that God is immaterial. Because if God were material God would change, there is no apparent need to argue any further for divine immateriality. But just on historical grounds Plantinga is in trouble here. David of Dinant and Hobbes are not, as he thinks, the only philosophers who have defended divine embodiment. As Plutarch attests, almost all the ancient philosophers, including Plato, believed in God as the World-Soul who animates the world-body. These examples, along with Hartshorne's lifelong defense of the Platonic World-Soul, are noteworthy omissions in Plantinga's historical gloss.[15] Once again, my point here is obviously not to demonstrate the strength of the belief in divine embodiment, but rather to show the intellectual and historical thinness of the assumption made by analytic theists, in this case by Plantinga, that God must be completely immaterial, in order that they might preserve belief in divine immutability. The process theist suggests that by taking Hartshorne seriously, and by thinking carefully about holy change and about nature as sacramental, one may treat the theodicy problem, the environmental crisis, etc., in a more fruitful way than is possible in even the most technically proficient varieties of classical theism. Most of the traditional problems in classical theism are found in analytic theism, problems which stem in large part from the belief in God as a supernatural being who does not change. For pragmatic reasons alone, there should be an incentive to examine the assumption that God is this sort of being.

Second, Plantinga agrees with Swinburne (against St. Thomas, Stump, Kretzmann, and Mann) that God's eternity is not timeless, but rather consists in endless and beginningless duration, i.e. in sempiternity or everlastingness. From this claim, however, Plantinga does not make the understandable move toward process theism, but tries to hold on to the classical theistic belief in a God whose knowledge is not "temporally limited" (45). God, for Plantinga, right now knows even the remote future in minute detail, *but* God is not timeless, whatever that means. God in some peculiar way acts in time and does some things before others, but is not affected by time or change (45-46).

Plantinga has a very strong sense of God as absolutely omnipotent, of God as in control of everything, or as Hartshorne would put it, of God as Oriental despot. Hartshorne would agree with Plantinga that the notion of God as maximal power is "non-negotiable" (134) from the perspective of theism, but what it means to have maximal power differs in the two thinkers, with Hartshorne (see *Omnipotence and Other Theological Mistakes*) claiming that *omni*potence in the classical theistic sense conflicts with belief in human freedom, the statistical nature of scientific laws (à la Peirce), and creates the nastiest problem of evil. The point I want to make here, again, however, is that Hartshorne has spent a great deal of energy criticizing in detail the concept of omnipotence, and analytic theists have spent a great deal of time ignoring these efforts. Moreover, from Hartshorne's point of view, their unquestioned assumption that immutability is integral to theism is connected to their overly strong view about divine omnipotence. For, in their view, if God were not omnipotent He (the masculine pronoun is needed here) would not be in control and could be pushed around (i.e. *changed*) by others.

The beginnings of a dialogue

Whereas Mann, Stump, and Kretzmann assume *simpliciter* that God is immutable, Plantinga (with Swinburne and Wolterstorff) offers at least some indication, however inadequate, of why immutability should be attributed to God. Richard Creel, in his book *Divine Immutability*, is perhaps alone among analytic theists in arguing in depth for his classical theistic assumptions regarding immutability. It should be noted that Creel is primarily concerned with God as "impassible" (*apathes*), which is not necessarily the same as "immutable," in that an immutable being must be impassible but an impassible being does not have to be immutable, say, if it changes itself. Because much of Creel's analysis affects immutability as well as impassibility, his book is the most fruitful sign that bridges can be built between process theism and analytic theism. But these are difficult bridges to build when one considers that for Hartshorne it is only the dead (or the insentient aggregates of sentient constituents) that truly can be said to be impassible.[16]

The dialogue is facilitated by distinguishing four senses of "impassibility" used by Creel.

(1) Regarding the impassibility, indeed the immutability, of God's *nature*, there is no disagreement between Hartshorne and Creel. God always exhibits maximal power, goodness, and wisdom; and God exists necessarily and hence not contingently. In this sense Hartshorne agrees that God is immutable.

(2) There is some agreement also in Creel's account of impassibility of *will*. He correctly notes (60-61, 87) that in Hartshorne's theory God's memory of the past, although all-embracing, must change due to the influence of later stages of process, just as each new generation of human beings must rewrite their history books, i.e. God's knowledge of the past is in a way passible for Hartshorne. For the most part, however, there is quite a distance between Creel and Hartshorne on impassibility of will. Creel wants to hold that God's response to creatures does not entail that God change; it is perhaps more accurate to call these responses "presponses" or "indesponses" (16, 209). There is no real re-sponse on the part of God because God decides independently of our actions what he will do. God has already decided what he will do when we choose. This is what allows Creel to hold the oxymoronic (Hartshorne would say inconsistent) classical theistic claim that God is both *apathes* and loving (18, 26).

It should be obvious that Creel's position regarding impassibility of will depends on God knowing the future. God knows all possibilities (34, 62), according to Creel, but to know a possibility thoroughly is to know what an actuality will be like that instantiates that possibility (46). This is what allows Creel to hold that God not only knows all possibilities, but also all actualities, *including* future actualities (35), hence allowing God to be impassible in will in that God can will his "indesponse" before the creature acts.

But this view sidesteps altogether Hartshorne's critique of Whitehead's theory of eternal objects as well as Hartshorne's claim that omniscience consists in knowing all actualities as actual and all possibilities as possible. To know a future contingency as actual is to misunderstand the meaning of contingency and is thus not consistent with maximal knowledge. Hartshorne would wonder how a future event could be actual, for if it were actual it would be here already. Future events, he thinks, must be potential (even those for which there is a very high degree of probability) for them to remain future. This is not to say that God was once ignorant of anything actual. God has *always* known the actual, but future contingencies are not actual.

One gets the suspicion that Creel, despite his wishes, is defending an eternal duplicate of this world in God's mind which will eventually be actualized exactly as God's knowledge indicates it must. This odd version of Platon*ism* differs from Hartshorne's more judicious use of Plato,[17] and it leaves the analytic theist with most of the traditional problems of classical theism. Creel's concessions leave the major problems about divine immutability and impassibility untouched.

(3) Creel's position regarding impassibility of *knowledge* is similar to that regarding will. But it is here that the fundamental tension (or contradiction) in his thought surfaces most clearly. On the one hand, he holds that God is impassible and immutable since God knows the realm of possibility (the plenum) *exhaustively* (80, 86), hence he knows how every possibility, if chosen, will be actualized (again, 35, 46). On the other hand, God's knowledge of "concrete possibilities," i.e. of actual individuals, is temporal, passible, and mutable (86-87). The latter part is a concession to Hartshorne, the former to classical theism.

One wonders if Creel can have it both ways. Consider this quotation from him:

> Hence even if his knowledge of what I *will* do is impassible, his knowledge of what I *am* doing must be passible, i.e. subject to influence by what I am doing (88).

Clearly Creel *thinks* he can have it both ways, but if he is correct in saying that by virtue of knowing a possible world God knows what I will do if he actualizes that world (179), then there simply is little or no room for his concession to Hartshorne that God's knowledge of actual individuals is mutable. In short, Creel has not met the process theist halfway; rather he has taken a step or two in the direction of process theism, whereas if Hartshorne were to agree with Creel's position regarding impassibility of knowledge he would have to jog several miles.

This same tension can be found in Creel's view of eternity. On the one hand, he criticizes the Boethian "eternalism" found in Geach (as well as in Mann, Stump, and Kretzmann) because, as we have seen, he thinks God's knowledge of the future is passible. That is, he agrees with Hartshorne that there are no individual determinables, that there are no individuals apart from determinateness. Relying on Wolterstorff as well as on Hartshorne, Creel holds that God only knows possible individuals before they become actual (96-99). On the other hand, Creel admits that he is closer to the classical theistic stance on divine eternity than to process theism because he believes that "time can pass without change" occurring (102-103). This is an odd position, to say the least. It does not suffice merely to *say* that God has (temporal) duration but not a successive existence; one must, in addition, indicate how this could be so without stretching human concepts of time to the (Boethian) breaking point.

At other points in his book Creel quite explicitly states that God is unchangeable, atemporal rather than temporal. "He simply is," without past or future (104). But this is precisely the Boethian view which Creel earlier criticized. Creel's only concession to process theism here is that we can make temporal statements about God, e.g. that "God existed" (105-106). But God has all of *his* life at once (106-107). Hartshorne would wonder how, on Creel's view, God could have all of his *life* at once if living entails temporal change and adaptation from moment to moment: responding to at least the immediate past, savoring the fleeting present, and anticipating at least the immediate future. Creel is quite understandably forced into the old Thomistic trap of claiming that all relations are external to God (109). I find unintelligible his own novel formulation of this: "changes in God's knowledge of actuality make a difference *in* him [Then why not say that God has internal relations?] but not *to* him" (111—my insert).

(4) Creel believes that God is impassible in *feeling* for several reasons. First, in response to the claim that *personality* requires passibility he uses Stoic *apatheia* as an example of a type of personal awareness which deëmphasizes passibility. Stoic "impassibility," however, is obviously a mask (literally one of several *personae*) worn by a passible, feeling, human animal. That is, not even an Epictetus could, strictly speaking, be impassible. Second, Creel rejects the idea that *love* requires passibility, as when he claims that:

> I see no problem with assuming that an emotionally impassible being could *feel* about and be disposed toward the welfare of someone else (117—my emphasis).

But if the Greek word *pathe* by definition means feeling in the sense of being passive with respect to something, how can there be a feeling being who is *apathes*? Creel's view seems to be that divine feeling is merely a disposition to feel rather than the ability to have feelings in a strong sense, i.e. really to react to creatures. Further, Creel's rejection of divine passible love is integrally connected, as we will see, with the traditional classical theistic theodicy, which has made the case for theism so untenable for thinking (and feeling) people over the last several centuries. He says that:

> We cannot, then, rule out the possibility that God knows something about our destiny that renders it unnecessary and inappropriate for him to be disturbed by our suffering in this life (121).

But this plays right into the hands of a Humean or a Camus-like thinker who would accuse God of sadism.

Third, Creel does not think that *omniscience* requires passibility; he does not think that to know suffering is, in a way, to suffer. Creel's view here is based, however, on the view that God does not know any of our feelings directly (129); and this view is based on the (again, as in Plantinga's case, unexamined) assumption that divine embodiment makes no sense (25, 85). It also denies that God can be "sympathetic" in the strongest sense of the word. Creel is correct that there is a difference between one's own feelings and those of others, but if God is sympathetic with creatures (literally, sym-pathy), as he sometimes admits, then the gap between divine and creaturely feeling is bridged, as in my feeling pain because cells in my finger have been burned.[18]

And fourth, Creel does not think that morality or *theodicy* requires passibility. He admits that on his view God is omnipotent pure activity (68), and because of God's omnipotence God is directly or indirectly responsible for all suffering; but suffering, he thinks, is an instrumental ingredient in redemption (147). That is, God can "counter-balance or cancel out" any evil (189). Hartshorne, by way of contrast, agrees with Wordsworth that "what having been, must ever be." There is no way that innocent suffering can be completely canceled out, as Creel thinks (149), because any being with memory, especially the greatest conceivable memory, would be pained to recall, e.g. that some innocent being sometime before had been tortured. In that Hartshorne's God is not omnipotent (although Hartshorne's God does have the most power logically compatible with free creatures) it is not his God who can be accused of coöperating with the Holocaust (138), because the concrete pole of the divine nature is not entirely up to God, as Creel incorrectly alleges of Hartshorne's view (166).

Yet if God is, as Creel alleges, an omnipotent pure activity, then one can quite legitimately accuse this "God" of coöperating with the Holocaust. It is easy to allege this coöperation because of Creel's claim that God does not take pleasure in, nor is God pained by, each creature intensively but only extensively (144). What this means is that God merely counts the number of beings who experience pain without divinity being pained. Is *this* a morally supreme being? Creel thinks so, comparing his God's impassibility to Buddhist compassion (158), but exactly what sort of compassion could this be? An incomprehensible compassion, I think, just as incomprehensible as the claim made by Creel that God did not choose this world because it is the best possible one, but rather this is the best possible one *because* an omnipotent and impassible (in effect, immutable) God "chose" it (203).

Conclusion: Plato

As indicated in the introduction, this article is an attempt to enter a dialogue with those analytic theists who have largely ignored Hartshorne's work and hence who have assumed with equanimity that God is immutable. It is also an attempt to continue the beginnings of a dialogue already in progress between Creel and process theists, a dialogue which has only scratched the surface of the differences between the two, and perhaps of similarities which I have not emphasized. The differences, however, are not due, as some would think, to Creel and other classical theists inheriting the Greek tradition of immutability while Hartshorne and process theists eschew this Greek tradition in theology. Rather, the differences seem to be due to two separate modes of appropriating the Greeks, particularly Plato.

There are two significant ways in which Plato talks about God (*theos*). First, he inherited from Parmenides the notion that being is eternal, immutable, and self-same. This notion was the starting point for the tradition of classical, monopolar theism, a tradition kept alive, with few changes made, by the analytic theists I have treated in this article. "The extent to which Plato is committed to such an absolute schism between *being* and *becoming* ... would seem to dictate for him a similar exclusion from divinity of all shadow of change."[19] This tendency is evidenced in Book Two and elsewhere in the *Republic*, the *Phaedo* (78-80), and the *Symposium* (202-203).

Second, however, there is no textual foundation for the popular identification of Plato's God with the transcendent form of the good, nor even with the world of forms, either as a whole or in part.[20] Even when talking about divine eternity and immutability (in the limited dipolar sense), the Platonic locus for divinity is *psyche* or *nous*. It comes as a shock to some readers of Plato who have read only the *Republic*, *Phaedo*, and *Symposium* that in the *Phaedrus* (245, etc.) Eros is claimed to be divine. Here Plato discovers, according to Leonard Eslick, a new, dynamic meaning for perfection, similar to the one Hartshorne defends. The perfection that is dynamic is the perfection of life itself, treated not only in the *Phaedrus* but in Book Ten of the *Laws* as well.

In the *Timaeus* and the *Sophist*, both poles in Plato's theism are brought together: the perfection of divine immutability and the perfection of divine life. The former is identified in the *Timaeus* with the Demiurge, who eternally and without change contemplates, but is not identical with, the archetypal models, the eternal forms. The latter is identified with the World-Soul, whose essence is self-motion, but whose motions include both actions and passions. In fact, in the *Sophist* reality is identified with *dynamis* or power, specifically the power to affect or be affected by others. Aristotle attests to the fact that reality (even divine reality) for Plato is the joint product of the One and the Indefinite Dyad.[21] Unfortunately, Aristotle's own notion of God as completely unmoved loses the second tendency in Plato's theism, and the mesmerizing influence that Aristotle has had on the history of theism (through Plotinus, St. Thomas, et al.) has prevented progress from being made in the Platonic project of bringing the two poles or tendencies in God's nature together.

It is the appropriation of the former tendency in Plato, as filtered through Aristotle and the classical theistic tradition, which supports analytic theism's denigration of divine change and divine embodiment.[22] And it is Hartshorne's appropriation of both tendencies in Plato (not the latter tendency only)—tendencies which represent the mature Platonic metaphysics—that supports Hartshorne's defense of God as the World-Soul of the body of the world, a World-Soul which is nonetheless happy in the midst of the tragedy it experiences (contra Creel—137). Perhaps the best way to explore the extent to which analytic theism's version of classical theism and process theism can agree is for both analytic theists and process theists to reread the *Timaeus* and *Sophist*. In these dialogues, the two tendencies in Plato's theism are brought together, a synthesis which underlies these profound lines from Whitehead, lines which indicate in a short space how a mutable, tragic God is nonetheless a perfect being worthy of worship:

> At the heart of the nature of things there are always the dream of youth and the harvest of tragedy. The Adventure of the Universe starts with the dream and reaps tragic Beauty. This is the secret of the union of Zest with Peace:—That the suffering attains its end in a Harmony of Harmonies. The immediate experience of this Final Fact, with its union of Youth and Tragedy, is the sense of Peace. In this way the World receives its persuasion towards such perfections as are possible for its diverse individual occasions.[23]

The belief in divine immutability is often a veiled theodicy, as is made explicit in Creel, but is implicit in all of the authors I have treated in this article: there is ultimately no need to be troubled by evil and pain in the world since God, who is not changed by these, makes everything turn out fine in the end. Hartshorne and Whitehead, however, in their mode of appropriating Plato, as opposed to that of the classical theists, are also interested in appropriating the Greek sense of life, even divine life, as tragic but worth living nonetheless.

NOTES

1. I am referring to his paper titled "Analytic Themes in Whitehead's Metaphysics," presented to the Eastern Division of the APA in 1987.
2. *The Journal of Philosophy* **78** (1981): 429-458.
3. *International Philosophical Quarterly* **23** (1983): 267-276.
4. My criticisms of Stump, Kretzmann, and Mann apply as well to the earlier work of Geach and Ross, writers who also assumed that God is immutable. See Peter

Geach, *Providence and Evil* (Cambridge: Cambridge University Press, 1977), p. 22. And James Ross, *Philosophical Theology* (N.Y.: Bobbs-Merrill, 1969), p. 63, although Ross is quick to point out that there are nonetheless contingent attributes that God has, but they are not due to any agent other than God. I will not be treating nonanalytic Thomists in this article, e.g. those like Norris Clark, who have indeed entered into debate with process theists.

5. Colin Gunton, *Becoming and Being* (Oxford: Oxford University Press, 1978), p. 11.
6. Among Hartshorne's books that I will be using in this article are: *Beyond Humanism, The Divine Relativity, Reality as Social Process, Philosophers Speak of God* (hereafter: PSG), *The Logic of Perfection, Anselm's Discovery, A Natural Theology for Our Time, Creative Synthesis* and *Philosophic Method, Insights and Oversights of Great Thinkers*, and *Omnipotence and Other Theological Mistakes.*
7. I realize this is an assumption on my part, nor is it made with equanimity. Also, my treatment of divine attributes below should give special treatment to Mann, who conflates the divine nature with divine attributes. Finally, I admit that the permanence-change contrast is used both as an instance of a non-invidious contrast and as a generic heading for all of the other instances of non-invidious contrasts listed.
8. For Hartshorne, God must be as great as possible at any particular time, or else God would not be the greatest being. But new moments bring with them new possibilities for greatness, which God must realize in the best way possible if God is the greatest, or better, the unsurpassable. This means that God is greater than any being who is not God, but God can always surpass previous instances of divine greatness. It does not mean that God's earlier existence was inferior, because it was at that particular time the greatest conceivable existence, the greatest existence logically possible, and greater than any other being.
9. This does not mean that there are no historical roots to Hartshorne's dipolar theism. See his PSG and *Insights and Oversights of Great Thinkers.* Also see an excellent article by Leonard Eslick, "Plato as Dipolar Theist," *Process Studies* **12** (1982): 243-251.
10. Let me emphasize once again that the purpose of Mann's article is to show that God as simple and immutable can also be a person. The question I am asking is: Why should we assume that God is immutable? The purpose of Stump and Kretzmann is to elucidate the concept of eternity, but in their elucidation they betray the same assumption as Mann. Also, the reader who is interested in Hartshorne's treatment of the theodicy problem, God as creator, divine omnipotence, etc., can easily find his thoughts on these matters. God is not a watered down divinity in Hartshorne's thought. For example (contra Mann, Stump, and Kretzmann), God as a perfect knower would not have to mean that God would eternally know every actuality, but rather could mean that God would know what can be known; God's omniscience means that God would perfectly know actualities as actualities, and future contingencies as contingencies. To "know" a future contingency as an actuality is to know imperfectly. Just as there is no highest number, there are some values, such as knowledge, which do not admit of a maximum in a temporally changing world. See Robert Carr-Wiggin, "God's Omnipotence and Immutability," *The Thomist* **48** (Jan., 1984): 44-51, where the author admits that God's failure to change would be for the worse, yet

God may still be immutable in the sense that God is always omniscient and perfect, at $time_1$ and $time_2$, etc. Another article that criticizes Stump and Kretzmann is by Delmas Lewis, "Eternity Again: A Reply to Stump and Kretzmann," *International Journal of the Philosophy of Religion* **15** (1984): 73-79. Also see John Zeis, "The Concept of Eternity," *International Journal of the Philosophy of Religion* **16** (1984): 61-71, and George Shields, "Davies, Eternity, and the Cosmological Argument," *International Journal of the Philosophy of Religion* **21** (1987): 21-37. However, for a defense of immutability see Theodore Kondoleon, "The Immutability of God: Some Recent Challenges," *The New Scholasticism* **58** (1984): 293-315.

11. Alvin Plantinga, *God and Other Minds* (Ithaca: Cornell University Press, 1967), pp. 174-180.
12. See Hartshorne's *Existence and Actuality.* It is clear from Plantinga's *The Nature of Necessity* (Oxford: Oxford University Press, 1974) and other works that Plantinga is somewhat familiar with Hartshorne's work on the ontological argument, but there is no written evidence of which I am aware that Plantinga is familiar with Hartshorne as a process philosopher.
13. Alvin Plantinga, *Does God Have a Nature?* (Milwaukee: Marquette University Press, 1980). Numbers in parentheses in the remainder of this section on Plantinga refer to page numbers in this book.
14. I have dealt with Swinburne in some detail in "Does God Have a Body?," forthcoming in *The Journal of Speculative Philosophy.*
15. Ibid. Also see my "Hartshorne and Plato" in the forthcoming Hartshorne volume in The Library of Living Philosophers series, as well as additional comments in a chapter with the same title in *Hartshorne and the Metaphysics of Animal Rights* (Albany: SUNY Press, 1988).
16. Plantinga's views on divine immutability rely heavily on Nicholas Wolterstorff, "God Everlasting," in *God and the Good*, ed. Orlebeke (Grand Rapids: Eerdmans, 1975). Richard Creel also seems to rely on Wolterstorff. See Creel's *Divine Impassibility* (Cambridge: Cambridge University Press, 1986). Also see a fine review of this book by James Keller in *Process Studies.*
17. Again, see my article on "Hartshorne and Plato" as well as the conclusion to the present article.
18. See my article titled "An Anticipation of Hartshorne: Plotinus on Daktylos and the World-Soul," forthcoming in *The Heythrop Journal.*
19. See Eslick, p. 244.
20. See P. E. More, *The Religion of Plato* (Princeton: Princeton University Press, 1921). The position which identifies the form of the good with God relies on the neoplatonic (actually the neoaristotelian) interpretation of Plato popular in late antiquity.
21. Metaphysics A.
22. Other factors also enter into the reluctance of some to abandon divine immutability, e.g. the classical theistic tradition of male bias in theology, which favors a rigid God devoid of emotion; and the classical theistic tendency to think in substantial rather than in process terms, a tendency which should be as antiquated in theology as it is in geology, biology, and physics.
23. A. N. Whitehead, *Adventures of Ideas* (N.Y.: Free Press, 1967), p. 381.

BIBLIOGRAPHY

I have used the following works by Hartshorne:

Beyond Humanism (Lincoln: University of Nebraska Press, 1968). Originally published in 1937.

The Divine Relativity (New Haven: Yale University Press, 1948).

Reality as Social Process (Boston: Beacon Press, 1953).

Philosophers Speak of God (Chicago: University of Chicago Press, 1953).

The Logic of Perfection (LaSalle, Ill.: Open Court, 1962).

Anselm's Discovery (LaSalle, Ill.: Open Court, 1967).

A Natural Theology for Our Time (LaSalle, Ill.: Open Court, 1967).

Creative Synthesis and Philosophic Method (LaSalle, Ill.: Open Court; and London: SCM Press, 1970). A new edition has been published (Lanham, Md.: University Press of America, 1983).

Insights and Oversights of Great Thinkers (Albany: SUNY Press, 1983).

Omnipotence and Other Theological Mistakes (Albany: SUNY Press, 1984).

Existence and Actuality: Conversations with Charles Hartshorne (Chicago: University of Chicago Press, 1984).

The other works I have used are:

Carr-Wiggin, Robert. "God's Omnipotence and Immutability," *The Thomist* **48** (Jan., 1984): 44-51.

Creel, Richard. *Divine Impassibility* (Cambridge: Cambridge University Press, 1986).

Eslick, Leonard. "Plato as Dipolar Theist," *Process Studies* **12** (1982): 243-251.

Geach, Peter. *Providence and Evil* (Cambridge: Cambridge University Press, 1977).

Gunton, Colin. *Becoming and Being* (Oxford: Oxford University Press, 1978).

Kondolean, Theodore. "The Immutability of God: Some Recent Challenges," *The New Scholasticism* 8B(1984): 293-315.

Lewis, Delmas. "Eternity Again: A Reply to Stump and Kretzmann," *International Journal of the Philosophy of Religion* **15** (1984): 73-79.

Mann, William. "Simplicity and Immutability in God," *International Philosophical Quarterly* **23** (1983): 267-276.

Plantinga, Alvin. *God and Other Minds* (Ithaca: Cornell University Press, 1967).

———. *The Nature of Necessity* (Oxford: Oxford University Press, 1974).

———. *Does God Have a Nature?* (Milwaukee: Marquette University Press, 1980).

Ross, James. *Philosophical Theology* (N.Y.: Bobbs-Merrill, 1969).

Shields, George. "Davies, Eternity, and the Cosmological Argument," *International Journal of the Philosophy of Religion* **21** (1987): 21-37.

Stump, Eleonore and Kretzmann, Norman. "Eternity," *The Journal of Philosophy* **78** (1981): 429-458.

Wolterstorff, Nicholas. "God Everlasting," in *God and the Good*, ed. Orlebeke (Grand Rapids: Eerdmans, 1975).

"Mutable God": Hartshorne and Indian Theism

Stephen H. Phillips

Introductory and historical remarks

This paper is part of an ongoing, fieldwide endeavor to integrate Eastern thought into a single world history of philosophy. My aim here is to reveal conceptions that unite, as well as issues that divide, Western process theism and Indian theism. After surveying the relevant history, I shall focus on, in particular, Charles Hartshorne and the Indian philosopher, Aurobindo, as representative figures.

In the context of comparative efforts concerned with process thought and Eastern systems, this essay enjoys notable antecedents. Charles Hartshorne has identified certain Buddhist conceptions as closely consonant with his own, including views on causality, identity over time, empathetic cognition, and an ontology of "occasions" as well. There is also a similarity between Hartshorne's "rationalist" methodology and that advanced by Buddhists who subordinate "revelation" to reason and experience.[1] This along with the conceptual consonances identified has facilitated much thoughtful dialogue between process theologians and modern Buddhist theorists—the latter chiefly several Japanese professors of the "Kyoto school."

In contrast, there has been much less mutual study and dialogue between process thinkers and Indian theists. Since Whitehead and Hartshorne are theists, one might have expected that the long and rich tradition of theism in India—now that for decades many of its central texts have been accessible in translation—would have spurred process philosophers to lively comparative and evaluative efforts. Similarly, one might have expected, in reverse, many modern Indian theists to have taken a keen interest in Whitehead and Hartshorne. But in fact, there has been to date, with one outstanding exception, little work along either line.[2]

Now Hartshorne himself has made excursions into "Hindu" thought, criticizing the venerated eighth-century monist and illusionist, Śaṅkara, for instance.[3] He has even identified the theology of the (moderately obscure) sixteenth-century Bengali Vaiṣṇava, Jīva Goswāmī, and his "Bengali school," as espousing a concept of God closely resembling his own.[4] But his mentions of Jīva Goswāmī are disappointing. They seem casual, and Hartshorne's discovery that the Bengali joins him in espousing a "mutable God" (who "feels all feeling") serendipitous only.[5] To my knowledge, neither Hartshorne nor any process theologian has tried to draw an extended and illuminating comparison. None has tried to engage the Indian theist, of whatever stripe, Bengali-Vaiṣṇava or any other, classical or modern, in comparative and philosophic debate.[6]

There are serious obstacles to such engagement. Jīva Goswāmī, for example, is one of the more "systematic" of Vaiṣṇava theologians in the late classical age. But he turns—as do also his most immediate predecessors, Vallabha (c. 1450) and Caitanya (c. 1500)—to revelation, and not reason, as the grounds for his theological views. Jīva Goswāmī sees his several "scriptures"[7] as "suprarational," as presenting views that not only are beyond what reason, unaided, can achieve, but that also are not strictly comprehensible (*acintya*) by the rational faculty or "*buddhi*." The views are not so much to be defended, or even "believed," as they are, in their very incomprehensibility, to guide the soul of the devotee to a suprarational and "mystic" comprehension—in a trance devoid of intellection.[8] Hartshorne commends Jīva Goswāmī for seeing, and he does see—much better than most in his tradition—that from the supposition that God is continually creative, that Bhagavān upholds the world at all times as immanent in world processes and directs the broad lines of change, it follows that God changes, too—at least in God's "consequent state." (Jīva Goswāmī posits a dual nature for God, and holds that "in essence" [*svarūpe*] God does not change.) But the suprarationalism the Vaiṣṇava endorses remains a block to extended engagement between the two theological points of view.

Methodologically, the Naiyāyikas ("Logical-Realists") offer process theists the best entrée into classical Indian philosophic theism. But again there are obstacles to "engagement." Udayana (c. 1000) presents several "clusters" of argument for the existence of God, all broadly speaking "cosmological." The premier "Navya" Naiyāyika, Gaṅgeśa (c. 1325), develops some of these, reformulating them in the refined terms of his revolutionary "New" Logic. Gaṅgeśa's reasoning is also exclusively cosmological. I know of no "ontological argument" put forth by a Naiyāyika, of either the Old School or the New.[9] But it is not primarily this absence that presents a block to meaningful engagement with the Naiyāyikas on the part of a theologian of Whitehead's and Hartshorne's camp. The Naiyāyikas are thorough-going "Aristotelians," and uphold concepts of enduring "substance" as ontologically fundamental. Historically, the Naiyāyikas are the chief antagonists of the Buddhist "process theorists."

Furthermore, it is these "substance theorists," and not the Buddhist "*kṣaṇabhaṅgī*-s," "proponents of continual change," who—in the Indian context and "historical judgment"—clearly win. The Buddhists fail to see that some wholes are more than their constituent parts, and are unable to explain "emergent" attributes. They insist on dividing a realm of experience and a realm of concepts (all concepts are considered "abstract"), and are unable successfully to rejoin them. And they stumble in their analyses of self-consciousness and of recognition ('This is the same Devadatta I saw yesterday'), imperiled by, and ever about to succumb to the skepticism of their influential left wing, the Mādhyamikas (e.g. Nāgārjuna), or to the phenomenalism of their right wing, the early logicians (e.g. Vasubandhu and Dignāga). The Naiyāyikas score on all these issues, and others as well, particularly in epistemology, offering a theory perceived to have greater power of explanation, and one less in conflict with common sense. The Naiyāyikas carry the day argumentatively, and their victory may be counted as one factor in the eventual disappearance of Buddhist philosophic traditions in India.[10]

Of course, process philosophy avoids many of the mistakes of the Indian Buddhists, and shows e.g. in its analysis of an "occasion" surely much more sophistication than the Buddhists with respect to their "*kṣaṇa*," i.e. "momentary event." But in an attempt to take on the Nyāya, process theorists would in general find themselves (bored) rehearsing their arguments (based on science) against what Hartshorne calls (Western) "classical metaphysics"; or, in an effort to appreciate the Naiyāyika objections to "event-talk" in their own unique context, the (non-sanskritist, non-specialist!) process philosopher would encounter a (frustrating) system of technical terms seemingly impossible to decipher. Nevertheless, Nyāya's blend of theism, refined logical apparatus, and familiarity with Buddhist "process" theory remains a spur to the interest of theologians of the Hartshornean camp.

At this point in the history of scholarship, a process philosopher would do best to focus on a modern representative of Nyāya, for example, B. K. Matilal.[11] But unfortunately, Matilal—who is almost alone among scholars of Nyāya in trying outright to defend it, though many try to present the school in a favorable light—is not much concerned with the *theistic* claims of the classical reasoners. This is true of most other scholars as well. These moderns apparently see the epistemological and ontological accomplishments of the Naiyāyikas as separable from the theological. (It may be they think such separation makes Nyāya more palatable—more about this below.) I know of no prominent twentieth-century theist who has digested, or works from, classical Naiyāyika suppositions.[12] But we may hope one appears soon.

I have said that Buddhist "process philosophy" disappears in the later periods of classical thought. But this is not entirely correct. Much disappears as "Buddhist" but reëmerges as "Tantric," recast and assimilated to Hindu ideas. The problem with Tantric thought is that though rich conceptually it lies outside the mainstream of philosophic debate in Sanskrit. Scholars believe that particularly in Kashmir, where Mahāyāna remained strong much longer than in most centers of population and culture, Buddhist thought helped shape Tantric views. Nevertheless, Tantric writers appear largely unschooled in the centuries of reflection that precede them.

Further, while Tantric texts are not, to be sure, devoid of argument, even the most theoretic usually seem to belong to a genre other than "philosophy."

(Works by Abhinavagupta [c. 1050] are exceptions, as are some by Appayya Dīkṣita [c. 1550], and by a few others as well.) Most experts in the philosophic traditions have ignored them. Whereas Naiyāyikas argue with every sentence, Tantrics tend simply to propound a world view, and that with much admixture of myth, legend, and "spiritual advice."

In this respect, Tantric thought is, on the whole, worse than Vaiṣṇava theology, and has much less right to be counted as philosophic theism.[13] On the other hand, Tantric "metaphysics" is dominated by a concept of a mutable God, much more so than Vaiṣṇava theology—a "Shiva" who, one with a creative energy or "Shakti," self-transforms and exceeds continuously in time a false "perfection" of a state of "static transcendence." Thus I would think a process theologian would find herself more at home in this tradition than in any other that is both theistic and Indian, the odd and parvenu qualities of Tantrics—in the context of the broader history of Indian culture—notwithstanding. Some interesting work could be done here, especially with regard to Abhinavagupta and the more intellectual of his followers.[14]

I mentioned that I know of no "ontological argument" advanced by a Naiyāyika, the "mainstream" philosophic theist in classical times. But classical Indian thought does contain "proofs" of a "necessary being." These seem particularly fecund for comparative analyses. The influential eleventh-century metaphysician, Śrīharṣa, puts forth, in a variety of formulations, an ontological argument as the centerpiece of the positive side of his reasoning.[15] (Śrīharṣa is more famous for his "destructions" of others' views.) But Śrīharṣa and the other classical proponents of such a proof are (at least to my knowledge) all (or almost all) Advaitins,[16] espousing a concept not of God, but of *brahman*, the Absolute and the One, as the "necessary being" proved. That this "Absolute" is a Creator is categorically denied. Further, that "worship" is not the appropriate attitude towards *brahman*, many in the tradition make plain. In this way, the Advaitins distinguish themselves from Indian theists properly so-called.[17] Nevertheless, the Advaitins' "ontological proofs" deserve close inspection by Hartshorneans, and all those who are interested in the similar arguments proffered in the West.

In the sections below, I leave the classical tradition to take up the thought of Aurobindo, who, to my mind, invites scrutiny from a process-theological perspective as much as or more than any other twentieth-century Indian theist. Modern Indian thought, particularly that expressed in English, presents some obvious advantages over the classical tradition. But there are still obstacles. The contemporary Indian religious scene is dominated by theism, and a theism as multifaceted as might be expected in a nation of eight hundred million persons with culturally diverse regions and states. But there is also a peculiar feature of "Hinduism" that may be seen as in large part responsible for the variety in current theological opinion, i.e. as generating distinct theological points of view. This is the phenomenon of the "guru," who, credited by disciples with unchallangeable authority, makes, by selection and emphasis, his/her own sacred tradition, almost invariably expounding his/her own unique view. Most of the religious philosophies of the classical period survive in the twentieth century in some form, and numerous recent "spiritual preceptors" have modified, reformulated, and/or combined earlier perspectives into a multiplicity of current religious world views. To just which modern Indian theist should the process theologian target an effort of meaningful comparison and philosophic engagement? I intend to answer this question. But the plasticity of Indian theism, and the virtual singularity of any and all spokespersons, must be kept in mind.

Further, one must distinguish between the philosophy of university professors and that of "spiritual preceptors." Professional philosophers in Indian universities espouse as wide a range of positions as do philosophy professors in the West. They are all trained in the history of Western thought, and their medium of expression is almost exclusively English. Among them are found creative Marxists or "humanists," phenomenologists, neo-Kantians, existentialists, analytico- (or "piecemeal") metaphysicians, and others, taking their philosophic orientations from the West. Some address aspects of the classical, or contemporary, Indian religious scene; but, with the outstanding exception of one group, none tends to speak *from its heart*, so to say. The exception is modern Advaita. Sarvepalli Radhakrishnan, K. C. Bhattacharya, T. V. R. Murti, P. T. Raju, Kalidas Bhattacharya, and T. M. P. Mahadevan are exceptional among a host of eloquent twentieth-century academicians who have found new ways of defending—or have originated philosophies in close consonance with—the classical monism and illusionism of Śaṅkara. Indian theism is much, much less well-represented in the universities (though there are now some "Aurobindonists" and a few others as well[18]). This is surprising in the face of the prevalence of theism in the broader culture. But it is not so surprising in the face of the "Europeanization" of Indian universities, the sense that theism is *passé* (or falls, in its Indian varieties, to objections familiar in the West), and the attraction of the uniquely Indian quality, and the "clear austerity," if I may coin a phrase, of Śaṅkara's system (it is so clear that the world disappears!) In general, one has to look beyond the universities to the "folk" tradition of the "spiritual preceptors" to find the best spokespersons for the theism today.

Hartshorne and Aurobindo: two modern theists, Western and Indian

In this and two other sections, I shall compare, along certain lines, the theologies of Charles Hartshorne and the twentieth-century "guru," Aurobindo. While drawing out conceptual and justificational similarities, and some significant dissimilarities as well, I shall try to make a few points of assessment. But no summary evaluation of either view will be hazarded.

I assume the reader of this volume is familiar with Hartshorne's life and thought, but not with Aurobindo's. So let me begin with a few facts about the Easterner's life.

Aurobindo was born Aravinda Ghose, in Calcutta, in 1872, the son of a Bengali physician. Aurobindo's father was a ardent anglophile, and sent "Aravinda Akroyd" along with his two brothers to Manchester when Aurobindo was seven. Without returning to India, Aurobindo completed a Western education at King's College, Cambridge University (as a student, nine years Whitehead's junior), where he held two scholarships. The young gentleman returned to his native land in 1893 with much knowledge of Western culture but little of Indian. A nationalist and early proponent of independence, he supplemented a political activism with a personal cultural activism, mastering Sanskrit and several modern Indian languages. Aurobindo read widely in Sanskrit, but his study of philosophy was much more limited than his study of the epics, drama, and religious literature of the classical civilization. He especially delighted in the profuse religious imaginings of the *Mahābhārata* and the Purāṇas. He did read works by the great Advaitin, Śaṅkara, and carefully examined treatises by Śaṅkara's followers as well, some of them quite late (and thus tutored by Naiyāyikas). But Aurobindo learned little directly about Nyāya, nor about the Nyāya/Buddhist debate. After a career as a journalist and a nationalist politician, which landed him in jail for more than a year, Aurobindo declared himself a "*yogin*," a mystic, and exiled himself, in 1910, in the French colony of Pondicherry, in South India: there he would be both undisturbed by his British adversaries (a fresh warrant for his arrest was issued soon after he was released from prison) and at leisure to pursue his personal spiritual quest. He began publishing works of "spiritual philosophy" in 1914, and wrote voluminously the rest of his life. He died in 1950, in Pondicherry.

As a representative of Indian theism and a target for meaningful engagement from a process-theological perspective, Aurobindo presents particular advantages and disadvantages. Most encouraging is the wealth of concurrence in at least the broad lines of the world views, as Satya Prakash Singh has made plain with respect to Whitehead and Aurobindo.[19] Further, like Hartshorne and Whitehead in the context of traditional theology in the West, Aurobindo is a breath of fresh air in the Indian context. In marked distinction from all classical theists, save certain Naiyāyikas, he accepts no "scripture" as unfailingly true, guaranteed as spoken by God. He may be termed, like Hartshorne, a "natural theologian," although, like the classical Buddhists and unlike Hartshorne (who does not, I think, take up the question), he includes "mystic" perceptions among the data from which a metaphysician builds. His mysticism restores his place in the mainstream of Indian theism, which his naturalism might otherwise challenge. Like other "gurus," he is eclectic, viewing several "scriptures" as "holy"—because they are, he interprets, the records of mystical experiences had by his spiritual predecessors. Aurobindo is eclectic or, to use a less negative term, "synthetic" in a larger sense as well, recognizing the success of science and endorsing various views originating in the West.[20] One has to distinguish sharply between all classical theists and such moderns as Aurobindo, chiefly with respect to science and the encounter with the West. In this, he has more in common with university philosophers than with the "folk" tradition, though on the whole we must say he belongs to the latter.[21] Further, Aurobindo is no exegete, while all the classical theists, again with the exception of the Naiyāyikas, see their principal task as writers to be illumination of sacred texts. Nevertheless, I repeat, Aurobindo stands firmly in an unbroken continuum of Indian theism because of his mysticism, and because through his mysticism he finds himself able to endorse many ancient and classical conceptions. The ideas Aurobindo uses to interpret his special experiences are almost exclusively Indian and theistic.[22]

Allow me now to state frankly the obvious and significant differences between these two theists—Hartshorne and Aurobindo—as *writers*, differences that are reflected in their philosophies and that will help us to see quickly the one view in the other's light and vice-versa.

Charles Hartshorne is a modern professional philosopher. He has worked out in detail a world view that connects with science and is deeply "categorially coherent."[23] Or, to downplay his originality, we might say he is a leading spokesperson for a world view that is one of a very few metaphysical systems alive among professional philosophers in our time, a veritable contender in the current metaphysical arena—including "anti-systematic-metaphysics" metaphysics. Though he has a talent for addressing a popular audience (and teaching those untrained in philosophy), he writes chiefly as a professional for other professionals. And while he has failed to convince every colleague of his process theism—his "ontological arguments" are seen by some as successful only within a conceptual frame that is not theirs—he obeys the canons of professional discourse, I say to set up a contrast, revealing patient scholarship and an acumen informed by scholarship, to speak more directly to the point. Hartshorne's texts, as philosophic texts, are much more refined—by professional standards—than Aurobindo's.

Even in the Indian theist's most abstract work, *The Life Divine*,[24] where he spends more than a thousand pages laying out, with explicit argumentation, his world view, Aurobindo writes as a "spiritual preceptor," in a long tradition of intellectual, but hardly academic, "gurus." Except for his layman's command of science, Aurobindo as a metaphysician is more like much earlier figures in Western philosophy than any twentieth-century professional.

To speak for myself, Aurobindo's appeal lies not directly in his philosophizing, but in his philosophizing as informed by his mysticism. He gives us a free-thinking mysticism and a putatively *empirically* based (religious) world view. It is a theism that faces special problems as a mystic philosophy, to be sure. But the question of the "cognitive value" of mystical experiences is an open question, and a good one, I believe. In my opinion, some such "trans-sensual" empiricism may be called for in matters of religious belief. Aurobindo's philosophical talent is his singular ability to generalize the evidence of *mystical* presentations. And in such a project, he takes himself to speak philosophically for a long line of "spiritual" theists.

On the other hand, whatever one may think on the issue of the value of "mystic information" for philosophy, and whatever one may think about a mystic propounding his own metaphysics, I must add—to be fair—that Aurobindo, despite his lack of philosophic professionalism, is surely an unusual mystic in his ability to argue, an ability he displays in some places with great skill. Although motivated to read Aurobindo by his reputation as a mystic, I have become interested in his reasoning, finding several arguments worth abstracting, reconstructing, and examining at length. Further, Aurobindo claims that what he calls "pure reason" is able to arrive at (many of) the "spiritual" truths he feels he has mystically discovered (though personally I am dubious about this, so far as I understand it). And his world view has an extraordinary "categorial coherence," especially given his ideative context. His philosophy, like Hartshorne's, is an attempt to explain every experience and fact, connecting, like Hartshorne's, with science. And he addresses issues—free will, causality, particulars and universals, matter and mind, appearance and reality—that have engaged metaphysicians of both East and West over the centuries, although the breadth of his treatment of long-standing Western problems is surely deficient compared to Hartshorne's.

God as "self-knowing"

It is impossible to expound fully in a short paper either Aurobindo's or Hartshorne's world view. I shall focus on the two theists' concepts of God and of God's mutability.

Both philosophers discern a fundamental distinction of "nature," or "aspect," in God, "primordial" and "consequent" with Hartshorne, "essential" and "manifest" with Aurobindo.[25] Both also see God as mutable: Hartshorne holds that God has accidents in God's consequent state; Aurobindo holds that what he calls "evolutionary manifestation" is a manifestation *of* God. Both believe that God "includes" or "contains" our world of "becoming," and that God changes as it changes. (For both, it is a necessary truth that everything is "within" God's awareness, "prehended" by God.) But concerning the sense in which God is *im*mutable, there is sharp disagreement: the concepts of a "primordial God" and of an "essential Divine" are hardly a neat match. Once this is clear, it will be seen that, despite the similarity at first blush, each conceives "divine mutability" quite differently, too.

The key differences may be brought out with respect to ideas on "God's creativity" and an argument Hartshorne makes. For Hartshorne, God not only necessarily is but also necessarily creates. Aurobindo, in contrast, believes that God need not have created anything at all.

Hartshorne believes that the notion of a Creator without a creation makes no sense. But he should not be construed as holding simply that the terms 'Creator,' etc. connote a relational complex. The issue, he doubtless would admit, could be framed in a neutral way—for example: Is God necessarily a Creator? or: Could God have existed without creating? Indeed, Hartshorne supports his view that God is necessarily creative with several interlocking lines of argument, framed in the interlocking terms of his system.[26] As with Whitehead, the concept of "creativity" is with Hartshorne as central as that of "God." (Whitehead: "In the philosophy of organism this ultimate is termed 'creativity'; and God is its primordial, non-temporal accident."[27])

The argument on which I shall focus—as particularly well-suited for contrast with Aurobindo—hinges on Hartshorne's view that a characteristic of "perfect knowing" is intrinsic to God. (That is, we must conceive God as necessarily a perfect knower.) Hartshorne then asks: What would there be for God to know if there were only God's "own existence?"[28] For Hartshorne, God's "own existence" would lack a sufficiently rich content to qualify an exclusively "self-cognizing" God as a knower. The idea makes no sense. "Existence" is an abstraction from the actual. Without characteristics, what would there be to exist, much less to know? Note that Hartshorne's own concept of a "primordial state" of God is, in his view, an abstraction from God's actuality, that "aspect," namely, that prefigures "infinite potentialities of being."[29] God does not "know" even (Whiteheadian) "eternal objects" (such as numbers) *apart from* knowing the world. (Though "thicker" than a concept of bare "existence," "Primordial God" is in no way prior—conceptually or in any other way—to God as God is actually. The "primordial," "consequent," and "superjective" aspects each presuppose the others, as does "knowing perfectly" as well.) Indeed, "knowing perfectly" is an abstraction from God as God fully is. But we may take Hartshorne to say that it is by focusing on this aspect that we can see what nonsense is the idea of a merely "*self*-cognizing God."[30]

Let me add that while God is considered necessarily a perfect knower, not everything about God is so construed. Much of God's knowledge is contingent on contingent events. Further, what is contingent is, in Hartshorne's view, what might not have been. But contingency is not itself contingent, since the idea of a perfect knower demands that "Contingency must be *somehow* actualized, but just *how* or *in just what* it is actualized: *that* is the contingency."[31]

Aurobindo's "self-existent" (*svayambhū*) God, or "Brahman,"[32] has a triad of necessary, or "essential" characteristics.[33] The mystic uses the Upanishadic term '*saccidānanda*,' "Existence-Consciousness=Power-Bliss," to characterize this "essential nature" (or "*svarūpa*"): Brahman is self-existent and self-creative (*sat*), self-conscious and conscious of a power to ''loose forth'' contingencies (*cit* or, in an alternative formulation—indicating Tantric influence—*cit-śakti*), and blissful in itself (*sānanda*).

To understand Aurobindo's position, we need to review a concept of ''knowledge by identity'' that is expressed early in Indian thought, and that has known marked importance in several Indian schools: in Sanskrit, ''*svayamprakāśamāna*,'' literally, a ''self-illumining.''[34] Aurobindo holds that a capacity for such a ''non-dual'' knowing is an intrinsic characteristic of a ''self,'' whether God or a contingent being. He claims this ''self-knowing'' is continuous but ''subconscious'' for most humans at most times, and clearly evident during a type of self-absorbed meditation, i.e. in a mystic trance facilitated, he says, by *yoga*.

Perhaps it does violence to English usage to call such a state a ''knowing.'' But Aurobindo could respond that is it a peculiar ''awareness'' or native ''potentiality of awareness.'' It is presumed an awareness devoid of sense-mediated, affective, and mental content—''mental'' not in a sense of ''cognitive'' but in the psychological sense of ''thinking act.''[35]

Now Aurobindo holds that Brahman is not only necessarily existent (*sat*) and aware of its self-existence (*saccit*), but also intrinsically blissful (*sānanda*) and aware of its supreme bliss (*ānandacit*). Brahman is presumed to have necessarily a hedonic tone in its self-existence and self-awareness, an essential (and non-relational) ''ecstasy'' or ''bliss.''[36] The importance of the *ānanda* attribution in our context is that it allows—supplementing Aurobindo's claim about ''knowledge by identity''—the Easterner to make at least something of a response to Hartshorne's argument: ''divine self-knowing'' need not include knowledge of actual contingencies while having more content than of a bare ''own existence.''

But two questions would arise immediately in an ''engagement'' with Hartshorne: (1) Is it, all things considered, really conceivable that there be a ''knowing,'' or an ''awareness,'' that has as content nothing other than the ''self-knowing'' together with a hedonic tone of non-relational ''bliss?'' and (2) Why should one attribute such powers, or characteristics, to God ''essentially?'' Hartshorne sees God's knowledge as the ''intimate'' type we have of our own bodies. God is not an aloof witness, watching the events of the world like a movie. But the Westerner's ''body-in-mind'' metaphor falls short of the absolute ''intimacy'' of God's ''self-cognition'' on our Easterner's theory.

For Aurobindo, the two questions are difficult questions, though a response to the first is not too difficult to reconstruct. One would be unable successfully to challenge Aurobindo, or any mystic attesting to the personal experience, about the possibility of *something like* ''knowledge by identity'' and ''non-relational bliss,'' that is, about the possibility of the extraordinary (yogic) experiences that are taken to make an unmediated self-awareness and *ānanda* evident. The response would be that actuality proves possibility. Of course, one might rightly challenge the correctness of these and whatever characterizations were offered. But surely the basic move—namely, that an actual human state, albeit exceptional, demonstrates a divine possibility—is a good one. The move may nonetheless appear inadequate to a Hartshornean—and, apart from systematic considerations, for a reason I suspect it would seem perplexing to anyone who is not a mystic of Aurobindo's yogic type (it is perplexing to me!) Can a non-mystic make sense of such claims, not having an analogue in her own experience? I have probed the issue in another work,[37] and do not wish to repeat the entire argument. My conclusion is that, with certain restrictions, a non-mystic can understand such claims, but also that the lack of personal acquaintance gives her a reason to be especially dubious about putatively "mystically warranted" propositions. In any case, the latter question (2) takes us more directly to the heart of both philosophies, since it pertains to methodology. I shall presume that Aurobindo could answer the first satisfactorily, and that the dialogue could move on from "meanings" to "reasons."

But first note that if we allow this presumption, then Hartshorne's argument does not go through. Aurobindo's response would block Hartshorne's complaint, the Westerner's contention that divine knowledge could not possibly be limited to God's own being. Aurobindo conceives God's necessary aspects as richer than just a "bare existence," though not as rich as Hartshorne's "perfect knowing." And he would insist certain human experiences demonstrate the possibility of such a non-relational "knowing" and "bliss." If Hartshorne's reasoning hinges on the inconceivability of a "knowing" restricted to God's own being and character apart from creation, it would seem to fail.

Consider now (2) above. The short answer is, as I read Aurobindo, that certain mystical experiences require, to be intelligible, the *saccidānanda* characterization of an essential Divine. But let us not go so fast. It is important to see that methodologically Aurobindo and Hartshorne do not much disagree.

Both theorists advance converging lines of argument about why a theistic world view should be embraced. Both hold that a philosophy of (a divine) creativity provides the best explanation of the way the world is, as well as why there is anything at all. Aurobindo, unlike Hartshorne, offers no explicitly ontological argument.[38] But with regard to the theory of God's nature, both proceed on at least these two fronts: (a) the theory must be sufficiently rich to explain the broad lines of world phenomena (including "mystic phenomena," with Aurobindo), and (b) once we have accepted a set of interlocking explanatory concepts and claims, we may reason out analytically their implications. There seems to be also a third front with Hartshorne, and apparently with Aurobindo, too: (c) we may unpack the notion of God analytically with respect to what a "Perfect Being" must be. Just as we may conclude that God necessarily exists by examining this concept, so also we may tease out God's necessary aspects by inspecting our (Anselmian) idea of "that than which nothing greater can be conceived."

Personally, I am most dubious about this third line (c). We do not all have the same concept of God. Thus with regard to a teasing out of divine characteristics from the idea of a perfect being, I would feel at a loss to adjudicate a dispute: I have inherited no pellucid idea of divine perfection! Should we not be open to altering any concept whatsoever as facts demand, that is, any concept used in either a characterization or an explanation of actualities?—in other words, any concept that is not *merely* abstract and formal? (This is not to say there are no necessary truths about things, but only that we may not be entirely sure we have discovered them.[39]) Indeed I believe we should be prepared to make conceptual modifications as we review our explanatory propositions with regard to what we know and to the logical relations among them. Thus I see Aurodindo's best response to (2) to be that the "self-knowing" and "*ānanda*" attributions are required to explain certain lines of mystical experience. And I do not believe that a *purely* analytic defense can be decisive here.

Let me place these observations in a wider context, the context of the intellectual pluralism that obtains today, even (or especially!) in academia, and even (or especially!) among professional philosophers. Although I would not wish to restrict in some general way the possibilities of dispute, in some areas a pluralism of theory appears unmitigable. In the metaphysical arena in particular, it seems in certain cases that not only do the fundamental principles advanced in one theory compete only indirectly with those of another, but also that views that do compete as wholes cannot be decisively assessed without begging a "criterion" question. This is not a new point. But it does appear that especially with the highly abstract conceptions and explanations typical of metaphysical systems, there can be more than one good way of conceiving and explaining phenomena. And my sense is that this, whether just or not, has been the main thrust of the opposition to Whitehead and Hartshorne.[40]

Of course, not any theory will wash. Coherence considerations sometimes give a view an advantage. Also, there must be an epistemic route from experience to theory, as well as a route back. We rule out views, even some metaphysical views, because they lack sufficient support, or because their implications are in conflict with what we know. Physicists have good reasons for preferring a Riemannian geometry of physical space to Euclid's, for example. And we have discovered that a whale is not a fish. To my mind, many claims of Hartshorne's "neoclassical" theism exhibit similar advantages over "classical" theism. (The old thinkers did not have science to inform their world conceptions; thus they stand at a severe disadvantage vis-à-vis Hartshorne in conceiving God's relation to the world.[41]) Further, in the breadth of its integration of science, and of contemporary outlooks in the humanities as well, Hartshorne's theism has a marked advantage over

Aurobindo's, too. But Aurobindo's mysticism may well recapture some of this advantage. The mystic philosopher claims an arsenal of (putatively) empirical reasons for this or that position, reasons that Hartshorne ignores. Thus while the response to Hartshorne, "That's one way of looking at things," may be unanswerable, such a response may miss the mark with Aurobindo.

Yet despite this (vague) possible disadvantage with respect to mysticism, there are routes open for Hartshorne decisively to show his view of God, and specifically of divine creativity, to be superior to Aurobindo's. Our initial question was—given the confines of our imagined dialogue and "engagement"—whether God should be viewed, with Hartshorne, as having to create some world or other, or, with Aurobindo, as not having to create at all. To bring the disagreement into sharper focus, we reviewed Aurobindo's concept of an "essential Divine" and the imputed attributes of a "self-knowing" and a "supreme bliss." We discovered a reason to reject—from an Aurobindonist perspective—Hartshorne's attack on the contingency of God's creating: the argument presupposes "requirements" on a "divine knowing" that the Indian theist does not accept as true requirements. (Inheritors of Indian theologies work from a [complex of] concept[s] of God distinct from the Western, and some have empirical reasons, Aurobindo believes, to prefer the *saccidānanda* characterization.) Nevertheless, there remains here, it seems, a problem of coherence inviting Hartshornean attack. Or, to put matters less contentiously, a Hartshornean could try to patch up one significant disagreement between what are, after all, two largely concurrent views, by pointing out an incoherence in Aurobindo's notion of an "essential Divine." To have (and one may only think one has) special, mystic reasons for a position does not exempt it from requirements of overall coherence. Aurobindo's theory that God is necessarily, and is necessarily aware of, a power to *create*, to "loose forth" particulars that need not be, seems the attribution—and not the two we have so far reviewed—that makes here the Hartshornean case. How could this be "essential" to God, and God be only contingently creative? How could there be such awareness without God's actually creating some world or other? And since Aurobindo's project is to provide a comprehensive explanation of the way things are (at least on my reading), what point could there be to presuming God aware of a power of creation without necessarily creating something or other? To these questions, let us now turn.

God as Creator

Let me supply a bit more of Aurobindo's ideative context, his "philosophic problem-space," so to say. Our Indian theist spends tens of pages in *The Life Divine* attacking the Advaitin Śaṅkara and his concept of *brahman*. Time and again, Aurobindo asks why Brahman, conceived broadly in line with

Advaita, should be thought *incapable* of "finite, contingent self-manifestation." Aurobindo considers several responses, revealing understanding and sympathy for the tradition; but of course he rejects each.[42] One appeal made by Aurobindo seems to be to a (culturally) deep-set notion of Brahman's perfection: an incapacity to create could not belong to "the One who is Perfect." For myself, this reasoning is indecisive, because, again, I fail to see the validity of isolated conceptual analysis if one is trying to explain actualities. But often Aurobindo's sympathy for Advaita appears to grow out of a conviction, and putative experience, that a mystic can realize her identity with *brahman* apart from all other contingent determinations. Then within this frame of (mystically) empirical agreement, Aurobindo argues that the Advaitic "identity" experience does not support Śaṅkara's "incapacity" attribution.

But vis-à-vis Hartshorne, Aurobindo would line up with the Advaitins: the paradigmatically "Advaitic" mystical experience provides a reason to regard Brahman as possibly existent without creating. The fact of world phenomena is the premier reason the Advaitins are wrong, Aurobindo holds.[43] We must suppose Brahman actually a Creator to make sense presentations intelligible. But we should not suppose Brahman to be necessarily a Creator, Aurobindo would argue against Hartshorne.

Yet it would seem right for a Hartshornean to reply—if only with a mind to patch up the disagreement—that Aurobindo's position here is incoherent. To repeat: on the one hand, Aurobindo attributes a power to create, and an awareness of the power, to God essentially; on the other, he denies what this entails, namely, some actual creation or other. Aurobindo appears guilty of "reifying" an abstraction, and this contradiction is a mark of the fault. The solution would be simple and would not involve Aurobindonists in much theoretic emendation: God should be conceived as a unity, and the notion of a Brahman that could have remained "self-absorbed" should be excised.

Aurobindo does not appear to be unaware of the "contradiction," or "conceptual tension," if a tension it be. One may read his theory of "Supermind" as put forth to show it resolved. The problem is long-standing in Indian theology, as old as the *Īśā* and other Upanishads. Indian theists have typically wanted to view God both as essentially immutable (*svarūpe*) and as the author of changes in Herself—in "loosing forth" the world as Her body. The problem is long-standing, but much in Aurobindo's "Supermind" theory is his own contribution.

According to Aurobindo, Supermind is God's faculty of creation and creative awareness. (The concept is somewhat like that of a "Divine Logos" found in the West.) Supermind is the bridge between a Divine that must be what She is and finite, contingent "manifestations." All potentiality is governed by what God is: not every (humanly) conceivable possibility is inherent in *saccidānanda* (for example, a world of unending pain is not really possible, since it is incompatible with the intrinsic *ānanda*, Aurobindo reasons[44]). But within the set of infinite possibilities compatible with (or in a sense "inherent in") *saccidānanda*, things that need not be come into being through an (atemporally conceived) "series" of choices:[45] "first" (or "most fundamentally") on the part of God as God is in God's self,[46] "next" by Supermind, and finally (within a spatio-temporal "manifestation") by finite things (such as human beings) all endowed with (at least a minimal) creative power of their own. (Like Hartshorne, Aurobindo sees every contingent thing as potentially creative, and God's power over events as limited by a "surrender" to the wills of finite things.[47]) God, as God is necessarily, is presented with a single timeless choice, the option to allow Supermind to emerge or not.[48] With an affirmative "choice," Supermind (timelessly) emerges, and creates, or not, further inessential determinations. Timelessly "choosing" Supermind, God comes to be Supermind and to know as Supermind all that Supermind knows (namely, again, possibilities of further inessential "manifestation" compatible with God's intrinsic nature as *saccidānanda*, and all the realities that Supermind "looses forth" as well).

Further, Aurobindo appears to hold that given that Supermind has created, or is creating a "world," a spatially and temporally extended manifestation of Brahman, it is possible that God revoke the primordially affirmative choice. Our world would then disappear—to speak metaphorically—and not even God would be aware that it had been. (In a sense, it would not have been, because a temporal perspective would not be.[49])

Thus for Aurobindo, God's "immutability" amounts to a timeless status where God cognizes only God's own essence, including a continual (or timeless) option to become or not—and to become aware of or not—inessential determinations. God is necessarily "mutable" in that God cannot forsake being faced with the option of unfurling the divine body in, and as, our time and world. But God need not undergo such change. It is true that were God to recoil into a Divine trance of "self-absorption," destroying the world, that also would be, in a sense, a "mutation" in what God is: God's choosing not to change would itself be a change (timelessly figured). And so God is, strictly speaking, necessarily mutable, in Aurobindo's conception. But loosely speaking, God is, on his view, only contingently mutable.

To put this in terms more familiar in the West, we may say Aurobindo is a theological "voluntarist": God's "primordial" will is both inscrutable and, more importantly in our context, not determined by God's "mind."[50] Indeed, God's "mind," i.e. Supermind, is viewed as itself contingent upon a policy option. In a sense, God is necessarily mindful of possible creations: God is considered necessarily aware of an indeterminate "something more." But the full faculty of divine knowledge is considered itself (timelessly) contingent on God's will and positive choice. According to our Indian theist, God is a "force" (*śakti*) of creative will. She can hold Herself back, absorbed in what She is necessarily, or loose Herself forth and create "worlds."[51] To venture further into the realm of metaphors and to try one of my own: the emergence of Supermind may be figured as a "second," or more distant (but still "timeless"), round in a spiral of self-creation. In Her most fundamental "policy" enactment—that which makes possible everything else—God allows Herself to behold and become potentialities of Herself (as *saccidānanda*), through attending to, and at once "surrendering" Herself to, Her inherent Divine Mind, or "Supermind."

Clearly, all this is a far cry from the sense in which, according to Hartshorne, God transcends God timelessly: for Hartshorne, the "primordial state" of God is an abstraction from what God is actually, albeit an explanationally rich abstraction.[52] The problem seems to be that Aurobindo speaks too facilely of "timelessness" and "priorities" in the divine nature. Aurobindo, for his part, would insist that these are not abstractions, but realities demanding the metaphors he has used.

It is hard to say more without saying a lot more. To take Aurobindo at all at his word, the (imagined) Hartshornean charge of incoherence would have to be admitted correct: Aurobindo does hold that God—as God is in God's self—is aware of an indeterminate possibility of "something more." Whether God "chooses" to make manifest this "something more" or "chooses" not to do so, the option chosen would be in a sense created. Further, it would seem mute (at least without more context provided) to defend God's right not to be the Creator. What could be the point? On the other hand, Hartshorne's (imagined) complaint would be viewed by Aurobindonists as on the whole dismissible, in that they would take themselves to be able to conceive something like the "primordial choice," postulated by Aurobindo, as indeed governing the possibility of God's knowing our world, or any "world" so minutely determinate. And they would see the purpose of the concept as its rôle in the explanation of certain (mystical) experiences.[53]

Thus our imagined "engagement" would have to broaden to other areas of theory. To proceed otherwise would risk oblique speech, and a worry about common suppositions—whether these be sufficient to enable meaningful debate. Just the exposition required to complete a very much more telling "engagement" would demand a long book.

I have compared Hartshorne's and Aurobindo's theologies only in certain respects. Obviously, more can be accomplished. And I hope it will. Charles Hartshorne speaks for much of what is best in the traditions of Western philosophic theism and Western religion. Aurobindo, on his part, speaks for much that is of value and worth preserving in Indian theism and traditions of *yoga*.[54]

In a broader perspective, it is not an exaggeration to say the only "world religions" that are not Western (indeed, not Semitic) in origin are Buddhism and Hinduism. Since Buddhists deny there is a God who is a Creator, it is in the theism of Hinduism where one finds the most promising Eastern religious thought for reflection on issues in common with the religious philosophy of the West. Apart from the mystical dimension of Indian theism (an interest in Indian religious thought is necessarily in some part an interest in the mystical), there are especially several lines of "cosmological" argument, unexamined here, that deserve careful investigation. Of course, process theists can learn, as can anyone, from philosophers, such as the Indian Buddhists, who do not share their basic suppositions. But engagement between Western and Indian theists is bound to shed light on problems whose solution is critical to the survival of any "God-oriented" world view.

NOTES†

†I wish to thank Arabinda Basu of the Sri Aurobindo International Centre for Education in Pondicherry, who spoke at the Hartshorne Conference in Austin in February, for his gracious help with my work.

1. Prominent Buddhist writers—of all periods and Buddhist cultures—deny that scriptural tradition (*āgama*) is an independent source of knowledge, irreducible to perception and inference. The Buddha's statements are viewed as authoritative because they are taken to reflect a breadth and depth of personal experience (to include mystic perceptions) and great power of reason.
2. The exception is the fine book on Whitehead and Aurobindo by a professor of Sanskrit at Aligarh Muslim University, Satya Prakash Singh: *Sri Aurobindo and Whitehead on the Nature of God* (Aligarh: Vigyan Prakashan, 1972).
3. "Śaṅkara, Nāgārjuna, and Fa Tsang, with some Western Analogues," an unpublished paper read at the 1984 conference, "Interpreting Across Boundaries," sponsored by the Society for Asian and Comparative Philosophy, Honolulu.
4. *Philosophers Speak of God*, co-edited with William L. Reese (Chicago: University of Chicago, 1953), p. v, "Theism in Asian and Western Thought," *Philosophy East and West* **28**, no. 4 (October 1978), pp. 401-11, and *Omnipotence and other Theological Mistakes* (Albany: State Univerity of New York, 1984), p. 108.
5. Until recently (see note eight below), Jīva Goswāmi's views were largely inaccessible to non-sanskritists. Hartshorne read a University of Chicago dissertation, "The Philosophy of Śrī Goswāmī," by Mahanam B. Brahmacari (1938), which is what he quotes in *Philosophers Speak of God*.
6. As mentioned, there has also been little interest in the reverse direction—with the (most notable) exception of Satya Prakash Singh and his book noted above. Here I shall tend to write as a Westerner looking East, but I hope that some of what I say will be informative for future comparative efforts originating in India.
7. Jīva Goswāmī recognizes many texts as sacred and "revealed," but he argues that "for our age" the *Bhāgavatapurāṇa* is supremely authoritative.
8. Stuart Elkman has edited and translated one of the Vaiṣṇava's principal works: *Jīva Goswāmī's Tattvasandarbha* (Delhi: Motilal Banarsidass, 1986). See pp. 72-73, 127-33, and 162-68, in particular, for the "meta-"position described.
9. Since the tradition is, particularly in the later centuries of the pre-modern age, most extensive and largely unexamined by philosophers writing in the

contemporary languages of scholarship, it could be that one will be found. There is nothing in Nyāya that precludes such an argument, and the Nyāya concept of God is amenable to one.

10. Nyāya is far and away the greatest philosophic accomplishment of the classical culture. I say this because Nyāya is underappreciated. (Arguably, less centrally a religious philosophy than the Vedāntic and Buddhist schools, Nyāya has not enjoyed as much interest in our time as the more exclusively "religious" of India's philosophies.) The greatest of the Buddhist Logicians, Dharmakīrti (c. 620), rivals the greatest of the Naiyāyikas, Gaṅgeśa (or Raghunātha Śiromaṇi [c. 1500]). But there can be no question that the Naiyāyika tradition as a whole outpaces that of the Indian Buddhists. Such broad judgments, I realize, are hazardous, particularly since they are liable to be misunderstood. Western "philosophy" is a unique series of works and intellectual events, albeit one impossible to delineate without controversy. Indian "*darśana*," or "*anvīkṣī*," or "speculative, eristic, and metaphysical thought" is also unique. The comparisons implicit in the use of such a term as 'philosophical accomplishment' are therefore by nature risky. Still, I stand by my judgment.
11. In particular, Matilal's *Perception* (Oxford: Oxford University, 1986).
12. The technical apparatus of Navya-Nyāya proliferates throughout the intellectual world of late classical times—it is used by Advaitins trying to show their central claims compatible with Nyāya, as well as by authors in Hindu law, medicine, aesthetic theory, other areas, too. But it is not part of a modern Indian education.

    Here we may note two outstanding contributions to the study of Nyāya theology, both by Indian scholars (one, Vattanky, who belongs to the Society of Jesus and teaches at a Jesuit university in India, De Nobili College): John Vattanky's *Gaṅgeśa's Philosophy of God* (Madras: Adyar, 1984), and George Chemparathy's *An Indian Rational Theology* (Vienna: Gerold, 1972).
13. It is true that Tantrics and Vaiṣṇavas both rely on revelation more than on reason (with a distinct body of texts regarded as revealed). But the Vaiṣṇavas tend to know much more about the history of debate among Indian schools than do Tantrics, and to have profited by their study. (Even such a stellar figure as Abhinavagupta seems somewhat isolated from the wider ideative currents; this is less true of Appayya Dīkṣita.)
14. See Karl Potter's *Encyclopedia of Indian Philosophies*, Vol. I, rev. ed. (Delhi: Motilal Banarsidass, 1980), for a bibliography of Abhinavagupta's and Appayya Dīkṣita's works. Also, there are a few articulate modern defenders of a Tantric perspective, for example, V. A. Devasenapathi: *Śaiva Siddhānta* (Madras: University of Madras, 1958) and *Of Human Bondage and Divine Grace* (Chidambaram: Annamalai University, 1963) are among his principal works. (I hope that modern Tantrics soon will discover the resources of process theology—perhaps a more foreseeable development than an arising of interest in the opposite direction.)
15. Śrīharṣa's masterwork, the *Khaṇḍanakhaṇḍakhādya*, has been both translated and critically examined: Ganganatha Jha, *Śrīharṣa's Sweetmeats of Refutation* (Delhi: Sri Satguru Publications [reprint], 1971), and Phyllis Granoff, *Philosophy and Argument in Late Advaita* (Dordrecht: Reidel, 1978). See Jha, pp. 25ff, 44-46, 59ff, and 75-76 for Śrīharṣa's "ontological arguments."

16. Sarvepalli Radhakrishnan claims that Vyāsa's *Bhāṣya* on *Yogasūtra* 1.24 expresses an argument similar to Anselm's: *Indian Philosophy*, Vol. II (London: George Allen & Unwin, 1940), p. 369.
17. Indeed, Advaitins have even less right, in my own (albeit sweeping) judgment (the tradition is centuries-old and hardly monolithic), to be termed "theists" than have the Mahāyāna Buddhists who have sparked, more than other Eastern theorists to date, the interest of process theologians. (But of course, the classical Mahāyānins expressly declare themselves "atheistic," presenting, in the Indian context, a host of "refutations" of theism.)
18. One example is the Tantric, V. A. Devasenapathi, mentioned in note fourteen above. S. K. Maitra and Haridas Chaudhuri may be counted as the foremost of the academic followers of Aurobindo.
19. Singh, op. cit.
20. Though not schooled in philosophy, Aurobindo read widely in the history of Western thought, mainly in English, some in Greek, as for example Plato: Aurobindo was an accomplished classicist when he left Cambridge, having won University prizes for his work in Greek.
21. As mentioned, there are now a few Indian academic philosophers in his camp. But Aurobindo himself was no academic, though from 1899 to 1901 and from 1903 to 1905 he was a professor of English and French.
22. It should be noted that the practices of "*yoga*," "self-discipline," that Aurobindo took up are the time-honored practices of the Indian mystic—yet not exclusively of the theist: many of these bridge such divides as Buddhist/Hindu and illusionist/theist.
23. For a superb explanation of the notion, see the opening section of Whitehead's *Process and Reality* (New York: Free Press, 1969), pp. 5ff.
24. *The Life Divine* (Pondicherry: Sri Aurobindo Ashram, 1973).
25. More precisely, there is a triad of fundamental "states" with Hartshorne, as with Whitehead. God's "superjective state," according to process theism, would be, in Aurobindo's terms, an aspect of God's manifest nature, namely God's continual transcendence of Herself in time.

    As will become clear, Aurobindo is more subject to a charge of positing a division in the divine essence, than is Hartshorne or Whitehead. (See Hartshorne's defense of Whitehead against the charge: "Whitehead's Conception of God," *Actes: Segundo Congreso Extraordinario Inter-americano de Filosofía* [1961], pp. 163-70.)
26. These arguments appear in many of Hartshorne's works, and the concept of "creativity" is elucidated in several places: see in particular, *Creative Synthesis and Philosophic Method* (London: SCM Press, 1970), pp. 1-18, *The Logic of Perfection* (Lasalle, Illinois: Open Court, 1962), pp. 164-66, and a paper read originally in India, "The Idea of Creativity in American Philosophy," *Journal of Karnataka University* (Social Sciences) **2** (May 1966), pp. 1-13. The argument I shall focus on appears in *Omnipotence and other Theological Mistakes*, pp. 82-83.
27. *Process and Reality*, p. 10.
28. *Omnipotence and other Theological Mistakes*, p. 82
29. See e.g. "Whitehead's Conception of God," op. cit. p. 164.

30. We may note that our "neoclassicist" metaphysician sees God's necessary characteristic of divine knowledge as the "infallible power to know whatever in particular could exist, and the certainty of knowing its existence be this existence a fact." *Omnipotence and other Theological Mistakes*, p. 82.
31. ibid. p. 83.
32. For Aurobindo, the terms 'God' and 'Brahman' are interchangeable.
33. This "essentialist" talk should not be taken as "apriorist" in Aurobindo's philosophy. He believes certain necessary truths (in particular about God) are empirically—mystically—discovered. And let me say I agree in general with the approach: 'Pleasure is good,' 'The Morning Star is the Evening Star,' and 'Water is H_2O' are all necessary truths but empirically discovered.
34. The term '*svayamprakāśamāna*' becomes standard only in classical times. But the idea is as old as the *Bṛhadāraṇyaka Upaniṣad* (c. 800 B.C.E.), where at 4.3.9 the self is said to be "*svayaṃjyotir*," "illumined by its own light."
35. Aurobindo believes that the state is conceptualizable and "cognitive" in the sense of indicating the reality of a certain state of affairs. But he believes it involves no "thought." In an alternative psychological characterization, he borrows, as have many Indian mystics and mystic philosophers before him—Advaitic, theist, Buddhist, Jain, and others—a term central to the *Yogasūtra* (a classical manual on the practice of *yoga*), namely, '*cittavṛttinirodha*,' "the cessation of mental fluctuations," or, in Aurobindo's English, "mental silence."
36. Aurobindo follows a long tradition in his use of the term '*ānanda*.' In the Upanishads, the term has sexual connotations: it is used to express the bliss of conjugal union considered "non-dualistically," e.g. *Bṛhadāraṇyaka* 4.3.21-33 ("As a man in the embrace of a beloved wife knows nothing within or without, so this person in the embrace of the self-conscious Self knows nothing within or without.")
37. "Mysticism and Metaphor," *International Journal for Philosophy of Religion* **23**, no. 1 (1988), pp. 17-41.
38. But see the chapter in Book One of *The Life Divine* entitled, "The Pure Existent," pp. 71-79, where Aurobindo's reasoning falls just short of an explicit formulation.
39. See again note thirty-three above.
40. Hartshorne's "modal" argument for God's existence is a good example of the general problem. The argument relies on a premise that it is possible that necessarily there be a perfect knower. From this, Hartshorne reasons that it is not possible that a perfect knower not exist. (From $\Diamond\Box G$, it follows that $\Box G$—given the theorem, $\Diamond\Box p \equiv \Box p$. And from $\Box G$, it follows that $\sim\Diamond\sim G$.) But surely it is conceivable that there be a material universe with no consciousness or life, and no God. Thus I would deny *either* the premise *or* the modal system in which the inference is carried out.

    Of course, within the "world" that Hartshorne imagines this seemingly (to us!) possible world where God does not exist is not possible. Are there truths that are necessary in some possible worlds but not in others? I am no expert in modal logic, but I am tempted to say "yes." (Denial of $\Diamond\Box p \rightarrow \Box p$ would allow this, I think.) This would mean that our modal logic would permit "access" to Hartshorne's "world," but then Hartshorne with his modal system would not have "access" to our world. Thus I think the better option is to deny the theorem $\Diamond\Box p \equiv \Box p$, preserving only: $p \rightarrow \Diamond p$. (One would also deny $\Diamond\Box p \rightarrow p$. Hartshorne's opening argument in *The Logic of Perfection* appears to rely on the former theorem, but in other formulations he uses only this latter "entailment.") However, my contention is only that the possibility that God not exist is more intuitive than *both* (1) possibly necessarily God exists and (2) the modal theorem needed, viewed together—take your pick which to reject! (Cf. Robert Kane's discussion, "The Modal Ontological Argument," *Mind* **93** [1984], pp. 336-50.)

Note that Aurobindo believes that certain conceivable states of affairs are not "really possible"—e.g. a world of meaningless suffering—because they are not compatible with God as *saccidānanda*.

41. Hartshorne believes he has *a priori* reasons as well. But again, I see these as just as circular as the "classical" arguments he attacks (and thus as not cogent from a "neutral" perspective).
42. *The Life Divine*, pp. 441-78.
43. ibid. p. 472, in particular. Also, Aurobindo claims to have had personally the "Advaitic" experience "sublated" by a distinctly theistic mystical experience. See my discussion in *Aurobindo's Philosophy of Brahman* (Leiden: E. J. Brill, 1986), pp. 118-20.
44. *The Life Divine*, p. 605, in particular.
45. The best I can do to make the "atemporality" intelligible is to draw analogies that do not quite work. The divine choices seem to be something like social policies or practices that govern or make possible other practices. Or, consider the decision of person A to help B who is expressing pain. In A's particular choice, could there be implicit a choice of moral policy that is not localized to the particular moment, the encounter with B, or any set of moments of time?
46. On an alternative reading, this would be a choice in the highest "level" of Supermind, which then would belong, in this part, to the Divine as the Divine is necessarily.
47. Hartshorne holds that "creativity" is the "positive side" of contingency, *The Logic of Perfection*, p. 75. Aurobindo agrees: *The Life Divine*, pp. 86-88, 400, and 1037-38, in particular.
48. On the alternative reading, which has the highest "level" of Supermind as part of what God is necessarily, this would be the option of transcendently empowering, or not, Supermind to do what it will.
49. "World dissolution," *pralāya*, has been a prominent religious notion since the *Bhagavadgītā* (see esp. 8,18-19). Classical exegetes interpret it in several different ways, some agreeing with Aurobindo, and some not, that God has the power so utterly to absorb the universe as not to leave a trace.
50. Aurobindo sees that the "reason" God makes an affirmative choice has to be, strictly speaking, indeterminable. But his view would allow incorporation of a (roughly) Hartshornean thesis that greater value would be instantiated in the affirmative choice. And the Indian theist does speculate that the reason may be divine self-enrichment. See *The Life Divine*, pp. 91ff and 834-35.
51. Of course, Aurobindo is not as "voluntarist" as many in the West: he uses, for example, the notions "looses forth," "manifestation," etc., in conjunction with his view that "creation *ex nihilo*," is not possible even for God.
52. This type of "transcendence" is for Hartshorne distinct from a second (the two make up his doctrine of "dual transcendence"), namely, that God in time

continually exceeds what God was—a thesis that Aurobindo endorses, too.

53. The comparable "religious" strength of Hartshorne's view is, as the philosopher has often pointed out, that it would ground "worship." Who other than a perfect being would be worthy of this most fundamental, or most noble, religious attitude? Aurobindo, on the other hand, does not believe worship to be the best of human attitudes towards God. As indicated, the Easterner sees the point of his philosophy as providing intellectual support for *mystic* endeavors. Each theory's "categorial coherence" with these respective religious aims would have to be a key issue in a more broadly evaluative effort. But let us note briefly that Aurobindo's view would also ground religious worship. In fact, one might argue that since in the Indian theology God has the power to withdraw into unmanifest *saccidānanda*, the fact that God is not choosing that option provides an additional reason to worship, or at least to be grateful.

    Nevertheless, the Hartshornean position appears clearly superior in grounding worship: it would provide assurance that God takes seriously human values. To be sure, Aurobindo's view is only comparatively deficient on this score. For the Indian theist, God's essential nature as *saccidānanda* constrains what is a true possibility of inessential determination. I repeat that no world not in harmony with *saccidānanda* is really possible, according to Aurobindo. Indeed, he argues that our world would contain too much suffering to be compatible with the essential Divine were it not evolving—in part through the instrumentality of suffering—to a "diviner" life. Aurobindo breaks with his tradition in finding "meaning" for evil in the progressive accomplishment of a "diviner" life. However, the requirements on progressive betterment are surely stricter on Hartshorne's hypothesis, since the Westerner starts with a notion of a temporally perfect God, a God that necessarily becomes better at each moment to the fullest extent, and "better" according to human standards. The Westerner's conception of God's perfection would guarantee that God is maximally empathetic with human values, while Aurobindo would allow Brahman to neglect human fulfillments in the interest of another evolutionary goal. (He speculates in a few places that the human species may be "transitional" to a race of "more spiritual" beings, beings he envisages as realizing superior possibilities of divine manifestation.) Thus Aurobindo's theological voluntarism is inferior to Hartshorne's "perfectionalism" in grounding confidence that God is striving for what is—from a human perspective—the best that can be. Does this mean that Aurobindo's "Brahman" would not be worthy of worship? In some cases, perhaps indeed Brahman would not.

54. I see among the interesting topics—in additional to the crucial question of the veridicality of mystical experiences—views on "prehension" and "consciousness," theodicy, and questions of values, God's and the human as well.

Hartshorne and the Basis of Peirce's Categories

Kenneth Laine Ketner

Peirce's categories have not received a warm general welcome, either in his day or in ours. However, Charles Hartshorne is one master philosopher who has taken them seriously, and with revisions, used them in his own work.

I do not intend here to look into the categories as Peirce proposed them (initially in 1867) or as Hartshorne has revised them (1983 and 1984). Instead I want to consider the basis for them to be found elsewhere in Peirce's work. This distinction between the categories and the basis for them is one that some students of Peirce have missed, but which Hartshorne knows accurately: the categories are hypotheses within Peirce's metaphysics which are based upon certain suggestive results Peirce obtained in mathematics and the logic of relatives. (These results are hereafter mentioned simply as "basis" or "the basis.") I believe it can be shown that this basis has been misinterpreted by a number of students of the topic who also happen to be persons who may have influenced Hartshorne's understanding of this matter. After presenting and defending my interpretation of the basis, I hope Hartshorne can be induced to comment upon it, and whether it would change the way in which he understands and deploys Peirce's categories.

The categorial basis and cenopythagoreanism

After becoming aware a few years ago that Peirce's Existential Graph system of logic (hereafter EG) was a key for gaining an understanding of many basic points within his work, I began to seek for its roots. I believe I discovered them, in both the intellectual sense (reported in 1986a) and textual sense (reported in 1987b). Textually, the beginning of EG is found in *MS* 482 (following the cataloging system in Robin 1967), wherein Peirce developed it out of graph theory within topology. Under the heading of "Valency Analysis" (VA) I have isolated one aspect of the means for that development (1986a). This is a convenient name which I have coined; VA is not a phrase Peirce used, but it is consistent with his intent and practice.

For some time scholars have complained about being unable to find Peirce's proof for two distinctive theorems, which are (in uninterpreted form) as follows:

NONREDUCTION THEOREM:

No triad can be composed exclusively from dyads.

SUFFICIENCY THEOREM:

Tetrads or higher *n*-ads can be composed exclusively from combinations of monads, dyads, or triads.

In *MS* 482 these two theorems are established within VA, which consists of a formal system of uninterpreted graphs. An entity with one "loose end" is a monad, with two loose ends a dyad, with three loose ends a triad, with *n* loose ends a *n*-ad. The number of loose ends is a property that can also be described as the adicity of the graph. It is convenient to represent such entities with drawings like these.

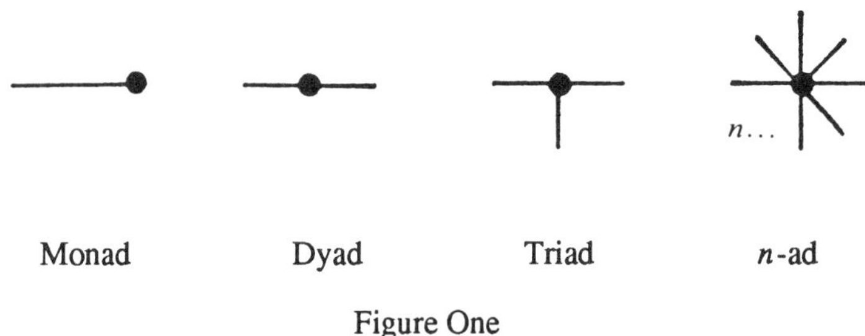

Monad Dyad Triad *n*-ad

Figure One

Loose ends are places in which any connection that is possible or permissible *may* occur. Connection of loose ends is by the process of bonding exactly two of them at a time. Within VA, one ignores material reasons for joining two loose ends to focus upon formal patterns of composition or rules associated with bonding. Two graphical entities are said to be "valency equivalent" if, no matter what other properties they possess, they have exactly the same number of loose ends. Thus all of the following four graphs are valency equivalent (valency of each is two).

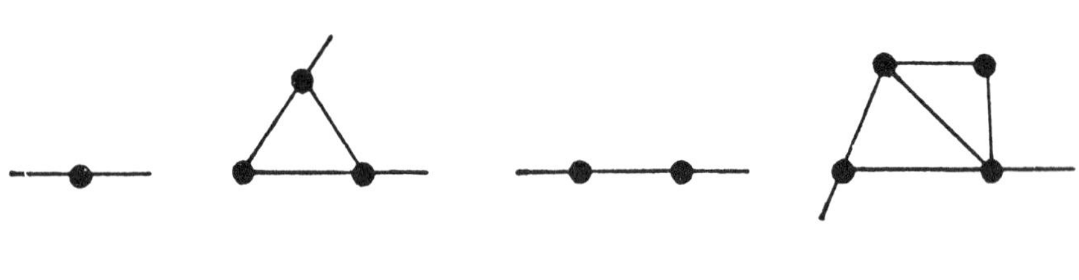

Valency = two

Figure Two

With these understandings, it is easy to prove that Nonreduction and Sufficiency are theorems *of VA* (proofs are in Ketner 1986:377-382). It is important to note at this point that these are not theorems about categories, because so far we are working with just an uninterpreted formal system.

Peirce's next step was to interpret VA over relations. He did it in this manner. He conceived relations rhematically, meaning that he first considered a relation sentence, then conceptually subtracted (precided) all noun-like aspects to produce what he called a rheme (a kind of partial sentence form). In that manner,

"George is a Bolivian"

becomes

"________ is a Bolivian";

"Excess current caused the resistor to melt"

becomes

"________ caused ________";

"Smoke represents fire to the priest in the tower"

becomes

"________ represents ________ to ________."

Peirce referred to the kinds of sentence forms (exemplified by the second of each pair above) as "relatives," from whence is derived his phrase "Logic of Relatives." I will avoid that phrase for now, because in his later philosophy, it became virtually a general name for his entire effort. Let us use a terminology similar to that Peirce employed before "relative" became such a general term for him. We may call these partially-precided relation sentences, for only the noun-like elements have been precided away. A fully-precided relation sentence is one in which the relating aspect is also generalized. That is accomplished by replacing the remaining words, the verb-like elements, with a big black dot. At this level of precision we find that monadic, dyadic, triadic, and n-adic relation sentences look just like corresponding graphs in VA. That is, the graphical entities of Figure One now mean respectively:

"Some object has some property"

"Some one object is in some dyadic relation to some second object"

"Some first object is in some triadic relation with some second object and some third object."

(Of course, 'object' is understood to range over "objects of discourse.")

Now it is clear that Peirce regarded that which we can know as consisting of relations. He rarely mentioned this important aspect of his system, but here are two clear instances (see also my discussion in 1988b):

> . . . Whatever we know, we know only by its relations, and in so far as we know its relations. (From a draft of 1868 in Moore et al. 1984:164)

> In reality, every fact is a relation. Thus, that an object is blue consists of the peculiar regular action of that object on human eyes. This is what should be understood by the "relativity of knowledge." Not only is every fact really a relation, but your thought of the fact implicitly represents it as such. (From a publication of 1892, in Hartshorne et al. 1935-58:3.416)

Once VA is interpreted over relation sentences, it has another contribution to make, for VA in conjunction with Peirce's long interest in the nature of scientific classification (described in Ketner 1981) inspired the Doctrine of Cenopythagoreanism.

> In classification generally, it may fairly be said to be established, if it ever was doubted, that Form, in the sense of structure, is of far higher significance than Material. Valency is the basis of all external structure; and where indecomposibility precludes internal structure—as in the classification of elementary concepts—valency ought to be made the first consideration. I term [this] the doctrine of *cenopythagoreanism*. (*MS* 292:34, 98)

Once VA is interpreted over relations, Peirce—looking with cenopythagorean eyes—found that all relations (and hence all knowables) divide into just three natural classes: monads, dyads, and triads. Dyadic relations so interpreted cannot be constructed from monadic relations; the Nonreduction Theorem shows that triadic relations cannot be constructed exclusively from dyadic relations; and the Sufficiency Theorem shows that relations of adicity *n*, where *n* is equal to or greater than four, are reducible to (are valency equivalent to) a combination of *n*-minus-two triadic relations. That is, a tetrad (adicity four) is reducible to two triads (four minus two is two), a pentad is reducible to three triads, a heptad is reducible to four triads, and so on. Furthermore, EG can be generated out of VA (summarized in Ketner 1986a:384-389). Roberts (1973) has shown that EG is consistent and complete for predicate logic with relations. From this point to the categories is but a short step, but one which will not be taken now, for I want to stay within the basis to see if it can be sustained. (Persons interested in reading two sound studies of Peirce's categories might consult Esposito 1980 and Krausser 1977; see also Peirce's intellectual autobiography in Ketner 1987a.)

Gallant charge of the ordered pairs

When I had what I thought was a good understanding of the topological foundations of Peirce's natural classification of kinds of relations via the Nonreduction and Sufficiency Theorems, it immediately occurred to me that these are important results. For instance, if the interpreted Nonreduction Theorem is correct, then all kinds of reductive explanatory strategies could be shown to fail. For instance, behaviorism or materialism in psychology, which are basically ways of reducing triadic relational phenomena to dyadic causal chains, would collapse. Here I am inspired by Walker Percy (1975), who is an independent re-discoverer of many of the conceptions about relations I have sketched above. Or, for another example, attempts to develop artificial intelligence only from deterministic resources would be doomed from the start (that thesis is defended in Ketner 1988a). I also quickly found that I was not alone in my researches, for two fine Canadian scholars were active in the same general area, Herzberger (1981) and Brunning (1981), of whom more later.

The first thing I wanted to know was what had happened in the logic of relations since Peirce's day. In talking with colleagues specializing in mathematics and logic, a number of persons mentioned that it was well known that Peirce was wrong about Nonreduction, and that triadic predicates could be reduced to dyadic ones. Inevitably I was referred to a paper by Quine (1954) where Reduction was said to have been achieved. That paper is a formal investigation, but it is clear Quine intended to interpret his formal results over relations. That point is further reinforced by some of his later comments (Quine 1981:201). It will be convenient to have the first two paragraphs of Quine's Reduction before us.

> Consider any interpreted theory Θ, formulated in the notation of quantification theory (or lower predicate calculus) with interpreted predicate letters. It will be proved that Θ is translatable into a theory, likewise formulated in the notation of quantification theory, in which there is only one predicate letter, and it a dyadic one.
>
> Let us assume a fragment of set theory, adequate to assure the existence, for all x and y without regard to logical type, of the set $\{x,y\}$ whose members are x and y, and to assure the distinctness of x from $\{x,y\}$ and $\{\{x\}\}$. ($\{x\}$ is explained as $\{x,x\}$.) Let us construe the ordered pair $x;y$ in Kuratowski's fashion, viz. as $\{\{x\},\{x,y\}\}$, and then construe $x;y;z$ as $x;(y;z)$, and $x;y;z;w$ as $x;(y;z;w)$, and so on.

To show that Peirce's Nonreduction Theorem is incorrect, and that Reduction is possible, it would be sufficient to show that there is at least one triadic relation that can be reduced to some collection composed exclusively of dyadic relations. It seems clear that Quine proposes to do that, not only for one triadic relation, but for all relations of adicity three or greater. And one of the essential tools he employed in the proof is the notion of an ordered pair. Let us take a careful look at "ordered pair."

The definition for ordered pair was given by Kuratowski in 1921 (see Kuratowski and Mostowski 1968:59), inspired by Weiner (1914). Pairs sound quite dyadic. However, I shall argue that the concept of an ordered pair is indeed a triadic relation. Therefore, use of it in a proof that many understand as breaking Peirce's Nonreduction Theorem would be a violation of the rules of the game. That is so because a proper reduction would have to constitute a triad from a collection of dyads only, not from a collection constituted by a bunch of dyads plus one triad. If ordered pairs are really triadic relations, then Peirce's Nonreduction Theorem, construed in terms of his definitions, is still standing in view of Quine's results. That is not to say that Quine's results are wrong; but it would mean that Quine's correct results do not break Peirce's Nonreduction Theorem.

Let us begin at a common sense level, and start with the notion of a set that is an unordered pair. I take that step, because a triadic relation seems to be buried even in the idea of a set that is an "unordered pair." I am trying to think of two widely disparate items such that nobody now considers them as a set or collection. Suppose that in the Arbuckle Historical Society Museum in Murray County Oklahoma there exists an object known locally as Mazeppa Turner's pocket knife, and that in Saint Tammany Parish Louisiana exists what people there call General Van Dorn's battle flag. A set is some number of objects of discourse brought together in our conception or imagination. I can say, "Collect or bring together in your imagination those two objects, Turner's knife and Van Dorn's flag; when you have done that, call the result of that process the set **H**." Since the process of bringing these two extremely disparate items together in imagination is an action of a person, a collector who puts a collection together, we can see that even the notion of a set that is an unordered pair presupposes a triadic relation. Based on our example, that relation would be represented in this sentence: "Robert Earl imagined a set composed of Turner's knife and Van Dorn's flag." That can be written rhematically as "________ imagined a set composed of ________ and ________," which is clearly trivalent.

Now let us consider the concept of "ordered pair." Suppose there are two particular rocks on a table in front of us. One of us notes their presence, then imagines them as a set. But suppose further that we wanted to designate one of these as the *first* rock a and another as the *second* rock b. That is, we want to move from an unordered set to an ordered set. To bring that about, I state, "I order a as first and b as second." That statement, considered as a partially precided rheme, becomes "________ ordered ________ as first and ________ as second." In other words, it is a triadic relation involving a giver of order to two objects which are thereby ordered. Its fully precided form is that of a VA triad (where **O** is the above triadic relation):

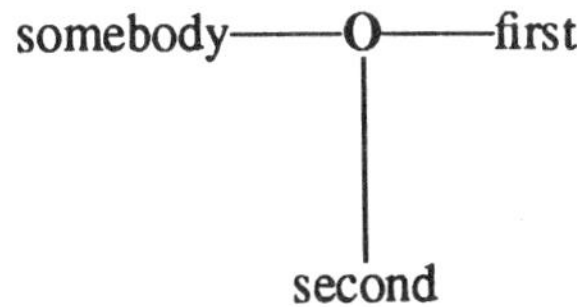

Figure Three

Here is an often-used way of defining an ordered pair (adapted from Halmos 1960:22). We can define the ordered pair *a;b* as the set composed of the set *a* and the set *a,b*, where {*a*} is simply the set one obtains at or before the first location in the order intended in *a;b*, and {*a,b*} is the set obtained at or before the second location in the order intended in *a;b*. This, however, is no better, for a triadic relation is evident in the definition of ordered pair, almost in the common sense way. Furthermore, the set {*a;b*} presupposed in the definition itself presupposes a triad as in the case of Robert Earl's unordered pair.

Some set theoreticians take a more simplified approach. For example Rubin writes (1967:47, adapted into Quine's notation):

> The actual technique used to define an ordered pair is unimportant. . . . What is important, however, is that it is a set and it has the one property that an ordered pair must have to deserve its name. That is, $(x;y) = (u;v)$ implies that $(x = u \;\&\; y = v)$.

This definition also presupposes Robert Earl's triad. But let us hold that card in reserve, and consider the definition from another aspect. The definition could be understood as a way in which the equality relation can be used to produce the notion of order.

I take this definition to mean that if two ordered pairs are equal, then it follows that the first element of the first pair must be equal to the first element of the second pair (and ditto for the second elements of the two pairs), and that if this condition holds, we therefore have an ordered pair. But one cannot produce order in this way without implicitly introducing the above mentioned triadic relation. Consider two unordered pairs *p,q* and *r,s*. And suppose that we are talking about a universe of discourse that does not include the predicate of serial order. We now assert that $p = r$ and $q = s$. In so saying we have not introduced a concept of serial order into this serially orderless universe. However, if we now allow the predicate of serial order to enter our universe, for *p* to be equal to *r*, the two must be equal in all predicates, including the serial order predicate. And for a pair to be ordered, someone must combine them according to some principle of order. Therefore, it seems to me that this method of defining an ordered pair cannot smuggle in the requisite conception of order using the notion of equality, so it is no different from the first common-sense case.

Some set theoreticians simply avoid verbiage and get right to the point by unflinchingly biting the bullet in (it seems to me) an unavoidable manner, for example Selby and Sweet (1963:73): "A pair of objects, one of which is designated as the first component and the other as the second component, is called an ordered pair." Here clearly we are asked to consider a designator, a combiner, an orderer—whether a person, an intelligent algorithm, or a Martian—as being the agency which brings two components together and designates one as first and another as second. And if we imagine such a thing, what we are imagining is a triadic relation.

The process of producing a set, whether ordered or unordered, is indeed just that: a process. The process begins with no set present. A set-maker comes on the scene and puts two things together in imagination. At the end of that process we have something new, a set. This set is what Peirce would have called a hypostatic abstraction. By that he meant that it is often profitable within inquiry to give the result of a predictable and already known process a noun or substantive name, and thereby to refer to it as a fact. And to refer to such substantives routinely sometimes leads researchers to forget the original process. Perhaps that has happened in the case of set theory. I believe that one could add a small footnote to Peirce's notion of a hypostatic abstraction by saying that when science is intimately involved in studying a problem for the first time, the language of research is typically full of process phrases. Once a piece of research is complete, known, dependable, often the language of research becomes noun-like in regard to those items just recently mastered, so one can handily refer to the previously established results in the context of the new problems at hand.

One paragraph in *Naïve Set Theory* (Halmos 1960:24-25, adapted to Quine's notation) strikes me as prophetic.

> However important set theory may be now, when it began some scholars considered it a disease from which, it was to be hoped, mathematics would soon recover. For this reason many set-theoretic considerations were called pathological, and the word lives on in mathematical usage; It often refers to something the speaker does not like. The explicit definition of an ordered pair [$((a;b) = \{\{a\},\{a,b\}\})$] is frequently relegated to pathological set theory.

I would not use the term 'pathological.' There is nothing wrong from my point of view about the concept of ordered pair; however, there is good reason to think that there is something inappropriate about conceiving it as being a dyadic relation. Therefore someone who uses the notion to reduce triadic relations is really reducing a triad to a collection composed of dyads plus one triad (ordered pair)—or plus two if one adds Robert Earl's triad. Obviously I have not advanced anything like a formal proof that ordered pairs are triadic. I have tried instead to appeal to the level of reasonable considerations.

Abraham Fraenkel ended his article on set theory for *The Encyclopedia of Philosophy* (1967, 7:426) with these words:

> ... the modern development of set theory seems to shatter mathematics altogether, at least in its analytical parts. New axioms apparently need to be introduced, corresponding to a deeper understanding of the primitive concepts underlying logic and mathematics. Yet nobody has so far succeeded in discovering even a direction in which such axioms might be sought.

One wonders if Peirce's logic of relatives, which accepts triadic relation as a primitive, might be a direction that Fraenkel has considered. In any case, these words seem to suggest that set theory is at a revolutionary phase of its development. Perhaps one of the reasons it has reached a dead end is its almost studious elimination of triadic relations in its explicit fundamentals; one hardly finds overt discussions of triadic relations anywhere in treatises on set theory, and never, as far as I can see, as a primitive element. It is as if they were not real. This means that set theory as it is now constituted harbors a serious implicit metaphysical bias, which might be some part of the cause of its apparent self-limitation.

Other suspicions about Peirce's two theorems

The first case to be considered now may have provided Hartshorne with a false lead in his dealings with Peirce's categories. In 1934, Eugene Freeman published what is still a solid treatise on the subject. Hartshorne wrote its preface. There are a number of prescient insights in this work, an important one being Freeman's recognition that Peirce was a mathematical empiricist (1934:3, where the term is attributed to "my teacher and friend, Professor Charles Hartshorne, under whose inspiring guidance this study was undertaken"). Freeman realized that valency was important in the basis of Peirce's categories, and he proceeded to give an outline of the matter (1934:15). After a good start, however, he made some mistakes. After introducing the graphical forms of monads, dyads, and triads, he forgot to mention that all bonding occurs two at a time. And when he began to present diagrams of actual compositions (bondings) of graphs and relation sentences, he made additional mistakes. For instance (1934:16), composition of two monads is represented as:

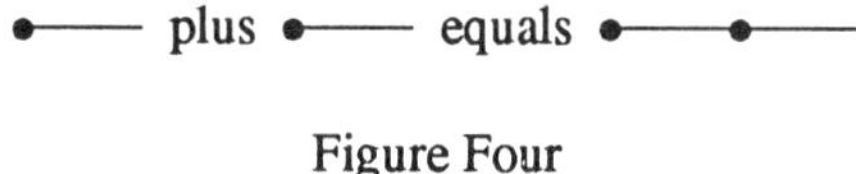

Figure Four

This shows a bond at a place Peirce did not allow, and because of that, a result with the wrong valency is produced. Freeman's bonding of two monads produced another monad. Bonding of two monads in Peirce's system actually produces a medad, a zero-valent graph in which every loose end is bonded, thus:

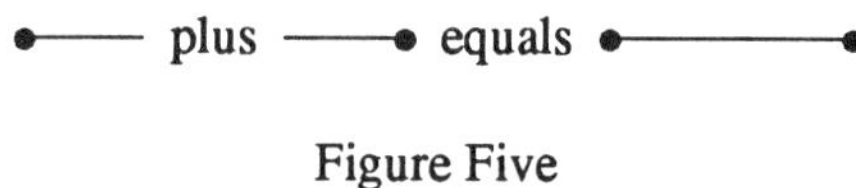

Figure Five

A similar mistake was made in Freeman's next example, which I draw here first in its erroneous form, followed by the correct form:

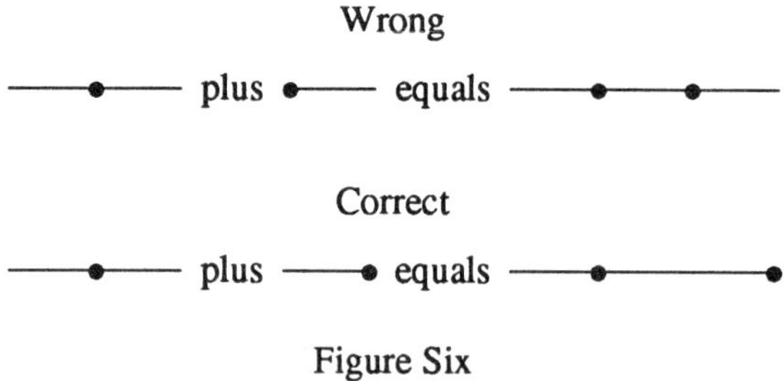

Figure Six

Three other graphs he drew are correct.

In Peirce's system, a monad bonded to a monad always produces a medad; a dyad bonded with a monad always produces a monad; a dyad bonded with a dyad always produces another dyad; a dyad bonded with a triad always produces another triad; a triad bonded with a triad produces a tetrad, and so on.

When Freeman turned from graphs to parallel English sentences, he again made some serious errors. I list below his first such form, followed by the correct form.

Wrong

> The monad "there is whiteness" plus the monad "there is hardness" gives the more complex monad "there is whiteness and there is hardness."

Correct

> The monad "something is white" plus the monad "something is hard" gives the medad "some white thing is a thing that is hard," or "Some white thing is hard," the Aristotelian *I* proposition, in other words (see Ketner 1986a:386).

He gave three additional examples like this one, incorporating relations of higher adicity. But in the additional three cases provided, bonding cannot occur in the way Freeman described, principally because most sentences in his examples are already medads—sentences with no "loose ends"—and hence not further bondable on Peirce's approach.

Freeman was aware that Peirce moved from this basis to a set of hypotheses about metaphysical categories, Firstness, Secondness, and Thirdness. But with this seriously erroneous grasp of the basis, his description of the transition from basis to categories must be suspect.

The next instance to be considered does involve more than a suspicion. Arthur Skidmore, another student of Charles Hartshorne, has argued (1971) for the incorrectness of Peirce's Nonreduction Theorem. His argument, illustrated below in graphical form, is that three dyads *can* be combined to form a triad.

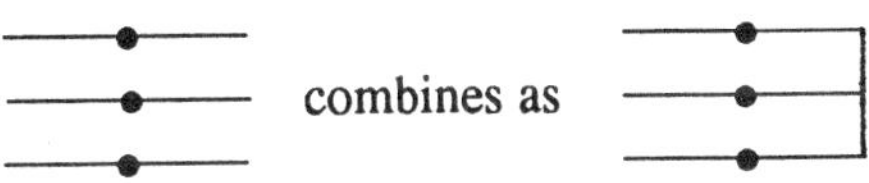

Figure Seven

That this is wrong from Peirce's point of view can be seen from either one of two standpoints. From one, the move is incorrect because it allows three loose ends to be bonded in one step. Peirce allowed two and only two loose ends to be joined in any single act of bonding. So this move would simply not be licensed by Peirce's VA system (Ketner 1986a). From another standpoint, the diagram in the right side of Figure Seven *can* be construed in Peirce's system as the composition of three dyads and one triad, thus:

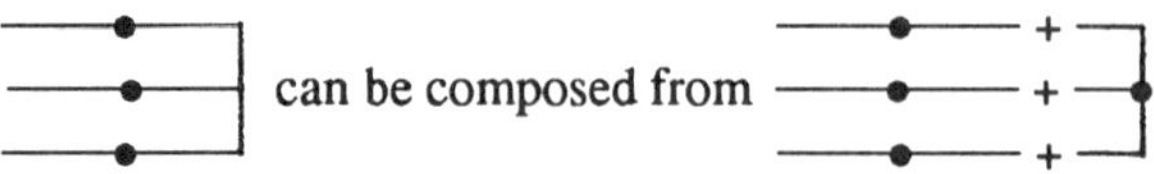

Figure Eight

This, of course, does not break Peirce's Nonreduction Theorem, for here one has composed a triad from three dyads and a triad. The point of triple junction was something Peirce allowed (which he called Teridentity), but he clearly recognized it as a triadic relation (see Brunning 1981). Herzberger (1981:55) has given additional reasons for rejecting Skidmore's account as inconsistent with that of Peirce.

Christopherson and Johnson (1981:241) are two additional persons with suspicions about the Nonreduction Theorem. The reason they give is by now familiar: "Set-theorists know that all relations can be treated as sets of ordered pairs, and that as a consequence n-place relations can be reduced to dyadic ones." This claim has been covered above. They go on to consider Thirdness with suspicion, but since this falls outside the basis, it is beyond my present scope.

Hartshorne's revision of Peirce's categories

In his revision of Peirce's categories (1984:77-78) Hartshorne characterizes Peirce's approach in this way:

> Peirce regards the single other as definitive of Secondness, and dependence upon two others (Thirdness) as essentially different, while dependence on more than two can, he holds, be reduced to cases of Thirdness. Thus he *counts the number of items* on which a phenomenon depends, defining Firstness as dependence on zero others, Secondness, on one other, Thirdness, on two others, and dismissing all higher numbers as reducible.
>
> My suggestion is that here Peirce misapplied the numerical model and thereby incurred needless trouble.... The number of items on which a phenomenon depends or does not depend is, I suggest, categorially irrelevant. What counts are the *kinds of relations* of dependence or independence.

Let us display in tabular form the basis Hartshorne attributes to Peirce alongside the basis Peirce actually used (where Roman numerals represent Peirce's categories).

CSH

I = depend on 0 other

II = depend on 1 other

III = depend on 2 other

CSP

I = kind of relations with monovalent external form

II = kind of relations with bivalent external form

III = kind of relations with trivalent external form

Again, I do not want to focus upon the categories proper (keeping them mostly in our peripheral vision), but I do want to inquire what kind of understanding about Peirce's basis Hartshorne might have, as exemplified in the remarks above. It strikes me that the first two sentences of the above paragraph are not at all what Peirce had in mind as the basis of his hypotheses about the categories. It would be helpful to know which passages from Peirce Hartshorne regards as supporting that interpretation. Counting the number of items upon which a phenomenon depends is something that Hartshorne has introduced, and it seems particularly foreign to Peirce's basis. This topic is repeated later in the paper (1984:84) where Hartshorne recommends, "He should not have been so fascinated, almost hypnotized, by the idea of counting, 'One, two, three.' " That is not the point at all within Peirce's basis, instead it is a question of topology interpreted over forms of relation. Simple counting is not the mathematical basis of Peirce's categories. Indeed, had Peirce (with his meticulous concern for terminology) proceeded in the way Hartshorne suggests, Peirce would have named his categories Zeroness, Firstness, and Secondness.

In a somewhat related essay (1983:3), Hartshorne seems to accept the dismissal, supplied by his student Skidmore (1971), of Peirce's Nonreduction Theorem. But he went on to say that his revision of Peirce's categories need not accept the Nonreduction Theorem, for he does not distinguish the categories by counting the number of terms in the dependence or independence relations. Now that seems strange, for the Nonreduction Theorem is at the heart of the basis of Peirce's categories. If one rejected that principle, which is so fundamental for Peirce, I do not see how Hartshorne can speak of a *revision*—it seems much more like a wholesale renovation, of the basis, at any rate. Perhaps in view of the previous discussion Hartshorne would not now accept Skidmore's proposed refutation of the Nonreduction theorem.

I have the impression that Hartshorne wishes to have a categorial set in which each category is separable from the others. That is to say that on his account there would be a clear and pure instance of Firstness (and of each of the other categories). But this was not Peirce's way, for he asserted in many places that his categories were universal: each one and all of them are to be found in any experience in some degree; there is no pure example of any one of them. Indeed, some experiences exhibit more strongly one or another of the categories. For instance, surprise is a favorite example of Secondness, but no experience of surprise on Peirce's view is lacking either in Firsts or Thirds.

That is why Peirce called them the Universal Categories: each of them is in every experience. The phrase 'Universal Categories' does not mean that "some category is to be found everywhere." The only way to gain some understanding of an individual category is to abstract each of them out of any given experience through clues such as valency. This means that to some extent Peirce was a rationalist—not an unexpected result, since his work incorporated a little bit of many things, usually combined in a brilliant new way.

Finally, Hartshorne tells us that what *really* counts are kinds of relations. That is precisely Peirce's point too. But the kinds Peirce had in mind were kinds of forms of relations; Hartshorne seems to have in mind material kinds of relations.

Would the above explorations in Peirce's basis make his approach more acceptable to Hartshorne, or influence Hartshorne to be less inclined to revise Peirce's categories, or perhaps bring him to accept them outright?

REFERENCES

Brunning, J. (1981). *Peirce's Development of the Logic of Relations*. Diss. University of Toronto.

Christopherson, Rosemarie and Henry W. Johnstone, Jr. (1981). "Triadicity and Thirdness," *Transactions of the Charles S. Peirce Society* **17**:241-246.

Fraenkel, Abraham A. (1967). "Set Theory," in *Encyclopedia of Philosophy*, ed. P. Edwards. New York: Collier Macmillan.

Freeman, Eugene (1934). *The Categories of Charles Peirce*. Chicago: Open Court.

Halmos, Paul R. (1960). *Naive Set Theory*. Princeton: D. Van Nostrand.

Hartshorne, Charles (1983). "Peirce's Fresh Look at Philosophical Problems," *Krisis* **1**:1-9.

——, (1984). "A Revision of Peirce's Categories," in *Creativity in American Philosophy*. Albany: State University of New York Press.

Hartshorne, Charles, Paul Weiss, and Arthur Burks, eds. (1935-58). *Collected Papers of Charles Sanders Peirce*. Cambridge: Harvard University Press.

Herzberger, Hans. (1981) "Peirce's Remarkable Theorem," in *Pragmatism and Purpose: Essays Presented to Thomas A. Goudge*, ed. J. Slater, T. Wilson, and T. Sumner. Toronto: University of Toronto Press.

Ketner, Kenneth Laine, (1981). "Peirce's Ethics of Terminology," *Transactions of the Charles S. Peirce Society* **17**:327-347.

——, (1984). "Peirce on Diagrammatic Thought," in *Zeichen und Realität*, ed. K. Oehler. Tübingen: Stauffenbrug Verlag.

——, (1986a). "Peirce's 'Most Lucid and Interesting Paper': An Introduction to Cenopythagoreanism," *International Philosophical Quarterly* **26**:375-392.

——, (1986b). *A Comprehensive Bibliography of the Published Works of Charles Sanders Peirce*. Bowling Green: Philosophy Documentation Center.

——, (1987a). "Charles Sanders Peirce," pp. 13-92 in *Classical American Philosophy*, ed. John J. Stuhr. New York: Oxford University Press.

——, (1987b). "Identifying Peirce's 'Most Lucid and Interesting Paper,' " *Transactions of the Charles S. Peirce Society* **23**:539-556.

——, (1988a). "Peirce and Turing: Comparisons and Conjectures," *Semiotica* **68**:33-61.

——, (1988b). "Toward an Understanding of Peirce's Master Argument," *Cruzeiro Semiotics* **8**:57-66.

Krausser, Peter (1977). "The Three Fundamental Structural Categories of Charles S. Peirce," *Transactions of the Charles S. Peirce Society* **13**:189-215.

Kuratowski, K. and A. Mostowski (1968). *Set Theory.* Warszawa: PWN Polish Scientific Publishers.

Mertz, Donald W. (1979). "Peirce: Logic, Categories, and Triads," *Transactions of the Charles S. Peirce Society* **15**:158-175.

Moore, Edward C. et al. eds (1984). *Writings of Charles S. Peirce.* Bloomington: Indiana University Press.

Peirce, Charles Sanders (1867). "On a New List of Categories," reprinted in Hartshorne and Weiss, eds. 1935-58.

Percy, Walker (1975). "The Delta Factor," *The Southern Review* **11**:29-64. Reprinted in *The Message in the Bottle*, New York: Farrar, Strauss, and Giroux, 1975.

Quine, Willard Van Orman, (1954). "Reduction to a Dyadic Predicate," *Journal of Symbolic Logic* **19**. Reprinted in *Selected Logical Papers*, New York: Random House, 1966, 224-226.

——, (1963). *Set Theory and Its Logic.* Cambridge: Harvard University Press.

——, (1981). *Mathematical Logic.* Cambridge: Harvard University Press.

Roberts, Don D. (1973). *The Existential Graphs of Charles S. Peirce.* The Hague: Mouton.

Robin, Richard R. (1967). *Annotated Catalogue of the Papers of Charles S. Peirce.* Amherst: University of Massachusetts Press.

——, (1971). "The Peirce Papers: A Supplementary Catalogue," *Transactions of the Charles S. Peirce Society* **7**:37-57.

Rubin, Jean E. (1967). *Set Theory for the Mathematician.* San Francisco: Holden-Day.

Selby, Samuel and Leonard Sweet (1963). *Sets, Relations, Functions: An Introduction.* New York: McGraw-Hill.

Skidmore, Arthur (1971). "Peirce and Triads," *Transactions of the Charles S. Peirce Society* **7**:3-23.

—— (1981). "Peirce and Semiotics: An Introduction to Peirce's Theory of Signs," in *Semiotic Themes*, ed. R.T. DeGeorge. Lawrence: University of Kansas Publications.

Wiener, N. (1912). "A Simplification of the Logic of Relations," *Proceedings of the Cambridge Philosophical Society* **17**:387-390.

Temporality and Transcendence

Lewis S. Ford

Process theism may be characterized as that revision of classical theism needed in order to overcome the objections of modern atheism. In proclaiming the death of God a century ago, Nietzsche meant to oppose those absolute immutable structures epitomized in the traditional understanding of the divine. It may be questioned, however, whether any of the divine features he rejected could be found in the view of God Hartshorne champions.[1] Certainly the classical notion of divine immutability has been rejected by both.

Hartshorne's basic argument against immutability develops from the implications of the nature of knowing. The knower is affected by the known, and not vice versa. The epistemic relation is internal to the knower, external to the known. This applies to the divine instance of knowing equally well as to any other instance. Moreover, future contingents are not yet knowable, since not yet determinate. Only as they become determinate, can they be known. This applies to divine as well as to other knowers. As the perfect knower, God is necessarily omniscient, knowing all there is to know, but God cannot know the unknowable (i.e. future contingents) until they become determinately knowable. If so, divine omniscience requires that God's knowledge increase over time.

This is clearly counter to the immutability of classical theism. Yet classical theism has a very strong argument for immutability based upon the necessary properties of a perfect being. Such a being must have perfect unity, and that unity could not have temporal parts such as that which is earlier and that which is later as would be required by any divine change. Therefore whatever knowing a perfect being has must be immutable. To insure this, the future must be in some sense already determinate and knowable to divine knowing.

This runs so strongly against powerful intuitions concerning the indeterminate future and our free power (partially) to determine it that this argument is often ignored. Yet it can be countered on its own terms by distinguishing between a perfect knower (whose knowing is perfectly contoured to what is known) and a perfect being which knows. Process theism can affirm the first while questioning the second. I have argued elsewhere that God is not so much the perfect instance of being as the perfect instance of becoming, and it is as becoming that God is the perfect knower of a future that also becomes.[2]

Once divine immutability has been effectively challenged in terms of omniscience, the way is clear to a revision of the concept of God on other points, such as the question of divine suffering, and the question whether God's power ought to be reconceived in ways that avoid most of the issues posed by the classical problem of evil.[3] In this essay I propose to go even further, making it my aim to treat *everything* divine as open to change and temporality.

Richard Creel has recently challenged these efforts to enlarge the scope of divine mutability.[4] He accepts Hartshorne's basic argument concerning omniscience, but then seeks to show what minimal adjustments this entails for classical theism. In particular no modification of strict divine impassibility is needed.

Some modification is required, however, and this is the sticking point with many traditionalists. For if immutability is modified at all, however, the way God transcends the world is called into question. Traditionally God transcends the world as the eternal transcends the temporal, and that which is not strictly immutable cannot be eternal. The immutable *does not* move or change, while the eternal *cannot* do so, since it has no distinction between before and after which alone makes change intelligible. In classical thought, God is conceived to be eternal, utterly timeless, in contrast to a purely temporal world. Xenophanes, Parmenides, Plato, Aristotle, Plotinus all agreed that the divine should be conceived as timeless. Plato contrasted the excellence of the eternal Forms with the flux of actualities, which are always coming into being and perishing and never really are.

Medieval theology, enamored of this Greek ideal of perfection, reshaped the Biblical image of the everlasting God, who was, and is, and is to be, from everlasting to everlasting, into a sheerly timeless being. Thus it is that the same word 'eternal' can mean both that which has the most time of all, everlastingly, and that which is utterly devoid of time, the timeless, the atemporal. In any case, however, timelessness became the very mark of God's transcendence of the temporal world. A changing and therefore temporal deity cannot transcend the world in this time-honored sense.

Most process theists, following the lead of Whitehead and Hartshorne, assert that God is at least partly eternal, but have sought to introduce a second, temporal nature as well. Yet will such a partial eternal nature express the way God transcends the world?[5] I shall argue that God should be conceived as wholly temporal, and that we need to express divine transcendence strictly in temporal terms.

If God has a temporal nature as well as an eternal one, some sort of relation between the two is needed. Hartshorne proposes that God's eternal nature be considered as necessary and abstract, the temporal nature as contingent and concrete. Can a nature which is inherently abstract do justice to divine transcendence, especially if this abstract nature is the defining characteristic of the society of divine occasions. In that case the abstract component is purely objective, whereas we might think of divine subjectivity as transcending such objectivity.

Here it may appear that a better way in which God as eternal could transcend the temporal world might be found in Whitehead's understanding of the primordial nature of God as itself subjective.[6] On occasion Whitehead clearly describes the primordial nature in subjectivist terms: "The 'primordial nature' of God is the concrescence of a unity of conceptual feelings, including among their data all eternal objects. The concrescence is directed by the subjective aim, that the subjective forms of the feelings shall be such as to constitute the eternal objects into relevant lures of feeling severally appropriate for all realizable basic conditions" (PR 87f/134).[7] If so, cannot God, even while having temporal relations to the temporal world, have an inherently nontemporal essential subjectivity. Could it not be by means of this subjectivity that God transcends the world?

This description assumes that it is possible to abstract from temporality and still retain subjectivity. In part this is achieved by restricting the objective content experienced to that which is timeless, in anticipation that its subjective counterpart will be timeless as well. Here, however, we have no clear warrant, for it seems impossible to distinguish between a genuinely nontemporal experience and a present immediacy exclusively characterized by a timeless content. Analogous problems beset the notion of an eternal present, which remains a present after all.

There would seem to be an inclination towards a nontemporal subjectivity were the eternal objects primary and uncreated, as Whitehead supposed (PR 257/392). Then God's subjectivity would be centrally expressed in a primordial envisagement organizing the eternal objects. Yet it is possible to conceive of their atemporality as merely apparent, stemming from the fact that their temporal origination has been abstracted from. Whitehead recognizes that actualities become objective only as past. We propose to generalize this by claiming that all objects are past, meaning that so-called "eternal objects" are derivative abstractions from past actualities, abstracting from all the circumstances of their origin. Just as Melchizedek, presented as without birth or genealogy, is taken to be eternal by the writer to the Hebrews (Hebr. 7.3), these derivative objects betray no hint of any temporal origination.

Emergent "eternal objects" can be seen as a result from a generalized ontological principle. Whitehead tells us that "There is no justification for checking generalization at any particular stage" (PR 16/25), but he himself limits the application of the ontological principle simply to the derivative existence of eternal objects, and not to their nature. Actual entities find their reasons for what they are in other actual entities and in themselves, but why should this not be true of other entities as well? If becoming grounds being in the case of actualities, why not other beings as well? In that case the being of an "eternal object," what it is, would be explained by its emergence.

Whitehead first conceived of "eternal objects" in terms of the sense-objects of his philosophy of nature. The early division into objects and events is purely a phenomenological description of what is: the spatiotemporal happenings and that which characterizes them. "Eternal" (i.e. atemporal) simply described the relation these characteristics have to time and temporal events (EWM 25f). In the Lowell Lectures of 1925, which form part of *Science and the Modern World*, these eternal objects were purely immanent, existing only in events, but they acquired a transcendent status in the addition on "Abstraction" as Whitehead wrestles with the implications of his newly devised epochal theory of time (EWM 67-70). As transcendent, the eternal objects were at first separately existing Platonic forms, only some of which were admissible for actualization by the principle of limitation, as Whitehead then conceived God to be. Later, however, perhaps after the adoption of the reformed subjectivist principle, God became the ontological ground for the eternal objects, which by the general Aristotelian principle possessed a derivative existence dependent on the primary existence of God.

Whitehead finally speaks of a primordial envisagement of all the eternal objects whereby they are all evaluated in terms of divine subjective forms (PR 31f/46f), but he stops short of arguing that the eternal objects could be created (PR 257/392). A primordial, nontemporal creation poses problems of intelligibility.[8] How is there a before in which the eternal objects are not yet unified as they will be in God, and an after when they are, if there are no temporal dimensions to the primordial act? Moreover, there might be the lurking suspicion that in creating the eternal objects God could be taken to be the creator of the world, even if indirectly.

Since for him then the eternal objects were uncreated, Whitehead could see no way of extending the ontological principle to explain their nature. But the ontological principle could be so extended if we suppose that the so-called "eternal objects" are temporally emergent. Such "emergent objects" would only appear to be timeless because we would have abstracted from, and then ignored, their mode of origination.

Such abstraction could be achieved by the fourth category of conceptual valuation, if this category is conceived in more active terms than Whitehead uses (PR 248/379). It would account for all the functions Whitehead assigns to the eternal objects, except for novelty and for the way God influences actual occasions by means of initial subjective aims.[9] Novelty, in particular, cannot be explained in terms of abstraction derived from past actualities. How can the new come from that which is exclusively old? These functions will be explained later in the exposition of this essay, without requiring any primary role for atemporality. I see the temporal as alone primary and concretely real, with all forms of the atemporal, the eternal or the nontemporal as derivative abstractions.

Whitehead's nontemporal subjectivity, moreover, depends upon there being a present everlasting concrescence. Otherwise it could not be integrated with divine temporality. Yet a concrescence that never perishes cannot be objectified, and hence cannot be prehended. How would God then influence the world temporally? Confronted by this problem, Whitehead recognized that he had not solved it.[10] Hartshorne's modification, whereby God is reconceived as an unending series of divine occasions, does show how God can influence the world in the very same way any other actuality does, but it must treat whatever primordiality God has as strictly objective.

Hartshorne's emendation would be difficult for Whitehead to accept. Whitehead's "everlasting" consequent concrescence is explicitly defined as "devoid of 'perpetual perishing' " (PR 347/527), while Hartshorne's divine occasions would be perpetually perishing all the time. This is less of a problem for Hartshorne, simply because he does not endorse this notion of "perishing." In noting the points on which he differed from Whitehead, Hartshorne wrote: "I never could see in the 'perishing' of actual entities anything more than a misleading metaphor which, taken literally, contradicts the dictum, entities 'become but do not change.' "[11]

To be sure, once a being becomes it cannot perish in the sense of changing.[12] If becoming is seen as the dynamic part of being, it too would then not perish. On the other hand, if being and becoming are exclusive categories, then it would be possible for the becoming of an actuality, which is a dynamic process of unifying the past multiplicity prehended, to cease in the attainment of its final unity of satisfaction. The perishing of becoming could then be a condition for being.

Whitehead states this very cryptically in the principle of process: "Its 'being' is constituted by its 'becoming' " (PR 23/34f). Interpreters differ as to its meaning. Hartshorne, Leclerc, and Sherburne take it to mean that becoming is to be identified with (a part of?) being, while I find Jorge Nobo's interpretation that becoming produces being more convincing.[13] Hartshorne's identification of being and becoming is consistent with his denial of perishing, but elsewhere in criticizing Paul Tillich's notion of being as embracing both rest and becoming, he argues that becoming includes being and not vice versa.[14] If so, becoming should be something more than being, having an aspect not to be identified with being.

If there were real perishing, would not something be lost for a divine knower. If so, how could God be omniscient? Yet the issue at stake is the status of present subjectivity. In the case of the future Hartshorne argues that what is indeterminate is unknowable. Whitehead extends this unknowability of indeterminacy to apply to present subjectivity. God knows all there is to know, but subjectivity is not part of this, for it has no being, only becoming.

Whatever being an occasion attains is objectively immortal, surviving to influence superseding actualities, including the omniscient being.[15] In reflecting upon Locke's notion of time as "perpetual perishing" against the backdrop of "objective immortality," Whitehead came to realize that the temporal shift from present to past marked a qualitative, ontological transformation from subject to object. This was a real transformation which could only be expressed by the perishing of the subject itself. But that does not signify complete and total perishing, for whatever could be objectified would be in terms of objective immortality. In this context "perishing" is always shorthand for "subjective perishing and objective immortality."

Hartshorne also recognizes that the subject-object structure is also a present-past structure (cf. e.g. TPP 94). Yet because there is no "perishing," this is not so much an ontological transformation as a shift in point of view. The actuality could have the same definiteness (and hence knowability) as subject that it has as object, since nothing has perished for a perfect knower.

Perhaps the primary reason our two thinkers diverge with respect to "perishing" can be found in their contrasting theories of actualization. Hartshorne, with Peirce and Weiss, sees actualization primarily in terms of "definition," the process whereby possibility, which insofar as it is indefinite includes many alternatives, is rendered more and more definite. The indefinite becomes fully definite and actual when it has excluded all alternatives. The final act transforming possibility into definite actuality occurs all at once, for Hartshorne subscribes to Whitehead's doctrine of the atomicity of becoming. Yet Hartshorne accepts this doctrine largely in order to meet Zeno's paradoxes, not because it is essential to actualization.

Hartshorne is committed to a purely formal approach to actuality. Consider the alternative, as expressed by his disciple Gene Peters: "To deny that a thing qua actual is its full definiteness or particularity is to commit oneself to the position that [sheer] actuality is a totally featureless something, a sheer surd—even for an omniscient knower."[16] If only the purely formal character of actuality were sufficient, concrete particularity could be replaced by eternal objects. For Whitehead there *must be* something more, something by which eternal objects can pass from being unactualized to actualized. This something cannot simply be another eternal object.

Whitehead uses the quantum of time in order to explore the interiority and subjectivity of an occasion, an analysis which becomes focussed upon how determinate actuality comes into being. The process of definition is an important factor in actualization, but it is not the only factor. Definition is described in terms of the successive modifications of the subjective aim (PR 224ff/342ff) until its final form is reached. This is not enough in Whitehead's eyes, however, to constitute actuality. For the past actualities of the world as physically prehended at the outset must be synthesized together in a final contrast. The final subjective aim provides the formal means whereby the multiplicity of past actualities can be unified, while the actualities enable the form to stand out from among its near alternatives as the form actualized in that particular instance.

These past causal conditions play a role on Hartshorne's account, but only to serve as the means for achieving increasing definiteness. For Whitehead the past causes serve primarily as the content, or as we might even say, the matter of the final actuality. They are its matter, for it is out of these past actualities that the new occasion is made. In the end they provide no formal features, for these are all already contained in the final form, but they provide the matter which transforms the final form from being a timeless possibility into a particular actuality.

While Whitehead does not use the term, we may properly characterize his as a theory of dynamic hylomorphism. It requires something more than form, and this "something" can be seen to be the matter out of which the actuality is formed. It is the difference between unactualized and actualized form.

Sometimes, Whitehead is quoted in support of the claim that mere definiteness is actuality.[17] Actually, what Whitehead wrote is that "*definition* is the *soul* of actuality" (PR 223/340). The soul or inner activity is more like the subjective aim, while the rest of the concrescence (i.e. the continuing physical prehensions) functions as its body. Definiteness is an essential part of actualization, but it alone does not constitute the determinateness of actuality.[18]

In Whitehead's terms, if definiteness were sufficient, then actuality could be exhaustively analyzed in terms of conceptual prehensions. There would be no need for physical prehensions as well. The distinction seems necessary for there to be any divine temporal experience, because it is quite possible for a purely nontemporal actuality to know all the eternal objects. A timeless physical prehension is impossible, for it depends upon both the temporal emergence of the actual occasion prehended, and on the temporal subjective activity consequent to that emergence. Would Whitehead have come to affirm God's consequent nature had he not been already committed to a hylomorphic analysis requiring both timeless conceptual and temporal physical prehensions?[19]

Moreover, if actualization were only the progressive definition of the indefinite, then one stage would be as knowable as another. It would be subjective for its own process of actualization, while being objective for all others. But if concrescence is as complex as the hylomorphic account requires, then then there would have to be intermediate stages of concrescence.[20] We have no evidence that such intermediate stages can be experienced as objects by others, and this would violate the rule of relativity physics that only what is past can be prehended. Intermediate stages also lack the full unity required for objectification, having only the unity of propositions. Finally concrescence has the ontological status of becoming and hence is imprehensible, since only beings can be prehended.

None of these Whiteheadian reasons apply to Hartshorne's theory of actuality. Thus Hartshorne originally argued that God could even know contemporaries. Since the 1950's, however, he gave up this view, not because contemporaries as subjective were unknowable, but because relativity physics seemed to require it.[21]

As long as God was conceived as knowing contemporaries, divine prehension could be understood as strict inclusion. Whatever exists or existed, in the past or in the present, was included within the divine experience by means of prehension. This was strict panentheism, which Christian long ago argued was quite foreign to Whitehead's approach.[22] Contemporaries cannot be prehended, not only because of relativity physics, but because there was nothing to prehend. What God could and does prehend, is the entirety of the past.

Let us review the contrast between actualization as formal definition and actualization as hylomorphic determination in terms of three classes of entities the discussion calls for.

(a) *Possibilities.* For Hartshorne a possibility is (relatively) indefinite, to be rendered definite in the process of actualization. For Whitehead each possibility is an absolutely definite eternal object, which is formally the same whether actualized or unactualized. It is absolutely definite, since there is no possibility of its becoming any more definite if all eternal objects are uncreated. Emergent objects, on the other hand, can be rendered more definite through further emergence, and hence can function much as do Hartshorne's indefinites.

Possibilities, phenomenologically considered, often do function in the vague and indefinite way that indefinites do. I can entertain the possibility of raising my arm, but there are manifold ways of actualizing this possibility. Vagueness of possibility may be the rule rather than the exception.

Thus in Whiteheadian theory many conceive an initial subjective aim to be the totality of eternal objects which could be actualized in that particular situation, as valued by God, while the occasion's own freedom can be understood as the power of selection from this multiplicity. Yet the multiplicity could equally well be conceived as a single indefinite possibility rendered more and more definite in the process of concrescence.

Any indefinite can be conceived as a "clustering" of eternal objects, that is, as the dense infinity of absolute definites collectively constituting its range. Then the process of rendering an indefinite definite simply separates one eternal object from its neighbors. Then it lies in the nature of possibilities that unactualized eternal objects "cluster." Yet why this should be so is difficult to fathom, unless we derive all definites from indefinites, so clusters of definites are understood as indefinites.

There is also a particular internal problem which the notion of absolute definites poses for Whitehead's theory of the extensive continuum, as Hartshorne pointed out a long time ago.[23] Is the continuum composed of absolutely definite points or are these points derived from the continuum itself? The method of extensive abstraction, whereby points are defined as the resultants of converging inclusive sets, argues for the latter. If so, the definite is derived from the indefinite, and not vice versa. All these considerations favor the emergent object as indefinite over the eternal object as absolutely definite.

(b) *Actualities.* As the outcome of a process of definition, the actuality for Hartshorne is both definite and particular. A single eternal object, however, as absolutely definite, can be the form of the actuality, yet it in itself is still a universal. Moreover, given the inherent clustering character of eternal objects, it is not separated from its neighbors unless realized, i.e. unless serving as the form of unity for an actual exemplification.

Now the actuality is particular, but particulars are still universal, according to the principle of relativity, whereby every "being" is a potential for every [subsequent] "becoming" (PR 22/33). As Whitehead writes, "every so-called 'particular' is universal in the sense of entering into the constitutions of other actual entities" (PR 48/76). We need a term for that which is really particular, and that Richard Rorty has supplied.[24] They are:

(c) *Unrepeatables.* Possibilities and actualities, universals and particulars, are all repeatables for Whitehead, according to the principle of relativity, and for Hartshorne, since nothing has perished, at least not for God. Whatever God includes is repeatable, for it once existed for itself, and now exists as part of the divine experience.

Rorty makes a strong case that only unrepeatables can function as the true particulars required by philosophical analysis. We can add to that the observation that only that which absolutely perishes can be unrepeatable, since what survives will be repeated by omniscience. What is unrepeatable for Rorty is concrescence, which is precisely that which absolutely perishes in the attainment of concrete particulars, i.e. actuality as repeatable.

There are strengths and weaknesses to both theories of actualization. A theory of absolute definites which somehow necessarily "cluster" to form general alternatives seems less plausible than a theory which derives relative definites from indefinites. Yet it seems necessary as long as we assume with Whitehead that eternal objects are uncreated, because we must have all the definites we will ever need at all times, there being no opportunity to acquire more. If we replace eternal objects with temporally emergent objects, however, all this seems quite unnecessary. Emergent objects can be as definite or indefinite as needed. In particular, no absolute definites are needed for subjective aims as providing the basis for dynamic hylomorphism. Thus it is possible to understand actualization in terms of the unifying of past multiplicity by means of a relatively definite form. Then its final determination requires the perishing' of the process of becoming in producing the determinate being. This appears to be the only way the actualization can be radically unrepeatable while obtaining concrete particular outcomes which are repeatable.

Now no matter what theory of actualization we adopt, God can only be conceived as purely temporal if whatever eternal (i.e. everlasting) features which have been ascribed to God can be shown to be temporally emergent.

On the face of it this seems to be utterly impossible. Those features thought to be eternal are so because they are necessary. If we think of necessary features as temporally emergent because they initiate the creative process, then they contravene the everlastingness of creativity whereby every event grows out of some past. If there were some past from which the necessity emerges, then in the past the necessity did not yet apply, contrary to its absolute universality (cf TPP 68). Moreover, what is necessary for Hartshorne has no conceivable alternatives.

It will certainly *appear* to us that what we take to be necessary has no conceivable alternative. Our problem, however, lies in discerning that which is absolutely necessary. Whitehead warned us of this by indicating how difficult it is to distinguish between metaphysical principles as absolutely necessary and extremely broad empirical generalizations.

This is no particular problem with respect to our "cosmic epoch," which is that large period of time in which the physical laws and constants now present hold sway. Conceivably this could be forever, but that seems highly unlikely. The fact that most of these are quantitatively expressed, suggesting alternatives, and are empirically discovered, points to their contingent character. They have alternatives, and thus could change.

How they change is differently explained by Whitehead and Hartshorne (TPP 75-77). For Whitehead the laws are generalizations of the average behavior of the simpler occasions of that epoch. There may be a weakening of the hold of a given physical law on its members, so that fewer and fewer of its members exemplify it. There may be a stage of relative chaos in which no law is exemplified by any strong proportion. Or members may start exemplifying some other law, thus inaugurating a new cosmic epoch. Thus the laws of nature are conceived as immanent in the world itself.

Hartshorne takes the laws of nature to be divinely imposed. "God's power to have any logically possible world," Hartshorne argues, should be defined "not as his freedom to choose that world, but as his freedom to choose the basic laws of such a world."[25] Thus "The only 'acts of God' we can identify (in spite of the lawyers) are the laws of nature."[26]

He finds this teaching in Whitehead. Whitehead does say that " 'God' is that actuality in the world, in virtue of which there is physical law" (PR 283/434), in a context that speaks of standpoints as being derived from subjective aim. Yet anything resulting from subjective aim involves creaturely activity supplementing and modifying the aim as provided by God. God is needed for there to be any physical law at all, and indirectly determines particular laws. But the laws themselves emerge from the activities of the occasions themselves.

The alteration of physical laws lies within the bounds of possibility. The laws are contingent and have alternatives. Since moreover it is possible for these laws to be modified by the occasions themselves, out of their response to God's aims, it does not seem necessary to explain any change in the law by means of divine imposition. It would seem that we should follow the general rule of not introducing God to explain that which the world can satisfactorily explain.

Yet if God imposes no physical law, it seems difficult to see how God influences the world, particularly if little use is made of divine persuasion in the way Whitehead conceives it. While that way of explaining divine influence in terms of particular aims for particular actualities is never rejected, it seems not to be centrally utilized either (TPP 77-79). This may well be due to Hartshorne's assumption (well founded if all other-causation is past causation) that *all* forms of other-causation limit creaturely freedom (OTM 118f). Then God's way of limiting our freedom must pertain to the general laws providing the context for our freedom rather than to aims which could inspire us towards greater novelty, enhancing and expanding our freedom.

The key issue concerns the bounds of possibility. Both thinkers agree that there are some general laws that God alone establishes, but differ as to which these are. Since the laws of nature are contingent, they should be changeable, Whitehead argues, and this can be accomplished by means of an altered average behavior in the basic physical actualities of the world. Direct divine activity should be the means of changing the laws of nature, Hartshorne argues, because otherwise God would have no influence on the world. No other general laws can be altered. For him, the basic metaphysical principles are *a priori*, without any conceivable alternatives (TPP 67-72). They need not be established by any divine primordial envisagement, as Whitehead claims (PR 31/46, 343f/521ff). Since the primordial envisagement is relevant to *all* actual occasions, there are no alternatives to the metaphysical principles which are actualizable.

If for Hartshorne's reasons we reject God's establishment of metaphysical principles, and for Whitehead's reasons we reject Hartshorne's divine imposition of the laws of nature, then it would seem that God cannot influence the world in terms of general laws. There is, however, another alternative in terms of temporal emergence. What *appears* to be absolutely necessary may turn out to be relatively necessary, that is, necessary for a particular "metaphysical epoch." What *appears* to be timeless may turn out to be an abstraction from the process of its emergence.

Likewise a metaphysical principle might *appear* to apply to all cosmic epochs. We have intimate knowledge only of our own cosmic epoch, however, and we can only vaguely conceive of neighboring ones. It is much more difficult to determine how well these principles may apply to epochs very distant from us. While our metaphysical principles may be most suitable to our epoch, and to those most relevant to us, we can know extremely little with respect to very distant ones.

As the epochs become more distant, and hence more different from our own, we might expect that the principles would become less adequate and applicable. Then it would seem that God would make the necessary adjustments, creating a new metaphysical epoch. There would be strong continuities between the two epochs, but some principles would be replaced. We can conceive that all or most could be stepwise replaced in the unimaginably distant future. Likewise, looking toward the distant past, we can conceive of the temporal origination of the principles governing our present world.[27]

This temporalistic revision of primordial envisagement allows for actualizable alternatives, those belonging to other metaphysical epochs. Yet it agrees with both Whitehead and Hartshorne that what is outside the domain governed by the metaphysical principles is not possible—although with the qualification that it is not possible within this metaphysical epoch. However, even on this alternative, there is still a place for that which permits no conceivable alternatives. There is still something uncreated, although it would be a bare minimum. The uncreated are the preconditions of creation, that which makes the emergence of anything whatever possible. Without them, nothing could be created, but by the same token it would be impossible for them to be created.

In particular, they are the preconditions for the emergence of metaphysical principles, for in terms of them the emergence of particular actualities is possible. This ontology of preconditions is probably quite a bit narrower than Hartshorne's metaphysics, which might include a good many principles properly belonging to this particular metaphysical epoch.

We have argued in this programmatic sketch that there is nothing eternal which is not derived from the temporal. What can we then say about the transcendence of God? This should eliminate all possibility of understanding this transcendence in terms of any eternal structure in God which contrasts with the simple temporality of the world. If so, God would have no distinctive essence, and Hartshorne's project of reconceiving divine occasions to be like actual occasions as much as possible would run into the difficulty of not providing for any no essential difference between God and the occasions. Any differences would be simply accidental and contingent. It would even be questionable whether the divine occasions could necessarily exist as required by Anselm's argument.

There is also, however, the second way in which God transcends the world according to Hartshorne's theory of dual transcendence.[28] Concretely God transcends the world as the whole includes its parts. God excels all particular actualities as that which contains them all. No other actuality does this, or could do it. Christian is quick to point out that Whitehead does not conceive of God in this panentheistic fashion: "God does not literally include or contain the world."[29] To be sure, God prehends or experiences the world without any exclusions or negative prehensions. The difference between prehending and including something concerns the nature of objectification. Does it as object have a different mode of being from the subject experiencing it? For Whitehead, this is the difference between the objectified past, and the subjective present prehending it. The temporal shift is expressed in terms of the metaphor of perishing, which Hartshorne rejects in order to insist that there are no limitations on divine inclusion. The more the concept of inclusion is insisted upon, however, so that inclusion in the way in which a whole includes its parts, the more divine subjectivity is lost sight of. Subjectivity requires something more.

We cannot here appeal to the abstract nature of God to safeguard divine subjectivity, since that is merely the defining characteristic of the society of divine occasions, and is purely objective. Divine subjectivity can only be expressed momentarily by each divine occasion, as long as its prehensive activity is not reduced to simple inclusion.

Hartshorne speaks of this inclusion as a form of transcendence, and so it is if transcendence is the way in which some "form of reality [is] exalted in principle above all others."[30] In this sense "God is unsurpassably inclusive and also unsurpassably integrated or unified. He is the all as an individual being."[31] Yet there is another meaning to transcendence: that what transcends be essentially other than what it transcends. This is impossible for a whole insofar as it is constituted by its parts.

The divine subject, to be transcendent, must be different in principle from the world. On the other hand, if God can no longer be conceived as transcending time, God must be found within time. God cannot be reduced to mere pastness, which is purely objective drained of all subjectivity. God cannot be purely present, then we lack any basis for distinguishing divine transcendence from the presentness we enjoy. God's pervasive and infinite activity, were it present, would usurp our own present activity, and undercut the sense in which God can act in a centered, unified way. If God were not able to transcend the present, God's omnipresence would simply degenerate into pantheism. If neither the past nor the present is appropriate, and the eternal is excluded, only the future remains.

Ordinarily we dismiss the future as merely a passive, empty domain upon which we project our hopes, fears, plans, and expectations. The future in this sense concerns what will be, i.e. what will someday be determinately past. It is the future according to the order of being. No determinate being occupies it as yet. The future as being contains little interest, but the future as becoming is quite a different story. It contains no determinate being, but it could contain an infinite, unified activity of becoming. Nothing is manifest, just as a mind is not directly manifest, and only indirectly manifest in the behavior of its body.

The future could contain the activity of a cosmic divine mind whose manifestation is to be found in the present and past of the world.

As Whitehead discovered in analyzing the character of a concrescence, the order of becoming is diametrically opposed to the order of being. According to the order of being, the earlier is determinate, the later indeterminate. According to the order of becoming, however, the earliest phases of concrescence are most like the indeterminateness of the future, while the latest phases has the determinateness of the past. If we extend this order of becoming into the future beyond the finite concrescence, we find this future to be an active instantiation of creativity, only monistically conceived, not yet pluralized into the many actual occasions of the present.

Thus divine transcendence can be conceived as the activity of the future, not of what will be, but of what might be. As future creativity, it is the whole domain of creativity in its future aspect, yet as a centered, unified activity. This activity is now going on, for it is in unison of becoming with our present selves. Unlike our contemporaries, however, God is located in the future we shall someday occupy. This highly indeterminate becoming will become our own becoming one present finite concrescence is initiated. The interface between the future and the present along the entire spatial extent of the world defines divine omnipresence without any of the dangers of pantheism with its denial of God's centeredness. The way future creativity pluralizes itself into the many finite present occasions of creativity is a modern way of conceiving how God communicates his *esse* to the world along Thomistic lines.[32]

NOTES

1. There may well be other features of Hartshorne's thought that Nietszche would question, such as his understanding of truth.
2. See my essay on "Process and Thomist Views Concerning Divine Perfection," forthcoming in *The Universe as Journey: Conversations with Norris Clarke*, ed. Gerald A. McCool, S.J., to be published by Fordham University Press.
3. I have argued in "The Rhetoric of Divine Power," *Perspectives in Religious Studies* **14**/3 (Fall 1987), 233-38, that we should reconceive the nature of divine power, not simply viewing divine power as a limited instance of currently accepted notions of power. (Were this so, a God having limited power would be surpassed by a God of unlimited power.) I assume Hartshorne agrees.
4. Richard E. Creel, *Divine Impassibility: An Essay in Philosophical Theology*. Cambridge: Cambridge University Press, 1986.
5. As Robert Kane pointed out with respect to the original version of this essay, Hartshorne conceives of God as transcending the world not only abstractly but concretely. Though most of my concern here is directed at the abstract, eternal form of transcendence, I will briefly consider concrete transcendence towards the end.

6. I have systematically developed this in "The Non-Temporality of Whitehead's God," *International Philosophical Quarterly* 13/3 (September, 1973), 347-76. It now appears that Whitehead himself may have held this view for only a few months, from the time he proposed the revised subjectivist principle (requiring all actualities as active syntheses to be subjective) as a generalized reflection upon his revisions (D) until he adopted a consequent nature for God (I). See my study, *The Emergence of Whitehead's Metaphysics, 1925-1929* (Albany: State University of New York Press, 1984; hereafter, EWM). It may be that with the adoption of the consequent nature Whitehead came to appreciate that all subjectivity, including the divine, must be temporal.
7. Whitehead's *Process and Reality* (PR) will be cited first according to the corrected edition (Press Press, 1978), then according to the original edition (Macmillan, 1929).
8. In "The Non-Temporality of Whitehead's God," section 10, I sought to develop two analogies which might render the notion of a nontemporal decision more intelligible. The first indicated the intuition guiding the generation of a postulational system, while the second concerned the personal integrity discernible in the "style," the "character," or the "underlying unity" of the personal decisions we make in response to the various situations confronting us. I have been unable to devise any further analogies, however, and I am no longer confident that these are sufficient.
9. These two exceptions were strong reasons for endorsing eternal objects. See my essay, "Whitehead's Differences from Hartshorne," pp. 58-83, in *Two Process Philosophers: Hartshorne's Encounter with Whitehead*, ed. Lewis S. Ford (Tallahassee: American Academy of Religion Studies in Religion 5, 1973; hereafter, TPP). More recently, however, I have moved closer to Hartshorne on this issue, because I think novelty and subjective aim are best explained in nonobjective terms.
10. A. H. Johnson, "Some Conversations with Whitehead Concerning God and Creativity," pp. 9ff in *Explorations in Whitehead's Philosophy*, ed. Lewis S. Ford and George L. Kline (New York: Fordham University Press, 1983).
11. Charles Hartshorne, *Whitehead's Philosophy: Selected Essays, 1935-1970* (Lincoln: University of Nebraska Press, 1972), p. 2. (Hereafter, WP.) Another difference obviously shows his more nominalistic approach to eternal objects: "I never cared for his 'eternal objects,' as a definite yet primordial multitude of 'forms' of feeling or sensation. . . ." Ibid.
12. While only the becoming perishes, its being can "fade": cf. PR 340/517. Using our terms somewhat differently, we might here distinguish between "subjective" and "superjective" perishing, recognizing that our concern here is solely with the former. See EWM 195f.
13. Jorge Nobo, "Whitehead's Principle of Process," *Process Studies* 4/4 (Winter, 1974), 275-84.
14. Charles Hartshorne, "Process as Inclusive Category: A Reply," *The Journal of Philosophy* 52/4 (February 17, 1955), 94-102.
15. This doctrine of "objective immortality" was established early, already in the 1926 essay on "Time" (EWM 305f=IS 243f). The notion of subjective perishing to attain objective immortality came later, when Whitehead drastically revised the basis of what he had written in Part II of *Process and Reality* (EWM

194-96).

16. Eugene H. Peters, *Hartshorne and Neoclassical Metaphysics* (Lincoln: University of Nebraska Press, 1970), p. 47, citing Hartshorne's *The Logic of Perfection* (La Salle, Ill.: Open Court, 1962), p. 165.
17. Ibid., quoting Hartshorne's *Reality as Social Process* (Glencoe, Ill.: Free Press, 1953), pp. 88 and 94.
18. See category of explanation 20 (PR 25/38), where determinateness is defined in terms of "definiteness" and "position." I have interpreted "position," i.e. "relative status in a nexus of actual entities" more concretely. That nexus is the past actual world of the occasion, the very multiplicity of actualities the occasion is called upon to unify in its final satisfaction.
19. As a graduate student Hartshorne was convinced by William Ernest Hocking, one of his teachers, that "the future must be open, partly indeterminate, even for God" (TPP 7). But the means for developing this insight in terms of divine dipolarity and the asymmetrical nature of relations depended upon Whitehead's *Process and Reality* (cf. TPP 6-9).
20. As the third and final point of difference, Hartshorne writes: "I never cared for . . . his analysis of the becoming of an actual entity (a concrete unit-happening) into 'early' and 'late' phases" (WP 2).
21. See Frederic F. Fost, "Relativity Theory and Hartshorne's Dipolar Theism," TPP 89-99.
22. William A. Christian, *An Interpretation of Whitehead's Metaphysics* (New Haven: Yale University Press, 1959), 403-409.
23. Hartshorne pointed this out to Whitehead in the 1930's, but it does not seem to have been written up anywhere. I discuss it in my contribution to the Hartshorne volume of the Library of Living Philosophers.
24. Richard M. Rorty, "Matter and Event," pp. 68-103 in *Explorations in Whitehead's Philosophy*, ed. Lewis S. Ford and George L. Kline (New York: Fordham University Press, 1983).
25. *Creative Synthesis and Philosophic Method* (La Salle: Open Court, 1970), p. 137.
26. *A Natural Theology for Our Time* (La Salle: Open Court, 1967), p. 102. See also the other references cited TPP 76f, and more recently, *Omnipotence and Other Theological Mistakes* (Albany: State University of New York Press, 1984), p. 18. (Hereafter, OTM.) See its praise for Whitehead's notion of divine persuasion, p. 22.
27. Delwin Brown in "Freedom and Faithfulness in Whitehead's God" (*Process Studies* 2/2 [Summer 1972], 137-48) argues that God would not alter his basic principles, while free to do so, out of faithfulness to his prior commitments. Yet those prior commitments were made to a world situation which presumably no longer exists. As long as that or analogous cosmic epochs prevailed we may expect God to honor prior commitments, but continued persistence of these principles in situations in which they become less and less appropriate would be counter-productive. In drastically altered cosmic situations the goodness of God requires the revision of metaphysical principles.
28. See *Creative Synthesis*, chapter 11, pp. 227-244.
29. Christian, *An Interpretation of Whitehead's Metaphysics*, p. 405.
30. *Creative Synthesis*, p. 227.

31. Ibid., p. 236.
32. Here see my essay, "Creativity in a Future Key," pp. 179-98 in *New Essays in Metaphysics*, ed. Robert C. Neville (Albany: State University of New York Press, 1987).

Our interpretation of divine activity as future may shed some light on the difficulties Schubert Ogden has pointed out with respect to Hartshorne in ascribing subjective experience to God analogically. (See his essay, "Hartshorne's Theory of Analogy," pp. 16-36 in *Existence and Actuality: Conversations with Charles Hartshorne*, ed. John B. Cobb, Jr. and Franklin I. Gamwell [Chicago: University of Chicago Press, 1984].) It may be that we should consider the difference between object and subject as a formal, literal, transcendental difference, as the difference between past and present. Temporal modalities thus become transcendental features. There could still be analogical differences with respect to degrees of mentality, which measure the degree of creative response to novelty, but the present/past distinction would be absolute. All present actualities would enjoy subjectivity, which is not a matter of degree. If so, we should not predicate subjectivity of God analogically, as we ascribe mentality. Subjectivity would be a transcendental property belonging to God literally, in virtue of the divine temporal modality, on the grounds that both present and future activity may be conceived as subjective, or at least as nonobjective.

Ogden's argument may be more radical, however. It may be that God ought not be considered as subjectivity at all. Here a simple subject/object dichotomy will not do, for God is surely not a past determinate object. We need a trichotomy such as the temporal modalities can provide. As future activity God is not so much subjectivity as the pre-subjective source of all subjectivity, providing both its creativity and its basic novel aims.

Transcendence, Temporality and Personal Identity: A Response to Ford

Robert Kane

I am not sure I fully understand Lewis Ford's provocative philosophical project, and these remarks are meant to evoke a better understanding. One thing seems clear: while Ford's work is clearly influenced by Whitehead and Hartshorne, it involves subtle modifications of their view and raises important questions about the nature of process thought in general. Some of my questions about it may be based on misunderstandings, but if so, I think the misunderstandings may be shared by others, and are therefore worth addressing.

Traditionally, the transcendence and eternity of God were closely related, as he says. As a timeless and immutable being, God existed over and above a temporal, changing world. But this simple alignment of transcendence and eternity cannot persist for a process view, in which God is temporal and changing. What then becomes of divine transcendence on such a view? Well, eternity does not entirely drop out of the picture. For Whitehead and Hartshorne, God is both eternal and temporal. One chooses both sides of this ultimate contrast, assigning them to different aspects of God. And the eternity of God is transmuted into the Biblical notion of everlasting life. Unlike finite creatures, God exists at all times, and always has certain properties like omnibenevolence, unsurpassed power, knowing all that is, and the like, which are essential features of God. In addition, eternity in the sense of everlastingness can account for the necessity of God. Thus, Hartshorne defends a temporalized version of the modalities which he finds in Aristotle (according to which, what exists at all times, is necessary), and which Jaakko Hintikka and his cohorts at the Finnish Academy have also found in Aristotle and some later medieval thinkers.[1]

But can eternity so conceived account for the *transcendence* of God? Ford thinks not. He says, "Hartshorne proposes that God's eternal nature be considered as necessary and abstract, the temporal nature as contingent and concrete. Can a nature which is inherently abstract do justice to divine transcendence?" Ford's answer to this question is "No," and this answer seems correct from a process perspective. Whitehead and Hartshorne would surely agree with the negative answer. The transcendence of God with respect to the world cannot be a matter of the eternal nature of God *alone*, for that is merely abstract, and in Whitehead's terms "deficient in actuality." (PR, p. 34) The transcendence sought must be, in Hartshorne's apt expression, a "dual transcendence."[2] God must transcend the world both eternally and temporally—in the excellence of essential properties and in the concreteness of temporal existence. This means, however, that while eternal divine properties are not sufficient to account for the transcendence of God, they are a necessary condition for transcendence. The word "transcendence" has several meanings. Roughly, it means "being above and beyond." But this "above and beyond" can be taken in several senses. In one sense, it may mean that God surpasses the world in the *excellence of God's nature.* In another sense, it may mean that God is above and beyond the world *in the reality of God's life.* For dual transcendence, both senses are meant and both senses are important.

My first question to Ford therefore is whether he would grant at least this much significance to the abstract nature of God as a contributor to divine transcendence. There is evidence that he would not, for he says that his aim is "to treat *everything* divine as open to change and temporality," and adds that this project would "eliminate all possibility of understanding . . . transcendence in terms of any eternal structure in God which contrasts with the simple temporality of the world." These strong claims provoke some interesting questions. Does he mean to dispense entirely with the notion of an eternal, necessary, divine nature which transcends "metaphysical epochs," or does he suppose that such a notion can be derived from the notion of God as "future creativity?" Are the excellences of the divine nature (omnibenevolence, etc.) to be conceived, like the laws of nature and other cosmological principles, as "temporally emergent," or are they among the "ontology of preconditions" which "permit no conceivable alternatives"—an ontology which is said to be "quite a bit narrower than Hartshorne's metaphysics?" If the latter is the case, Ford owes us a more detailed account of how and why the divine excellences belong to the ontology of preconditions. Why must it be the case, for example, that something conceived as "indeterminate" future creativity, is omnibenevolent, and in what sense does such a being "know" all things past? Ford owes us more explanation of these matters.

Assuming these questions about the abstract, eternal aspects of divine transcendence can be cleared away, we still face the central problem of Ford's paper: how does God transcend the world *concretely* and temporally—in the reality of God's life? On Ford's view, this question calls for some radical reconception. He says, "If God [as concretely existing] can no longer be conceived as transcending time, God must be found within time" and in such a way as to also transcend the world. But where in time and how transcend the world? His answer is that the transcendence of God cannot be found in the past, or the present, and therefore must be found in the future. "Divine transcendence [he says] can be conceived as the activity of the future, not of what will be, but of what might be." It is "the whole domain of creativity in its future aspect," conceived as a "centered, unified activity" which is nonetheless "highly indeterminate becoming."

He makes some insightful remarks in defense of these claims. But they are so unusual, they must give us pause. The questions that came to my mind about them are these. First, what does it mean to speak of "the activity . . . , not of what will be, but of what *might* be" unless it means activity that *might* take place in the future—in short, possible, but not actual, future activity. And if divine transcendence is merely possible future activity, how can it be something concretely real? Do we not have once again mere abstraction? Second, what does it mean to say that creativity is "in the future," unless it means that it *will* be. Let us grant for the sake of argument that creativity was past, is present and will be future; it is everlasting. But in what special way is it *actually* rather than merely potentially in the future? Third, in what sense is this future creativity a "centered, unified activity," if it is also "highly indeterminate becoming?" And what does it mean to say that indeterminate becoming is "in the future" over and above the commonplace that the future is indeterminate? I realize these questions are disingenuous. To ask them is to pose as something of a Luddite defending common sense in the face of what appears to be a revisionary metaphysical vision. But I think we must begin by asking just such questions if we are to understand Ford's view—and determine whether it is ultimately coherent.

His desire to find the transcendence of God in the future is proceeded by arguments eliminating the other two options. He says, "if neither the past nor the present is suitable [as the locus of temporal transcendence] only the future remains." On the unsuitability of the past as the locus of transcendence, his argument is that "God cannot be reduced to mere pastness which is purely objectivity drained of all subjectivity." This makes sense on a process view, and I have no quarrel with it. But the next step of his argument puzzles me. On the unsuitability of the present as a locus of divine transcendence, he argues that "God cannot be purely present, for then we would lack any basis for distinguishing divine transcendence from the presentness we enjoy. God's pervasiveness and infinite activity, were it present, would usurp our own present activity, and undercut the way in which God can act in a centered, unified way."

I do not see why these consequences follow. On Hartshorne's view, for example, the present experience of God is related to our present activities and enjoyments as the unified experience of a self or person is related to the cells of a supercellular organism. Such a view is reminiscent of the World Soul of Plato's *Timaeus* and also of certain Oriental views, perhaps that of Rāmānuja, according to which the world is God's body.[3] Now there are certainly problems with such World Soul images. But the point to be made here is that views which so conceive the relation of God to the world are not *obviously* subject to the objection just quoted. Such views can place divine transcendence in the present without lacking "a basis for distinguishing divine transcendence from the presentness we enjoy.'' For the presentness we enjoy is to the divine experience as the activities of the various cells of the body to the unifying experience of personal identity. The experience of the whole is conceived on this view as something ''over and above'' the activities of the cellular parts and is not merely the aggregate of them which provides no unifying perspective. It is an additional experience to them and so transcends them. Furthermore, the activities of the parts which this unifying experience unifies lie in its past, so the transcendence is also one of present to past, which in process terms amounts to the transcendence of subject to object.

Ford seems to reject this kind of ''panentheist'' view defended by Hartshorne and others when he says that what transcends must be ''*other* than what it transcends,'' and ''this is impossible for a whole insofar as it is constituted by its parts.'' But much depends on what is meant by a ''whole'' being ''constituted'' by its parts. If it means that the whole is not greater than the sum of the parts, as physical wholes may not be, then he is right. But the soul-body, subject-object relationship is not like the relation of physical wholes to physical parts. Or, putting it another way, a ''unifying experience'' is not ''constituted'' by its parts as is a physical whole. Thus, Ford's objections to the alternatives to his view, and in particular to Hartshorne's alternative, are not entirely convincing. But this does not mean the issues are settled against his view. As Ford has noted elsewhere, there is a growing feeling among process thinkers that the best known process accounts of God's influence on the world, notably those of Whitehead and Hartshorne, must be modified in some way—or at least rescued from inadequate interpretations. (For an alternative view of Whitehead, see the following essay of this volume by Jorge Nobo). Hartshorne's view is the best known process alternative to Whitehead's, but it is also contested by many. So Ford's alternative deserves to be given careful attention and a good place to begin understanding it is by asking some of the questions asked above.

To conclude this essay, I would like to address one further problem which is critical for both Ford's view and World Soul views of God's relation to the world, like Hartshorne's. The problem I have in mind is one of the oldest and deepest of metaphysics, the problem of personal identity. Is the experience of personal identity something more than the aggregate or bundle of particular perceptions that Hume and certain Buddhist thinkers took it to be? Or does the experience of being one unified person or self transcend this flux or aggregate, and if so how? What, in general, is personal identity, and in what sense is God a ''person?'' Answers to these questions are clearly central for any kind of theism, and they are difficult because we are far from having undisputed answers about the nature of personal identity even in the human case. For Ford's view, the problem can be stated this way: where and how does God's personhood, or personal identity, enter into the picture of God as ''future creativity'' on Ford's view? It is true that Ford speaks of this future creativity as a "centered, unified activity," but we have already questioned whether he is really entitled to call it such, given that he also speaks of it as "highly indeterminate becoming." Perhaps the "personhood" of God on his view is to be found in the "manifestation [of God] . . . in the present and past of the world" while the transcendent reality of God is future. But is this "manifestation [of God] . . . in the present and past" just the world process itself or something that transcends the world? If the former, then the world *is* the personhood of God, though not God's full reality (a highly unorthodox conception); if the latter, then there is another kind of transcendence to be countenanced which is in the present and past, not in the future, and which needs to be explained.

But the problem of personal identity is also a problem for views like Hartshorne's which conceive the relation of God to the world on the analogy of the relation of soul to body and see God as the World Soul. For such views, the questions asked above about personal identity are also directly related to issues about transcendence. Is the experience of personal identity something more than the aggregate or bundle of particular perceptions that Hume and certain Buddhist thinkers took it to be? Or does the experience of being one unified person or self (for God as well as for humans) transcend this flux or aggregate, and if so how? In the attempt to provide better answers to these questions from a process perspective, I think one can say something in favor of the future, and this will be my final point. I think the idea of personal identity in the more manageable human case is related, not only to how we unify our past, but also to how we project ourselves into the future by way of intentional action. Seeing ourselves as *agents* rather than merely as recipients of data is one of the keys to understanding personal identity. Hume was deficient in this regard and it is one reason he could not find the self in the flux of experience.

Though process philosophy is very un-Humean in many respects, nonetheless, in its treatment of experience, it has tended to focus on perception and memory, which represent the receptive, or input, end of experience—the influence of the past on the present. It has concentrated less on the output end of experience, the influence of the present on the future, by way of intention and intentional action. Concrescing experiences not only unify the past, they create "messages" in the form of intentions or purposes which constrain the future without determining it. Pertinent to this is John Searle's recent introduction of an idea of self-referential causation to explain intentional action and perception as well.[4] On Searle's view, the intentional object (in Brentano's sense) of an intention refers not only to a future event but also to the fact that the intention itself will causally influence that future event. In other words, the intending agent does not merely intend (that such and such an action will occur) but rather (that such and such an action will occur and *this intention* will be the cause of that (future) action). In such manner, the intentional object of a present experience can refer to the experience itself in its future causal role; and this would mean in process terms that when such an occasion of experience is prehended by a later occasion there would exist a kind of self referential relation whereby the present occasion prehends a past whose very meaning and purpose was to be prehended by the present occasion. This unique reciprocal and self referential relation between temporally successive events lies I think at the basis of the relation we call personal identity. In God's case on a World Soul view, the future directedness would be called providence, and it would be a defining feature of the personhood of God as well as a condition for the unity of the world. This would not bring the future into the picture in as strong a sense as Ford envisages. But, assuming that personal identity is one key to understanding transcendence, as I am suggesting, it does capture some of Ford's insight that the future must be factored into any understanding of transcendence on a process view.

NOTES

1. Hartshorne, *Insights and Oversights of Great Thinkers*. See the chapter on Aristotle. Hintikka, *Time and Necessity*.
2. *Creative Synthesis and Philosophic Method*, chapter XI.
3. See, for example, Hartshorne and Reese, *Philosophers Speak of God*, the introductory essay entitled "The Standpoint of Panentheism" and the discussions of Plato and Rāmānuja.
4. Searle, *Intentionality*, chapters 3 and 4.

BIBLIOGRAPHY

Hartshorne, Charles. *Creative Synthesis and Philosophic Method*. LaSalle. IL.: Open Court, 1970.

——. *Insights and Oversights of Great Thinkers*. Albany: State University of New York Press, 1983.

—— and William Reese. *Philosophers Speak of God*. Chicago: University of Chicago Press, 1953.

Hintikka, Jaakko. *Time and Necessity*. Oxford: Oxford University Press, 1973.

Searle, John. *Intentionality*. Cambridge: Cambridge University Press, 1983.

Whitehead, A. N. *Process and Reality*. Edited by David Ray Griffin and Donald W. Sherburne. New York: The Free Press, 1978.

God as Essentially Immutable, Imperishable and Objectifiable: A Response to Ford

Jorge Luis Nobo

Ford believes that "a concrescence that never perishes cannot be objectified, and hence cannot be prehended" (supra p. 159). Since God, according to Whitehead, is an actual entity whose concrescence never perishes, Ford concludes that God's influence on the temporal world cannot be consistently explained by Whitehead. In support of this conclusion, Ford reports that Whitehead, when confronted with this problem in a private conversation with A. J. Johnson, "recognized that he had not solved it" (supra p. 159). Ford's manner of paraphrasing Whitehead's remarks, however, is misleading; for it suggests, albeit unintentionally, that Whitehead admitted both to having tried to solve the problem and to having failed to find a solution. But what Whitehead in fact said was that he had not *attempted* to solve the problem (EWP 10). The difference is significant. That Whitehead did not attempt a solution does not mean that a solution is impossible. Moreover, the very fact that Whitehead did not even attempt a solution could mean that he did not consider the problem to be truly serious or major. After all, in his response to Johnson, he succinctly characterized the problem as "genuine," but gave no hint of thinking that it posed a threat to his conception of Deity or to the coherence of his metaphysical system (EWP 9-10).

Here it must be remembered that, in respect to the internal criticisms of metaphysical systems, Whitehead carefully distinguished between logical inconsistency and categorial incoherence (PR 5-9). By logical inconsistency he meant, of course, the existence of contradictory statements in the actual exposition of the system. By incoherence, on the other hand, he meant the arbitrary disconnection of categories or first principles—their failure to presuppose each the others. Only the latter form of internal criticism, Whitehead argued, is ultimately a serious threat to the acceptability of a system. "The reason is that logical contradictions, except as temporary slips of the mind—plentiful, though temporary—are the most gratuitous of errors; and usually they are trivial" (PR 9).

The problem posed by the objectifiability of the imperishable divine actuality is, I contend, one of logical inconsistency. To resolve it, we need only to redefine or clarify the systematic meaning of 'superject.' Thus, unlike Ford, I believe a Whiteheadian solution—one developed in terms of, and compatible with, the categories and principles of Whitehead's metaphysics—is not only possible, but also relatively easy to accomplish.

I do agree with Ford, however, although for reasons other than he presents, that Hartshorne's societal conception of God does not constitute an adequate Whiteheadian solution to the problem of God's objectifiability. Certainly, Hartshorne's societal conception parts company with many a Whiteheadian metaphysical principle and thus is, in that sense, non-Whiteheadian.[1] But even more importantly, Hartshorne's theory purchases the objectifiability of each completed divine actuality at an unacceptable cost: the necessary immutability of the divine essence.

My contention, in this last regard, is that the conception of God as a serially ordered society of divine actualities is incompatible with the attribution of any essential, or eternal, subjective character to God; for if God is such a society of actualities, then by God's eternal character no more can be meant than the divine society's defining characteristic—the set of characteristics shared by *all* of the divine society's constituent actualities. But this common denominator of the divine actualities must include certain forms of subjective definiteness and certain kinds of aims and purposes that are essential to any plausible concept of Deity—e.g. perfect benevolence and perfect universality of altruistic concern. Unfortunately, these defining characteristics of Deity must belong to each divine actuality either by reason of its objective inclusion of, and compulsive conformation to, an earlier divine actuality, or by reason of its own autonomous self-determination.

The second alternative seeks to ground the shared subjective definiteness of many successive individuals in the unique freedom of each such individual. In other words, it seeks to explain what is common to all members of the divine society by the free contingent decisions of each such member. In short, it seeks to base absolute necessity of subjective character on the relative contingencies of successive subjective autonomies. Accordingly, it must be rejected.

The first alternative fares no better and basically for the same reason. There is no principle in Whitehead's metaphysics necessitating that the subjectivity of a later member of a given society conform perfectly and in all respects with the definiteness of both the subjective form and the subjective aim of an earlier member of that same society. On the contrary, causal objectification necessarily abstracts from the full definiteness of the superject being objectified (S 25-27; PR 364). In addition, an occasion's conformation to the objectified definiteness of an earlier occasion is itself abstractive and, hence, only partial.[2] In Whitehead's metaphysics, therefore, the continued instantiation of a set of specified characteristics in each component of a linear succession of actual entities is necessarily a contingent fact. This conclusion, of course, is fatal to the societal conception of God; for with that conception the possibility remains open that a future member of the society denoted by the term 'God' may fail to exhibit the set of characteristics connoted by the same term. Were that to occur, the existence of God would come to an end.

But a God that may yet cease to exist is for Whitehead, as for Hartshorne, no God at all.

In Whitehead's metaphysics, the essential divine characteristics endure without fail precisely because God is a single, imperishable actual entity. This fact has been lost on Hartshorne because he has been unable (as indeed most Whiteheadian commentators have been unable) to make sense of Whitehead's doctrine of internal supersession—the doctrine that the becoming of every actual entity involves a real succession of creative phases (WP 178-79).[3] But the ways in which internal supersession differs from external supersession constitute a ground for the immutability of the essential divine attributes.

In each instance of the relation of external supersession, the earlier relatum and the later relatum are actual entities and thus are, strictly speaking, two different particulars, two different individuals. Also, in each instance of this relation, the influence of the earlier relatum on the later one is curtailed to some degree by the abstractions inherent in causal objectification and conformal prehension, and is deflected more or less by the autonomy of the later relatum. Thus the rule in external supersession is change and difference. It is to this rule that the societal conception falls victim.

In each instance of the relation of internal supersession, however, the earlier and later relata are phases in the becoming of one and the same actuality, one and the same particular. Moreover, in internal supersession, the earlier relata are absorbed into the later relata without loss or alteration (PR 225). The individual is becoming more definite, but is not changing. Thus, the rule in internal supersession is self-identity amid the self-diversity entailed by the process of self-definition (PR 38).[4]

It is this latter rule that provides a ground for the immutability and everlastingness of the essential divine characteristics; for, in the case of God, the essential divine attributes are the primordial ones. They constitute the definiteness of the primordial subjectivity whereby a conceptual synthesis of the entire multiplicity of eternal objects is achieved (PR 134). Also, they constitute the primordial phase of the divine becoming and are presupposed by every phase of God's consequent nature and by every worldly occasion (PR 70, 522). In one sense, they are always being absorbed, without loss or alteration, into the divine consequent nature (PR 19). In another sense, they are always absorbing the successive stages of the consequent nature into an unsurpassable synthesis of infinite conceptual appetition and finite physical enjoyment (PR 524). Thus, though there are always more entities for God to influence and be influenced by, to experience and be experienced by, to love and perhaps be loved by, his character remains ever the same—perfectly benign, benevolent, omniscient, and all-loving.

Whitehead's conception of Deity, then, unlike Hartshorne's, guarantees the immutability of the essential definiteness of the divine subjectivity. It now must be shown that Whitehead's conception can consistently and coherently explain the objectification of God in and for each of the worldly, or temporal, actualities.

In the organic philosophy, being a superject is a necessary condition for an actuality being causally objectifiable in and for other actualities. That much can be taken for granted. The real problem is, what are we to understand by 'superject?' Must every superject be devoid of subjective immediacy? A loud and clear no! is the answer implied by Whitehead's detailed formulation of the primordial nature of God.

Whitehead's characterization of God's conceptual pole as "a primordial superject of creativity" implies that a superject need not be devoid of subjective immediacy (PR 48). It implies also that a superject need not be a concrete actuality, but may be, instead, an abstract aspect of an actual entity; for the primordial nature, considered by itself, is an abstraction from the concrete nature of God as objectively interrelated with all temporal actualities (PR 50). Moreover, the primordial nature is clearly stated by Whitehead to be "an actual efficient fact" (PR 48). It has to be understood, therefore, as being causally objectifiable and as resulting from a primordial activity that "achieves, in its unity of satisfaction, the complete conceptual valuation of all eternal objects" (PR 48). Whatever else it may be, the primordial nature is a complete, even if only conceptual, synthesis of all the existential data available for the primordial creative activity (PR 64, 134).

Since a temporal superject is also a complete, if physical, synthesis of all the existential data available for the temporal creative activity from which it issued, I hold that by 'superject' we should understand "any complete synthesis of all the existential data available for the creative activity of an experiencing subject." In Whitehead's metaphysics, whatsoever is such a synthesis is causally objectifiable. Remember, however, that a temporal actuality has a finite subjective aim that is grounded in, and conditioned by, the very data it is to synthesize. The self-referential aspect of its aim is to derive a maximum of intensity of experience from its aesthetic synthesis of all the available data (PR 41). Thus, the complete actualization of its subjective aim necessarily coincides with the complete synthesis of its data. The actuality is then a superject. But, since the subjective immediacy of an actuality cannot endure beyond the complete attainment of its subjective aim (PR 129-30), it follows that a temporal actuality is a superject when, and only when, it is utterly devoid of subjective immediacy. In other words, a temporal actuality is causally objectifiable only when it has perished subjectively.

The metaphysical principles appealed to in explaining the causal objectifiability of a temporal actuality are not violated when we explain the causal objectifiability of the divine actuality. God's primordial nature is causally objectifiable because it is a complete conceptual synthesis produced by the primordial creative activity out of the infinite multiplicity of eternal objects—a multiplicity comprising absolutely all the existential data available for the primordial creative activity (PR 48, 134, 523). Moreover, each completed stage in the supersessional development of God's consequent nature is causally objectifiable because it constitutes a complete physical synthesis produced by the consequent creative activity out of all the attained actualities already in existence relative to the beginning of that stage of the divine development (PR 523-24).

In this account, the primordial nature and each already completed stage of the consequent nature represent each a specific, or relative, satisfaction of the divine concrescence. They represent God as fully made, or fully determinate, in respect to any set of determinate existents objectively available for his experience—any set, that is, other than the set he is currently prehending into the fullness of his experience. But from there being such specific divine satisfactions, it does not follow that God is ever completed, ever generically satisfied, ever an attained actuality; for God's primordial subjective aim, unlike any temporal subjective aim, is infinite and can never be fully actualized.

Remember, in this last regard, that God's primordial subjective aim is the comprehensive appetition that each of the infinite number of ideal possibilities he conceptually prehends be physically realized by actual occasions, each occasion realizing a subordinate divine appetition for its own enjoyment, for the enjoyment of occasions in its relevant future, and for God's own consequent and everlasting enjoyment (PR 134). Remember, too, that every completed occasion is causally objectified in and physically prehended by God and that, as thus prehended, it is synthesized with the specific primordial appetition whose realization it constitutes (PR 524, 134). Remember, finally, that there is always in God an infinite remainder of subordinate primordial appetitions having no physical or actual counterpart. Accordingly, God's primordial subjective aim is incapable of complete actualization. His subjective aim must be always in process of realization and, hence, his subjective immediacy will never perish. Given the proposed definition of 'superject,' however, the everlastingness of God's subjectivity is no impediment to the superjective functioning of those aspects of God in which he constitutes the complete synthesis of all available determinate beings—excepting those determinate beings currently being synthesized into the fullness of God's next specific satisfaction.

The objectifiability of God, we must conclude, is not the insurmountable problem Ford has made it out to be. Whitehead's metaphysics, after a suitable correction of the definition of 'superject,' provides a logically consistent and categorially coherent account of God as an eternal actuality that is subjectively imperishable, essentially immutable, and causally objectifiable. Through his superjective functioning, God is the stable metaphysical factor whereby order and progress are possible in the world; and, through the immutable perfection of his essential subjectivity, God is the legitimate object of religious worship.

NOTES

1. Hartshorne appears to believe that the societal conception of Deity is not only Whiteheadian, but also explicitly endorsed by Whitehead. He writes: "God is, as Whitehead agreed in a carefully noted conversation with A. H. Johnson, a linear sequence . . . of occasions—with the difference, as contrasted to ordinary personal sequences, that in God there is no lapse of memory, no loss of immediacy, as to occasions already achieved" (PSG 274). Hartshorne, however, is in error. In his conversation with Johnson, Whitehead allows that God is a society only in the sense that the worldly occasions "passing into God as consequent do provide a group or society of distinguishable components . . ." (EWP 9). But that God is a linear society of divine occasions, Whitehead explicitly denied in reply to a direct question by Johnson: JOHNSON: "Can you think of God (as consequent) as a 'society?' " Whitehead replied that he had considered the possibility since a society is what endures, and an actual entity passes away. But, WHITEHEAD: "The answer is no." (EWP 9)
2. My language here presupposes a difference between causal objectification and conformation. Most commentators confuse the two. I have argued for this distinction in WMES 56-57, 71-77, 94-99, 199-200, 353-57.
3. I have explicated the doctrine of internal supersession, and argued extensively for its importance, in WMES 44-48, 278-302, and in my "Causation and Supersession in Whitehead," an unpublished paper presented to the Society for the Study of Process Philosophy on March 12, 1987.
4. See WMES 285-300.

REFERENCES

EWP—Lewis S. Ford and George L. Kline, eds., *Explorations in Whitehead's Philosophy*. New York: Fordham University Press, 1983.

PR—Alfred North Whitehead, *Process and Reality: An Essay in Cosmology*. New York: The Macmillan Company, 1929.

PSG—Charles Hartshorne and William L. Reese, *Philosophers Speak of God*. Chicago: The University of Chicago Press,

S—Alfred North Whitehead, *Symbolism: Its Meaning and Effect*. 1927. Reprint. New York: G. P. Putnam's Sons, Capricorn Books, 1959.

WMES—Jorge Luis Nobo, *Whitehead's Metaphysics of Extension and Solidarity*. New York: State University of New York Press. 1986.

WP—Charles Hartshorne, *Whitehead's Philosophy: Selected Essays, 1935-1970*. Lincoln: University of Nebraska Press, 1972.

General Remarks

Charles Hartshorne

This is the fourth case of a sizable group of philosophers being asked to write critically about my philosophy, and of my being asked to respond to their commentaries. In the history of philosophy I do not recall any comparably abundant example of the idea—for which Paul Arthur Schilpp has to be given the credit—of arranging for a philosopher to defend or explain himself in response to definite written comments or criticisms by numerous other writers. It is the number of these others that is perhaps a record. Note that for this to happen I had to have passed my ninetieth birthday, indeed my ninety-first birthday. And I had to be at this age still functioning actively as a philosopher. For this in turn to be other than wildly improbable, modern sanitation and medicine had to have reached the level it now enjoys. Also there had to be parents comparable to mine in their longevity-favoring genes and also and above all the sanity of their living habits—no smoking or heavy drinking (in fact, none at all), reasonable exercise (not too much, not too little), moderation in fat-ingestion, and a few other health-serving traits. And finally I had to follow well or improve upon the role models they set before me. Like all good happenings it is a combination of good luck and reasonably good management in response to the luck.

I am grateful to my department, especially to then chairman Robert Causey, to Douglas Browning and Robert Kane for organizing the conference on which this volume is based, and to participants Kane and Stephen Phillips for their editorial help in its publication.

David Griffin

In writing this superb exposition and defense of my philosophy, Dr. Griffin has done me, and I dare to think the world, a great favor. I have for a long time thought that he understood me well, but in this essay I feel he has outdone himself, in a fashion outdone me. He repeatedly puts my case better than I have myself. True, he does it partly by extensive quotations from my numerous writings, but he puts it all together and orders it more tidily and forcefully than I have managed to do. My primary feeling is simply that of agreement and admiration.

I find no definite misunderstanding anywhere. I do not object to "panexperientialism" instead of "psychicalism," and see advantages in that terminology. I like "deep empiricism," and see the danger of my stress on "*a priori.*" "Radical empiricism" does have for me a danger in its Jamesian association with the silly ideas that "there might have been nothing" makes sense, and that there are no necessary ontological truths. Also James's use of "pure experience" in the famous essay seems more radically ambiguous than radically clarifying. James did convince me with his defense of human freedom. In that essay he struck gold. And he did see the fallacies in Royce's argument for a wholly absolute, immutable, and all-determining experience or will.

At one point my view is closer to Griffin's than he quite sees. In saying that he does not find the ontological argument (the OA) convincing, he almost duplicates what I sometimes say about it. Normal Malcolm defends the argument as though by itself it gives sufficient reason for belief. I have always denied this, if 'sufficient' means "apart from other arguments." What is convincing about the OA is that it shows the religious meaning of God to be incompatible with the idea that existence is in this unique case contingent; either it is a necessary truth that God, as defined in a given way, does not and could not exist, or it is a necessary truth that God as defined does exist. The basic question about God is the meaning question: does the idea make sense? As classically defined, God could not exist since the definition is incoherent; as neoclassically defined, it is at least not clear to me that the idea is incoherent, and the other arguments seem to me to show that if there is no coherent way to define God then neither is there a coherent way to clarify other comparably general ideas, without which we cannot think out the meaning of life. I have no use for playing favorites among the metaphysical arguments for God. Either they all, properly stated, establish something relevant or none do. That is the nature of metaphysical arguments. Here I am closer to Peirce than to Whitehead, though Whitehead himself has several arguments for God.

The question whether there is any coherent metaphysics brings me to what is most admirable and creative in Griffin's essay, his treatment of deconstructionism. I could not agree more than I do with what he says about this. And how well he says it! Whitehead's language about metaphysics, that it is the attempt "with our ape-like consciousness" to capture the most general truths (an attempt that is bound partially to fail), I take to mean that a view like Rorty's, who states the current fashions so forcefully, is something like a *quarter-truth* mistaking itself for a *whole* truth, while denying that there is *any* truth! Like all the extreme skepticisms, it is unlivable, and hence (Peirce) not genuinely believable. "We should not pretend," said Peirce, "to disbelieve in our philosophy what we believe in our hearts." I hold this as much as Peirce or James did. And Albert Schweitzer can also be cited to this effect.

I congratulate Griffin and thank him for his patient and ingenious way of explaining what I have been trying to say for so many years. I add a few remarks which, probably for reasons of space, he does not make. One is that much of my view was anticipated by Plato in his definition of psyche as what is self-moved, and in his view of God as Soul of the Cosmos. Other aspects were anticipated by Epicurus with his swerve of the atoms and his defense of freedom; others by Aristotle in his equivalence of the necessary and eternal and of the contingent and non-eternal, also in his recognition of the openness of the future. But Aristotle's "unmoved mover" was a calamitous mistake, misleading the world for century after century. Not often has one man misled so many for so long. (Philo, by misinterpreting Plato, had a similar effect.) Plotinus did not help either. They all worshipped eternity and unity, as though either had any value apart from time and diversity.

Jan Van der Veken

Dr. Van der Veken is a prime example of what I call the advantage of belonging to a small country. It is an advantage I cannot have, but I was helped to know about it by having one of my four grandparents French-Swiss, and also some relatives in Holland. In Belgium, where I lived for some months, two languages are taken for granted, Flemish and French. Van der Veken is also at home in English and American thought, his dissertation was on Merleau-Ponty. With what he says in this new essay I have scarcely any disagreement, but he does many things well that I have not done, or at best not done well. I add a few supplementary remarks.

Plato is not mentioned in the essay, but it was he who came closest to my panentheism before Peirce, Bergson, Whitehead and some other thinkers of the last thirteen decades or so. Plato took the cosmos as the divine body. Theism for him, though not for some of his followers, meant that the cosmos was be-souled; God was the Soul of the World, to speak analogically. The Neoplatonists missed the point here in a subtle and seldom correctly noted manner. (1) For Plato that is besouled which is "self-moved." I take this to mean—and there are other reasons for this interpretation—that Plato was not a determinist in his theory of causality. (2) Plato was absolutely clear on the point that the divine body is in principle unique, and hence so is the divine soul, since it is the only body that has no external environment. This body is not a fragment of the cosmic body as my or your body is, but is the cosmos itself. This difference is one of principle, not of degree. My chief difference from Plato is supported and partly explained by the history of science. Except for Epicurus, none of the ancient Greeks attributed freedom, self-movement in the causally significant sense that is incompatible with determinism, to the constituents of "inanimate nature." Epicurus guessed and science now knows that all of nature consists of self-moving actualities, or what I call "active singulars."

Had this been clear to Plato, he would not have accepted the mind-matter dualism by which he partly explained evils in reality. Allowing for extremely subhuman forms of "soul" or mind, he could have anticipated Leibniz's universal psychicalism and done so without falling into Leibniz's ultra-rationalistic fallacy of requiring strictly sufficient reasons for contingent happenings. Contingency, as Peirce saw, is precisely the absence of such reasons. Plato shows he is on the right side of this issue by his doctrine that disorder in the world comes, at least partly, not from mindless matter but from a plurality of minds, each with its own self-movements, that is, its own at least minimally free decisions. The question is not teleology or no teleology; chaos or disorder comes from the *many* ends, purposes, decisions, with no supreme end or decision to coordinate them. ("Too many cooks spoil the broth.") He argues for theism as the only way to explain what order there is in the world. "Inanimate" matter is irrelevant to *that* problem. The Ananke that limits the divine persuasion is not necessity but the opposite, chance, as the negative aspect of freedom, that what was done might not have been done. Translators have misled us here. Plural teleology means a plurality of purposes or desires, and makes conflict in principle, though not in detail, inevitable. On this issue the Stoics were simply wrong, and the other Greeks more or less wrong. Plato and Epicurus (who attributes freedom to the very atoms) might between them have arrived at the truth; the others were all too handicapped by deterministic presumptions.

Van der Veken says little about freedom and chance. Hence the above remarks. He is probably right that I tend to be too optimistic. Whitehead thought he had been—about Chamberlain at Munich, for example. I have had a sheltered life, even more so than Whitehead.

Barry Whitney

Dr. Whitney basically is justified in wishing that my writing about divine power had been clearer on the points he discusses. I have certainly been less definite on the idea of God as cosmic cause than on the idea of God as cosmic effect (God's consequent aspects). I have been unambiguous, I think, in arguing that divine power is adequate to *guarantee* that there can and will always be cosmic order sufficient to make the world a possible set of data for the divine prehensions. The divine body will never be incompatible with the divine psyche. God may suffer but not cease to be divinely good and wise. The world cannot degenerate either into hopeless chaos or hopeless monotony. If you feel unable to call this degree or kind of irresistible power anything other than coercive, then I suppose you will have to call it coercive. I, however, will not use this word to describe God's direct relation to any actual entity. Perhaps not all my readers have noticed that I have never said there are no miraculous divine interventions. I have said at most that we cannot know (for reasons Hume specified) that such interventions have occurred; also that we may not be able to be sure that such interventions are desirable. I do not claim to know they are undesirable. I argue that both intervention and non-intervention must have costs. Intervention implies a future even more unpredictable than the universality of freedom alone implies, and non-intervention makes such things as the holocaust all too possible, as it may well seem to us. If coercion means that any part of nature is made totally devoid of creaturely spontaneity, self-determination, self-movement (Plato), I regard this as impossible.

Indirectly laws of nature do bring about coercion. To slip, as I have several times done, on a greasy or slimy surface and fall with some violence is certainly to suffer coercion—not directly by God, however, but by the active singulars of "inanimate" nature acting according to physical laws. It is the meaning of laws, in combination with universal multiple freedom, that such things can happen. That there are accidents, some accidents or other, is not itself an accident but on my view is bound to occur, in any possible cosmic epoch. Mere puppets, both as wholes and in their parts moved only by others (or God) not by themselves, are metaphysical impossibilities. Epicurus alone among Greeks guessed this, but many recent thinkers have held such a view. Science no longer excludes it. Only the limited resolving power of human sensory awareness could make it seem that any part of nature knowably consisted of wholly unfree actions. The self-moving unseen cells, molecules, atoms, particles were always there, and the supposition they were not there was based entirely on ignorance.

The dualism of all Greek thinkers other than the materialists was based on this ignorance, not on knowledge. They did not know even minimally how matter on the small scale behaves, so of course they could not guess what it consisted of. We do know much about the behavior; we are in a position to explain the contrast between mind and matter as a contrast among degrees and kinds of mind or experience, not of two absolutely contrary kinds of stuff or process. Psychicalism, not materialism, is the reasonable solution of the mind-matter problem. The notion of "mere matter" is a non-idea. Only minded matter is alone knowably instantiated if we want to say what properties over and above bare mathematically expressible structures, what *qualities*, are there.

Materialism is either agnosticism or covert dualism. The former option was taken by Russell, also by Roy and Wilfrid Sellars. The latter option seems to me the common one. It is natural enough for physicists and chemists, though far from universal among them; rather less natural among biologists, and I think less common. William James hesitated between psychicalism and a radically ambiguous "pure experience."

Donald Wayne Viney

In Dr. Viney's essay two things are accomplished. Partly he is reflecting (what I hope is) light of truth coming from me (or perhaps in some cases Whitehead); partly he is doing historical scholarship about philosophic proponents of views opposed, and some not so opposed, to mine. Both accomplishments seem to me well done. The way he exhausts the forms which the doctrine of timeless divine knowledge has taken is at the least neat (one of my aesthetic terms) if not downright beautiful. No one else, I dare say, has done this job nearly so well.

Viney notes that classical theists sometimes argue that God knows what we do, not beforehand but timelessly. One reply to this move by classical theists is to put the trilemma: does timelessly knowing mean *always* knowing, *never* knowing, *or what*? If the knowing is "always," then there is foreknowledge. If it is "never," then what has it to do with us or we with it? When we *now* talk about God's knowledge what are we taking about if it is not now real, nor always real, nor yet sometimes-but-not-always real? If time is "outside" of God, then where or when are the relations between divine knowing and temporal realities? If the relations are only in the temporal then temporal reality includes divine knowing but not vice versa. (To include a relation is to include its term.)

If timeless knowing and temporal events are mutually outside each other, how can there be any truth relations between them? As Viney says, the classical view creates more problems than it solves. I suggest we should worship God, not timelessness or any other one-sided abstraction. Becoming is the concrete, mere being is the abstract, and hence (Aristotle, Whitehead) the latter is in the former, not vice versa.

If future contingent events cannot be known beforehand, much less can they be known eternally. We may almost know our next quarter-second's experience but not what we experience tomorrow, and to have known at no matter what past time is more obviously impossible. And never to know is not distinguishable from simply not knowing, so far as I can see. My thanks to Viney for his scholarly discussion.

Daniel Dombrowski

For one philosophical writer to demonstrate to another that he or she well understands the other's philosophy is to pay the other a fairly high compliment, for communication in that subject is a substantial part of the task. Another part is the ability to be communicated to. I have tried in my writing to say what I say as clearly as possible. Dr. Dombrowski is not the only reader who can be certainly communicated to. I can be and have fairly frequently been well understood, as these things go in our profession. It is true that I have not made as much use of the most sophisticated techniques of symbolic logic and its symbolism as some of those in command of these techniques think requisite. Although I am somewhat apologetic about this, I am also honestly convinced that there is a possibility of diminishing returns in *this* way of being meticulously clear. The basic issues of philosophy are not those of mathematics. I do hold with Peirce, and Whitehead as well, that symbolic logic is relevant: however, there are always aspects incapable of the transparently demonstrative cogency that distinguish mathematical truths from those of ethics, aesthetics, or philosophy of religion or politics.

I heartily agree with this commentator that my views need to be dealt with in more analytic ways than I have used. Now and then I have said, at least to myself, that had I been smarter I would have made clear long ago how much common ground there is between my way of philosophizing and those more commonly regarded as analytic. I have always agreed with Carnap, whom I knew rather well, that in philosophy the great question is about meanings not facts in the ordinary empirical sense. Especially in discussions about God, at least for me, or for anyone who accepts what I call Anselm's principle (which is one premise of the ontological argument, not the whole argument), the questions are about meaning, not existence as additional to meaning. If we are sure that we have a definite and coherent idea of God, then it is nonsense or contradiction to say that we do not know whether or not God exists. Nor is the idea of God the only idea which has this essentially ontological character. All ideas of what Peirce called "the highest rank of generality" have this character. It cannot be less certain that "something exists" than that "deity exists," for deity is not sheer nothing, but at least something, and something or someone worthy of worship.

Some definitions of deity fail to make coherent sense. Carnap and I agree that atheism has to mean that this is true of any explication of the word God that justifies the religious term, except perhaps some empirically testable hypothesis that science would have good reason to reject. My view is that theism is not, in a reasonable sense, empirically testable. No conceivable experience could disprove it. However, unless there are other valid arguments that do not presuppose meaning for the religious term, the argument by itself lacks cogency. It think there are such arguments. So did Peirce and Whitehead.

I find scarcely a sentence to quarrel with in this commentary. I do see a slight ambiguity in "God's memory of the past . . . must change, just as each new generation of human beings must revise their history books." As Dombrowski knows, but almost seems to forget, there is one difference in principle that is not quite clearly covered by the all-comprehensiveness of the divine memory. Human historians may revise either to take into account old facts that happened to be previously hidden from historians, such as a letter by Washington (I have one to an ancestor of mine) which perhaps no earlier historian happened to see. God's memory changes only because of facts also new, such as letters which are such that the decision to write them just took place. But this is implied by the "all-comprehensive" that I omitted from the quotation. So this is nit-picking. I have meant to say what Dombrowski takes me to say.

Stephen Phillips

If my metaphysics were somewhat different, I would probably regard as divinely predestined my having Dr. Stephen Phillips for a colleague in the philosophy department of which I have been a member (now emeritus) for twenty-six years. Actually I see it as a case of fantastic good luck. What he does is about what seems ideally desirable in relating my thought to the traditions of India. Who else could have done it so well? There is little space to say much about an essay so rich in knowledge that I do not possess. The knowledge that I have seems largely compatible with what he says. I hope it will be read by many who know more than I do. I will venture a few mild disagreements and some supplementary remarks.

My relations to the monk Mahanam B. Bramachari are not exhausted by my *reading* his dissertation. He wrote it under my direction and I knew him well. From the first conversation I saw how close in some ways our views were. He told me that in his religion what mattered was love. Asked what he meant by love he said, "I mean consciousness of consciousness, thinking of thinking, [perhaps] experience of experience, [perhaps] feeling of feeling." If the last, then for him as for Whitehead, love is sympathetic feeling, whatever else it may be. I believed something like this before I read it in Whitehead, or met this Indian student. Peirce or Bergson had related ideas. I partly got it from R. Waldo Emerson.

I have long been aware of Aurobindo and have regarded his views as somewhat congenial. *The Life Divine* somewhat bored me by taking so many words and pages to achieve a somewhat unclear result. I also met some disciples of this writer and guru in India. Phillips is very helpful in expounding the doctrines. Concerning mysticism, I have written one essay. Rufus Jones of Haverford, my first teacher who was a professional philosopher, was also a scholar in and reputed practitioner of mysticism. He was a pupil of Royce and a reader of Creighton (of the Cornell School of idealism) and eventually got me to read Creighton with profit. Jones held, and I found it impossible to disagree, that the difference between mystics and nonmystics cannot be absolute. The difference between—on some level of awareness—experiencing God and not on any level experiencing God cannot, I believe, be spanned by our common human nature. Indeed I, with Whitehead, go further. All animals, all active singulars (my term), all actual entities experience (prehend) God. They feel but may not think or know God. The question is: do the pronounced mystics when experiencing God really experience such propositional truths as that God could have refrained from creating? I see little reason to grant this. I doubt if Jones granted it.

My sharpest non-agreement with Phillips is with his statement that we can conceive "a material world without God." With a great company of idealists or psychicalists, beginning at least as far back as Plato, I hold that the idea of mere, dead, insentient matter, *wholly independent of mind*, is a non-idea. The Buddhist "mind only" doctrine is also mine. It was that of my teacher W. E. Hocking. Plato already had a proof for it, though he could not quite carry it through because of the state of science and common sense in his time. Mind or soul is self-moved and the source of all motion, yet there seem to be some things that are in themselves inert, such as grains of sand. We now know these consist of self-moving atoms. *Greek dualism was based on ignorance not knowledge.* So is modern dualism, but the ignorance is now avoidable. Moreover Plato gave an argument also for theism. If there are many self-movers, how understand the orderliness of the cosmos? In this form a cosmological argument arises. Without the idea of self-movement, which I take to mean self-deciding, self-determining anew each moment, the changes of physical reality (pervasive, low forms of psyche) are inexplicable, and without a supreme psyche their tolerably orderly, mutually compatible actuality, is inexplicable. Moreover the notion of a simply unordered world, as well as the notion of total non-being, mere nothing, are also words lacking any clear and coherent meaning. "Total non-being" tautologically is not. I am not saying that no one can disagree with this. Nothing very important in philosophy is so certainly knowable by our "ape-like" minds. But there is a case for it.

The ontological argument is, by itself, vulnerable mainly because the coherence of whatever definition of God is used is not transparently evident. Nevertheless, as I use modal terms, the necessity of the divine existence is not dependent upon what possible world states happen to be actualized. If the idea is at all coherent, one of its plainest implications is that possible worlds can only mean divinely creatable worlds. Necessity as only in this actual world, or better, cosmic epoch, is not wisely called necessity in a theological context. What the laws of our epoch entail is necessary in that epoch; laws require, as the Greeks mostly held and I hold, a lawgiver. And God "must be Lord of possibility as well as actuality" (John Findlay). The theism question is essentially one of meaning, not of contingent fact. Otherwise it is a "fetish," not God, we are discussing (Peirce).

Even trying to think it untheologically, a "world of meaningless suffering" seems to me unclear or incoherent: Aurobindo and I are apparently in firm agreement about this, and he seems to have drawn out implications somewhat similar to my views. Animals could not live simply to escape suffering, not living suffices for that. They live for the satisfactions in living. Some possibility of suffering is necessary as negative reinforcer but positive reinforcement must be the primary force. Skinner is metaphysically right about that. Love not hate, joy not sorrow, pleasure not pain are primary.

I admire and am grateful to Phillips for this immensely stimulating and knowledgeable essay.

Kenneth L. Ketner

How good it is to have a Peirce scholar of Dr. Ketner's caliber discuss my revision of Peirce's categories! I have never been really sure that the revision retains all the truth in Peirce's scheme. I am fairly sure that my scheme does have truth value and philosophical usefulness, additional to, whether or not instead of, Peirce's scheme.

Peirce did, I think, prove *something* about the importance of triadicity. My scheme has a basic triadicity in its three modes, in spite of their clear distinguishability, and I would argue that this is not in the least compromised by my scheme. The basic form of secondness or dependence is asymmetrical and presupposes the instantiation of firstness or independence. Looking in the opposite temporal (or serial order) direction—by my generalization of what Peirce insisted upon in one type of instance (that logical biconditioning is a special case of which the principle is one-way conditioning)—I hold that symmetry is secondary to one-way order. As for my third category, the way earlier experiences are related to later experiences or events is by something between sheer dependence and sheer independence: that there will be future events or experiences able to relate back to their predecessors as their conditions—this too is inherent in the events.

After all, both Peirce and I, in arriving at the categories, are doing phenomenology; we hold phenomena are temporal and causal. Purely timeless phenomena (all events given to a single perception or consciousness) are according to some theologies enjoyed by deity, but certainly not according to us. It seems to me, indeed, that Peirce is perilously close to classical theism when he defines Firstness as devoid of intrinsic relations ("regardless of anything else"). Oddly, he never mentions the fact that his definition sounds exactly like the (to me objectionable) concept of God as "the absolute." The definition also forces him to attempt the dubious experiment of trying to imagine an experience that presupposes no other experience as its condition, something that his own system of ideas makes impossible. Certainly no human experience can be that, for according to Peirce (and me) experience (in the form of feelings, strivings and functioning signs) is the presupposition of everything, except possibly "God as First, before all creation."

Partly because of conversations with him, I take my former student Skidmore's position to be more subtle and complex than that triadicity is reducible to dyadicity. It is rather that any criterion that makes triads irreducible will also apply to tetrads, quintads, and so on. Hence the three categories will not suffice. I am not entirely convinced of this, and see cogency in Peirce's reasoning about valency, and in his point that combinations, which are triads (x • y = z), can by combining z with two other entities, and so on, produce any degree of complexity up to infinity. In any case, my three modes of dependence-independence-probability are in some important sense modally exhaustive. The past is, in its particularity, necessary for the present, but the future is necessary only in some general respects. Evolutionary biology comes closer to fitting this pattern than physics, although according to some physicists, for example Prigogine, physics is moving in that direction. Certain dinosaurs had to be there in a quite particular fashion to leave the fossils and other still-existing traces. And a present with no future at all does not make sense in terms of experience and hence does not make sense—period.

I hold, as I think Peirce did, that modal logic is indeed basic. (According to Nicolas D. Goodman, who is my son-in-law, this obtains even in mathematics.) After all, "time is a species of objective modality" for Peirce, and I think it is *the* species, not just *a* species. The past is the sum of actual or "accomplished facts," and the future contains no entirely accomplished or fully particular facts—it is an irreducibly unparticular potentiality. When reduced to particulars, it will no longer be "future" but only "later." Peirce significantly said that "logic is not yet ready to take up the relations of truth to time." He also said that his categories have only a limited validity and are "more like tints or tones on conceptions" than conceptions. My categories are more definite.

I agree with Peirce that philosophy at its best presupposes the mathematically exact aspects of logic, and it seems evident that without both dependence and independence among propositions there is no logic amounting to anything, and that without probability (something between sheer dependence and sheer independence, or sheer necessity and sheer contingency) there is no exact logic useful in science. So I take these ideas and look to experiences, phenomena, for their ontological instantiations. Peirce's tychism is yielded more obviously by my version of the categories than by his own.

If, as is the case, logic must have both dependence and independence among propositions, how can there be merely dependence or merely independence in the reality which the propositions are about and by which they are made true or false? If time is objective modality, how could there not be modal contrasts between relations among phenomena in our obviously temporal experiences? If all science, as Peirce holds, is probabilistic, and if the meaning of temporal order for behavior is that the past is not open to decisions, but the future is at each moment being partly decided by them—if this is time's basic order—how does it make sense to deny (with Hume) any intrinsic relatedness (other than that derived from animal faith or pragmatic postulate) of present to past, while claiming (as Hume does) that science has shown the future to be strictly determined by the past? Phenomena have simply necessary relations to their predecessors as particulars, but no such relations to particular successors. To be sure, they do have necessary relations to some not wholly particular aspects of the future. But this is neither a matter of pure chance nor of any single (creaturely or divine) purpose; it is rather a mixture of both or all of these.

I share Ketner's profound admiration for Peirce. What a genius! In addition Peirce was, on the whole, basically good, dedicated to optimizing his contribution to the cosmic poem, or to "concrete reasonableness." With Plato and Whitehead, he is one of my three favorite philosophers. Peirce said of Plato, "he knew what philosophy is (or should be)."

Lewis S. Ford

A writer in philosophy is fortunate indeed to be understood as well as I find myself understood by Ford (by Griffin and other contributors here as well!). If Griffin devoted himself largely to expounding and defending my intellectual scheme, Dr. Ford, the meticulous scholar in the study of Whitehead, is more partial in his support of my position. The two essays together show, I think, the value of "scholasticism"—meaning discussion among adherents of a particular school of thought. The journal that Ford edits, *Process Studies*, has been a valuable medium for such discussion. It enables a group to focus on definite problems employing a common language with a minimum of self-serving polemics and a maximum of mutual benefit. To have brought together such able scholars as Ford and Griffin to promote such a purpose for serious students of Whitehead is surely an admirable achievement of John Cobb.

I grant to Ford that my system of ideas is not so trouble-free as I sometimes seem to present it. Like Whitehead, I think success in metaphysics can never be absolute. Language itself, and other limitations of our manner of experiencing and thinking, compared to what we conceive as divine psychical functionings, stand in the way of more than relative success. We do the best we can, and it can be worth doing, in spite of the extreme deconstructionists or skeptics.

My first remark, a mildly critical one, is historical. I deny that Plato held an unqualifiedly "timeless" view of deity. This all too popular view ignores Plato's contrast between the eternal God, the Demiurge, and the "God that was to be," the Soul of the Cosmos, which is the moving image of eternity. Textual evidence in the later dialogues that Plato attributed becoming, "self-motion," even to perfect being, seems to me conclusive. Here I follow Cornford, Levinson (a pupil of Paul Shorey), and still other scholars in Greek philosophy. Alas, most talk about "Platonism" has followed the wrong track on this point, misled by Aristotle and the entire Medieval tradition, along with much modern metaphysics, including Leibniz and Kant. I hold, with Richard

McKeon, that Neoplatonism was bad Platonism, and Aristotle was in this respect the first and greatest of the Neoplatonists and did much to mislead two millennia. This did not prevent Aristotle from being right in some respects, in comparison with his medieval followers in metaphysics.

My view about being and becoming is somewhat closer to Ford's own than he sees. I hold that divinity is the supreme kind of becoming. But in this sense the past too is an abstraction. In whatever present the past is given, it is less than that present and is included in it. Whitehead can be cited for the view that being an object is not different from being a subject, if the object is singular and concrete. Such objects are simply past subjects.

That becoming "produces" being for me simply means that we use the *word* being to cover the reality of past becoming. In this reality past concrescences are the most concrete constituents and whatever aspects are common to all past concrescences are the most abstract aspects. These will also be aspects of all future becoming. This is Aristotle: what never has come into being for the first time is necessary, not contingent. Ford and I seem to agree that possibility is vague, vaguer than Whitehead's eternal objects make it to be. However, it is *qualitative* eternal objects, like a definite pure blue, not purely structural, relational universals such as numbers, that I reject.

One real difference between Ford and me seems also to be a difference between Whitehead and me. It concerns laws of nature. At best I find the latter on this ambiguous; he seems to dismiss the idea of imposed laws, but then also to affirm it. (I have closely examined the texts on this in *Adventures of Ideas*.) I am quite unconvinced by Ford's idea that the creatures can simply by changing their habits, change the laws of nature. The obvious objection is, how can they produce anything but chaos if each is to decide toward what other possible law or habit than the prevailing one the change is to be? "The rule of one is best"—even a committee requires a chairman. I think natural laws require a lawgiver. As Sophocles said of them, "The power of God is mighty in them and cannot grow old." However, the ageless power can change its purposes. On this issue I find Peirce and Whitehead on the whole on my side, though neither is wholly clear. For both, the cosmos is a poem. True, the actual letters or words are self-creative creatures (Peirce: they act spontaneously, adding a new bit of contingency to reality), but there is a general style, unique to the cosmic epoch (Whitehead, not Peirce), and this forms the laws of that epoch. The trouble with mere creaturely habits as substitute for laws is that habits are individual. Hydrogen atoms are alike in behavior; this likeness implies something more than mere individual freedom as their origin, unless the individual is cosmic or divine. Of course, the creatures respond to God's aims; but if the aims do not change in God, how are the creatures all to agree in the direction of a change to new laws? I fail to see this.

I also am unimpressed by the idea that metaphysical truth is only valid for our cosmic epoch. What we mistakenly take to be metaphysical truth may be valid only in our epoch, but this means our metaphysical quest has to that extent failed. I define metaphysics classically as the search for universal and necessary truths, and with Aristotle refuse to distinguish the unconditionally necessary from the eternal. For truths limited to our epoch we have the idea of contingent laws. And we have the idea of empirical cosmology. To use the term 'metaphysics' for this seems to me a needless source of confusion. I value Karl Popper for being the first to define 'metaphysical' and 'empirical' properly (though Peirce came close to it). 'Empirical' does not mean "from experience," for no one, not even God, can know without experiencing. The possibility of conceivable *falsification* by experiencing a negative instance is the critical ground of differentiating metaphysics from everything else. Here too I am about as close, or a little closer, to Peirce than to Whitehead.

I prefer to take as my crucial difficulties about how to apply the theory of prehension to both God and creatures as coming to a focus in the problems of worldly time, as dealt with by physics and biology, in relation to what I incline to regard as divine temporality. And I have learned from Karl Popper on this topic. I agree with Ford that God is related to the future in principle otherwise than we are, for the divine future is all the future, and our experiencing will have its last instance in a few years or decades. Otherwise I do not quite know what to make of Ford's speculations on this head.

Robert Kane

I wrote my response to Ford before reading my colleague Kane's essay. His objections or questions to Ford cover much of the ground I tried to cover or thought of covering. By "transcendence" I mean primarily a value distinction. God is all-others-surpassing in excellence, and this excellence has two aspects. In whatever senses, and I hold there are such senses, it is logically possible to excel all other individuals in value and also possible to reach an absolute maximum of possible excellence so that the all-excelling individual logically could not in value excel even itself, God is excellent. This kind of excellence I have called absolute or A-perfection. Thus God is all-knowing or (they are the same in God) all-loving, meaning knowing all things ideally well. This is the classical idea of perfection. I accept it so far as God's knowledge, love and power are concerned. But there is another dimension of value in which no maximum seems logically possible, and this is the dimension of aesthetic richness. Aesthetic value is incapable of an absolute maximum, as Whitehead and I have argued. Berdyaev has a similar idea. Each new creature "enriches the divine life." Tillich too has accepted this doctrine and I find hints of it in Reinhold Niebuhr and Peirce, also W. P. Montague, under the influence of Peirce.

God is "the individual with universal functions," no other individual has such functions. God is the all-excelling individual, both excelled and, in one respect not excelled, by itself in other states. The importance of this complex meaning for transcendence is that it justifies worship and the definition of worship as loving with all one's being. Mere timelessness, mere infinity (the number series is that), mere absoluteness in the sense of independence or unchangeability, does not make something lovable with all one's being. Not at all. God, by my definition is the One worthy of worship by all others. I see no point in worshipping the mere word transcendence, or eternity, or immutability. Can the number three change? If I worship God, it is for definite reasons.

Kane is right in stressing the problem of identity in deity, and also in us. As the Buddha saw, human identity is a very relative thing, and is more definite in the bodily aspect of the person than in the personally conscious aspect. With sleep, insanity, multiple personality, etc., each of us is many concrete actualities in succession. Yet the gene structure is fixed after conception, and sleep does not stop the heart, lungs, and various other organs from operation. Well did a physiologist friend of mine call his book *The Unresting Cells*. The excellence of God must include an *ideal* form of self-identity, not sheer logical identity in the sense excluding all change, but in the sense excluding deterioration or decrease in content. The key change is in aesthetic enrichment. Shortly after I arrived at this conviction, an East Indian sociologist, Radhakamal Mukerjee, said this very thing in the University of Chicago chapel, and by good luck I was there to hear him. Did he derive this idea from Whitehead? Probably not. From Berdayev, ditto. Nor from me. The time simply was ripe for the thought; one more example of what I call "cultural change." To some extent the view is worldwide. Perfection, in the sense excluding change other than enrichment, or addition of new content, I call R-perfection, surpassable only in itself. I have long been proud of Kane, my colleague and fellow former-Haverfordian.

Jorge L. Nobo

That God is eternal (in the sense of being incapable of nonexistence) and actual, as well also "subjectively imperishable, essentially immutable, and causally objectifiable . . . and the stable metaphysical factor whereby order and progress are possible in the world" I am happy, with Dr. Nobo, to affirm. Where then are our differences of view? By "essentially immutable," I would mean changeable only in qualities not necessary to an individual's defining characteristics. God has always been and must always be God. Nobo speaks of supersession in the stages of the divine development. He also says the divine subjective aim is infinite and can never be completely satisfied. That seems to be what I hold. The divine capacity for value is indeed infinite in a sense in which no actuality can be infinite. This is why there must be becoming, and why there is no first or last instance of becoming. Always there could be more value, so the principle of divine life can only be, "let there be more." I too say that God's *character* is ever the same—perfectly benign, omniscient, and all-loving. Nobo speaks of the successive "phases" of the consequent nature, and I speak of successive "states" of that nature. How much more than verbal are these differences between us?

Perhaps the clue is the phrase, 'abstractions inherent in causal objectifications.' In non-divine causal objectifications, this inherence obtains, but I do not know the reason why it must obtain in divine objectifications. My view is that for God there is "loss" only in one sense, lost opportunities. I might have taught English literature, and this would have given the world and God some values, however modest, that in fact neither the world nor God will ever have. Otherwise I hold that God objectifies the entire value of actualities and thereby is influenced by them. Also God objectifies the divine subjective states actually achieved, of course without loss. The infinite divine aim comes with this. It has always been there and always will be. That each divine state has some freedom and so is contingent does not entail that the prehension of previous divine aims, all of which inherited the primordial aim, is merely precarious.

I sometimes say that God primordially has the consequent nature. Only the states or stages of that nature are contingent. God never could be or have been *merely* primordial. Although I am not very comfortable with the idea of successive phases in concrescence, I have not definitely rejected them. And certainly divine becoming could not be the fantastically contingent business it is in us. Divine properties are in principle only analogous to properties in us. Barth's "there is a kind of holy change in God," and similar statements by Berdayev, are signs of the cultural change that has occurred since the Middle Ages, beginning with Fausto Sozzini. But the essence of God of course does not change.

By rejecting the notion of eternal qualitative universals—because of the continuity of possible qualities as such—in contrast to the incurable discreteness of actualities, I do not mean, as Peirce did not mean with his similar doctrine, that there is no eternal divine aim. But as a continuum of space or time, or of anything else, is not a sum of definite points of instants or whatever, so the eternal aspects of possibility lack the definiteness of actualities. Definite pluralities imply definite singulars: the Leibnizian doctrine seems correct. Eternal "forms of definiteness" are not, as eternal, very definite: only as emergent do definite qualitative forms arise. Numbers I regard as eternal, but not "blue" or an exact feeling tone. Actuality *creates definiteness*, and does not merely instantiate it.

Contributors

David Ray Griffin is Professor of Philosophy of Religion at the School of Theology at Claremont and Claremont Graduate School, and Executive Director of the Center for Process Studies, Claremont, CA 91711. He is editor of the SUNY Series in Constructive Postmodern Thought, author of *God, Power, and Evil* and *God and Religion in the Postmodern World*, co-author of *Process Theology* and *Varieties of Postmodern Theology*, and editor of *The Reënchantment of Science: Postmodern Proposals* and *Spirituality and Society: Postmodern Visions.*

J. Van der Veken is Professor at the Institute of Philosophy of the University of Leuven (Kardinaal Mercier-Plein 2, B-3000 Leuven, Belgium), and is president of the European Society for Process Philosophy. An internationally known scholar, he has written widely about process philosophy, metaphysics, philosophy of religion and contemporary Continental and Anglo-American philosophy.

Barry L. Whitney is Associate Professor and Head of the Department of Religious Studies, the University of Windsor, Windsor, Ontario, N9B 3P4 Canada. He is author of *Evil and the Process God* (Mellen, 1985) and *What Are They Saying About God and Evil?* (Paulist, forthcoming), and is completing an annotated bibliography on theodicy. He has published chapters and articles on process thought in various books and periodicals: *International Philosophical Quarterly, Studies in Religion, Philosophy Research Archives, Horizons, Southern Journal of Philosophy,* etc.

Donald Wayne Viney is Assistant Professor of Philosophy at Pittsburg State University, Pittsburg, Kansas 66762. He is author of *Charles Hartshorne and the Existence of God* (SUNY, 1985), and has several articles in the areas of metaphysics and philosophy of religion. Dr. Viney is on the editorial board of *The Midwest Quarterly*, an interdisciplinary journal of contemporary thought.

Daniel A. Dombrowski is in the Philosophy Department of Seattle University, Seattle, WA 98122. He is author of many articles and four books, the latest of which is *Hartshorne and the Metaphysics of Animal Rights* (SUNY, 1987).

Stephen H. Phillips is Associate Professor of Philosophy, the University of Texas, Austin, TX 78712. A sanskritist by training as well as a philosopher, he has published several articles on classical Indian views, and others not confined to Indian traditions. He is author of *Aurobindo's*

Philosophy of Brahman (Brill, 1986), where he scrutinizes the metaphysics of the modern Indian philosopher whom he also discusses here.

Kenneth Laine Ketner is Charles Sanders Peirce Professor of Philosophy and Director, Institute for Studies in Pragmaticism, Texas Tech University, 304K Library (MS 2041), Lubbock, TX 79409. He is author of several articles on Peirce, is editor, *Comprehensive Bibliography of the Published Works of Peirce*, founder and general editor, *Peirce Studies*, a series published by Indiana University Press, co-organizer, Peirce Bicentennial International Congress (1976), Chairperson of Organizing Committee, Peirce Sesquicentennial International Congress, Harvard University, 1989, and Fellow (and formerly President) of the Charles S. Peirce Society.

Lewis S. Ford is Eminent Professor of Philosophy at the Old Dominion University, Norfolk, VA 23508. He is editor of *Process Studies*, and has also edited *Two Process Philosophers* (Scholars Press, 1973), and (with George L. Kline) *Explorations in Whitehead's Philosophy* (Fordham, 1983). He is author of *The Emergence of Whitehead's Metaphysics, 1925-1929* (SUNY, 1984) and *The Lure of God* (Fortress, 1978). He has written over eighty essays, mostly on process themes, including "Hartshorne's Interpretation of Whitehead," to be published in the volume of the Library of Living Philosophers devoted to Charles Hartshorne.

Robert Kane is Professor of Philosophy at the University of Texas, Austin, TX 78712. He is author of articles on philosophical psychology, philosophy of religion, theory of values and philosophy of science, which have appeared in more than a dozen philosophical journals, including "The Modal Ontological Argument" (*Mind*, 1984), selected by *The Philosopher's Annual* as one of the ten best philosophical articles of 1984. He is also author of *Free Will and Values* (SUNY, 1985).

Jorge Luis Nobo is Professor of Philosophy at Washburn University of Topeka, Topeka, KS 66004. He is a former student of Hartshorne, and wrote his doctoral dissertation under Hartshorne's direction. He is author of *Whitehead's Metaphysics of Extension and Solidarity* (SUNY, 1986), and co-editor of *The Individual and Society* (*Southwestern Journal of Philosophy*, 1978). His articles on process philosophy have appeared in *Process Studies* and *International Philosophical Quarterly*.

Charles Hartshorne is Professor Emeritus of Philosophy at the University of Texas, Austin, TX 78712. His fourteen books and hundreds of articles require no enumeration here: this volume as a whole stands witness to his accomplishments.